INSPIRATIONS FROM
ABROAD
FOR A HAPPIER LIFE
AT HOME

9 Countries, 3 Continents,
and What I Learned About Living a More
Joyful, Balanced, and Fulfilling Life

JUDITH FUHRMANN

For permissions and inquiry, please contact the author. Contact information can be found on the author's website: www.JudithFuhrmann.com

eBook: 978-3-9525449-0-7
Hardcover: 978-3-9525449-1-4
Paperback: 978-3-9525449-2-1

Cover Design and Illustrations: 100Covers.com
Interior Design: FormattedBooks.com
Editing: Debra Moffitt and Eva Saviano

Endorsements

Life begins outside of our comfort zone, and for a lot of people that comfort zone is limited to the place they were born and raised. For many people, leaving their hometown can be a challenge, let alone their home state or country. This leads to misguided opinions of the world at large. Fuhrmann looks to tackle that in this book, as she teaches us of the cultures around the world from a firsthand account. The stories she shares paint an amazing picture of the cultures and her in-depth research gives us an even wider view of these magical countries. A must-read for anyone looking to travel or better understand this world we live in.

—Dillon Barr, bestselling author of *The Happiness Gap*

📖

Culture can be a barrier, but it can also be a bridge; and Judith's book filled with personal anecdotes and in-depth research is a beautiful testament to such a bridge, reminding us that our diversity, varying customs, values, and beliefs bring richness and beauty into our lives—if only we let it.

—Eevi Jones, award-winning author and founder of Children's Book University™

📖

In a world of division, Judith Fuhrmann identifies what unites us and provides valuable cross-cultural tools for living a happier and more fulfilling life.

—Debra Moffitt, award-winning author of *Awake in the World*

📖

Judith Fuhrmann ignites our curiosity; inspires an appreciation for other countries, cultures, and people; and encourages open-mindedness and empathy when traveling. She reminds us it's only after we let our guard down and embrace our differences that we are able to connect with others on a deeper level.

When we learn, we grow; when we listen, we understand.

—Tanya Deke, writer, travel enthusiast, and blogger at <u>Taking-the-Time.com.</u>

📖

I really enjoyed discovering all the unique cultural insights Judith offered in her book. The book was a joy to read, and I felt I was part of her journey. And, I greatly appreciated the effort Judith went to on the chapter on Japan, to accurately and faithfully present the ikigai *concept to the reader.*

—Nicholas Kemp, Japanologist, Ikigai coach and founder of Ikigai Tribe

📖

Wow! This book not only inspires me to hold onto many of these principles and incorporate them into my life, but it also inspires me to want to travel more to learn from other amazing cultures.

—Penney Megginson, founder of Megginson Method, which combines mind therapy with total-body wellness

📖

It's a delightful book! I love the tone. So sweet, helpful, sharp, positive, empathetic, and lovely all around. Really, WOW! I love the story of ordering four ducks at the Chinese restaurant. I love all of the stories and quotes.

A must-read for all expats!

—Carmela Fleury, certified Holistic Health Coach and the organizer of Raising Happy & Healthy Mamas retreats around the world

FREE GIFT

Thank you, dear reader, for having chosen this book!

As a sign of my gratitude and appreciation, I would like to offer you my free accompanying workbook that will help you define your own tool-box for living a happier life at home.

You can get a copy by visiting:

https://judithfuhrmann.com/free-workbook/

DEDICATION

To Antoine, Noelie, and Elisa
My personal sunshines,
who bring joy and meaning to me every day

To my Parents and my Brother
Who lovingly provided me with roots and wings,
since the first day of my life and who are a constant
source of unconditional love and support

To my "Belle-Famille" and my "Wider Heart Family"
For adding joy and beauty to my life

CONTENTS

PREFACE

This book is like a third baby for me. It took time to grow and develop, and I am at once excited and anxious to release it into the world.

I started writing in the summer of 2019, and I completed the first draft about a year later. It took a lot of reflection and reminiscing to recall situations and pinpoint some of the things I really appreciated about the various countries I've called home during different periods of my life. And while I did my best to replicate the stories and conversations I mention as accurately as possible, I had to rely on my memory for the approximate word choices used during these conversations, especially when the dialogue took place years ago.

While revising my book and integrating feedback from friends and acquaintances, our planet underwent some profound changes. With the global COVID-19 pandemic in 2020, significant changes occurred in our ability to travel, and it also changed how many of us see the world. We have become even more conscious of how fragile our lives here on Earth are. And at the same time, it has been mind-blowing to see how large numbers of people in countries around the world have stepped up to help each other whenever and however possible. While views on the best way to handle this unprecedented situation vary, we can also observe more clearly what unites us all. Some of these things include the longing to live our lives in the best possible ways, to be able to work, to do what we love doing, and to meet and interact with people who are important to us. And while we might temporarily be restricted in terms of physical contact, we can still travel via books, movies, food, and music. And we can still communicate with family members, friends, and people around the world via other means.

I hope this book can help you immerse yourself in the countries I write about and pick up some inspiration for your own daily life. In the following chapters, I share how I try to integrate some of the positive mindsets and customs that I encountered in the various countries into my daily life. When I started writing, our elder daughter had just turned three and our younger one was a few months old. By the time this book is released into the world, our older child is five years old and our second "little baby" has turned into an active, exploring little girl. So, whenever I refer in the book to our three-year-old or our baby, it refers to the time when the passage was written.

With the pandemic situation, a lot has changed in our little family life, as well. In one chapter, I talk about how hard it was to have dinner together at times when my husband worked late or was away for business. Some of these situations have changed, and I point that out in the footnotes. But what has not changed, despite everything that happened in the past year, is that we can learn from each other, exchange views and experiences, and get inspired by people from around the world. And that is what this book is all about.

Switzerland, April 2021

START

Germany

U.S.

Netherlands

Mexico

France

Switzerland

Japan

China

India

Happier Life
at Home

VALUES

ATTITUDES

CUSTOMS

BELIEFS

MINDSETS

HABITS

INTRODUCTION

*Our homes are not defined by geography or one
particular location, but by memories, events,
people, and places that span the globe.*

—Marilyn Gardner

Bringing the World into Our Home

Have you ever wanted to keep alive the beautiful memories of a place you traveled to or lived in? You might decorate your home with travel souvenirs, create a photo album, or try to cook a meal you enjoyed in a particular country. Sometimes, we long to bring back home certain sensations or feelings we had when traveling or living abroad. Images, souvenirs, food, or even a specific smell can take us right back to the places we once visited. I certainly love looking at the beautiful photo books that my husband has created from our travels. When I look through them, I feel like I'm back there. They remind me of the people we met, the places we visited, the experiences we had, and the joyful—sometimes challenging and often funny—situations we ran into.

The amazing thing about traveling and living abroad is that it opens us to enormous learning and growth as we step out of our comfort zones. Curiosity and the desire to explore can be driving forces.

We encounter situations we might never have experienced before. We might discover customs, faith, and belief systems that are very different from our own. It can be challenging at times, and we might feel disoriented for a while. But in the long term, it can also be very rewarding as it opens up new perspectives on life. And the great thing is that we then have the option to integrate whatever resonates with us into our own daily lives—no matter where in the world we are living.

Once we start thinking like this, the world becomes a large, fascinating playground where we can encounter the most amazing people with the most varied backgrounds. Customs, belief systems, mindsets, and how we see the world might vary depending on the country, the culture, or the family we are born into—and on our own personalities. Yet, in the end, I think that we, as a human family, all strive for very similar things in life: love, connection, health, happiness; a sense of fulfillment and purpose, and understanding what our unique role in and contribution to this world can be. Of course, it ultimately depends on us. I believe that true happiness, fulfillment, and inner calm come from within us. And there is a lot that we can do to work on our inner self. The saying, "Nothing changes, until you change. Everything changes, once you change," by Julian Lennon holds very true in this regard. And at the same time, we can get inspired by seeing how other people and people from different backgrounds, cultures, or countries do things and deal with everyday situations.

That is what this book is about. It takes you on a journey to nine countries on three continents and provides you with a selection of concepts, customs, values, attitudes, and mindsets that stood out to me while living in these countries. I love traveling and started traveling at a very young age. So far, I have had the chance to visit almost 50 countries and to live in nine of them. Originally from Germany, I spent most of my childhood and teenage years in

Germany's Münsterland. Later, I spent a high-school semester in the U.S., a year and a half as a voluntary social worker in Mexico, several years in the Netherlands for my undergraduate studies, and I did a couple of language stays and a university semester in France. From there, I moved to Switzerland to pursue a Master's degree and then a Ph.D. in Development Studies; then I spent several months in India for my Ph.D. research. After that, my husband and I relocated to Asia together. For my husband's job, we spent a couple of years in China and then a couple of years in Japan before moving back to Switzerland. Each country impressed and surprised me in its own way. I also experienced moments of disorientation in each country, and sometimes I felt like hiding under my bedsheets for the entire day. Yet, there were also countless experiences and encounters that left me inspired in each place, and this book will focus on some of them.

How the Idea for This Book Was Born

For a long time, I thought it would be great to reflect on the lessons learned and the "aha" moments I experienced while living in different countries. Often, when I lived abroad and learned something new, I told myself: *"Wow, this is so interesting. I should take this behavior/belief/custom with me as inspiration when I leave."* Then life would get in the way, things got busy and I never really sat down to consciously go back and reflect on what it was that I had appreciated so much about the countries I once called home.

The impulse to do so—and, later on, to write a book about it—came after giving birth to our second daughter. It was early 2019, and my husband, our elder daughter, and I had returned from Japan to Switzerland a year and a half earlier. After four years in Asia, we thought that coming back to Switzerland would be a comfortable, smooth reintegration. My husband is Swiss, and I had lived in

Switzerland for five years before embarking on our adventure in Asia. Even though I knew that settling into a new place or a different country always involves an adaptation period, we were caught by surprise when we moved back to Switzerland in the summer of 2017. Settling back in and adapting to life in Europe again was more challenging than we had imagined. You often prepare yourself well when moving to a different place by gathering lots of information about the new environment and by learning about the various stages of culture shock. But for the reverse culture shock you can experience when coming back, we are often less prepared. When going through the mixed emotions upon our return, I thought of the difficult adaptation period I had faced years earlier. At that point, I had returned to my home country, Germany, after spending a year and a half in Mexico. Even though I had been delighted and excited to see my family and friends back in Germany again, it took me a good while to readapt to the German lifestyle. This time, with my husband and our daughter, we ended up settling in a little village on the outskirts of Geneva. The difference between this little village and the pulsing metropolis of Tokyo, where we had lived the two previous years, could not have been starker. We enjoyed being closer to our families and friends in Europe again, and the landscape surrounding us was exquisitely beautiful. Yet, for several months, we missed the way of life we had had in Asia—and I felt quite lost and uprooted.

Parallel to finding my footing back in Europe, I started to feel increasingly anxious, irritated, and helpless when watching the evening news. I have always been interested in following the news to get a glimpse of what is going on in the world. Yet, day after day, more negative news kept streaming in. Images of armed conflicts, hunger, violent and extremist movements, and increasing societal polarization kept showing up. Often, after watching the news, I felt a knot in my stomach. I wondered about the kind of world our two daughters had been born into. Even though there is, of course, good news, too, the majority of news channels highlight dysfunctions in our world and society. This might be the very nature of news. As the old saying goes: *"No news is good news."* Yet, in a way, this view can become biased when we hear day after day what is not working in our world. Certainly, it's very important to learn about the issues. I admire journalists who take significant risks to report about sensitive, yet important, issues that need to be addressed to help people. It is also necessary that, as individuals and as societies, we stand up against injustices that are often profoundly and systemically ingrained in our societies. I worked for several years on questions related to inequality, equity, poverty, and vulnerability when doing research in the academic realm. And I know that there is still a lot to be done in countries around the world to enable people to live a life of dignity, with their needs and human rights met. However, being overwhelmed with bad news on a daily basis can lead us to believe that we live in a crazy, dangerous world and that the majority of people have bad intentions. It can result in fear of the unknown. And negative headlines about countries we don't know first-hand, can put these countries in such a negative light that we might only have negative images in our minds when thinking of them and their people.

Between the irritation I felt when following the news and my nostalgia for the countries I lived in, I thought it might be a great experiment to consciously change perspective for a while. I aimed to focus on the good things and the beauty the countries around the world have to offer. In the quest to live a joyful, balanced, and fulfilling life, it can be a great asset to take into account different ways of thinking and living. It enlarges the plate of choices and tools we have at our disposal, so we can pick what suits us best. There is beauty to be found in every country, in every culture, and in every person. Sometimes, we just need to choose the right lens to see it. For my project, I started making a list of some of the major things that I appreciated in the countries where I had lived. Every country had provided me with some new insights and perspectives. I found pearls of wisdom when speaking to people or when observing how they acted or reacted to certain situations. Since I love learning about different ways to live a fulfilling life, I wanted to explore some of my positive observations more deeply.

For this, I engaged in a true marathon in terms of personal development and positive psychology techniques in 2019 and 2020. I joined networks, groups, online courses, talks, and seminars. I dived into countless books, listened to podcasts, and watched inspiring TED talks that dealt with integrating positive thinking into our daily lives. I learned that we can shift our mindset from negative to positive with regular training, for example, by using gratitude practices, by formulating positive affirmations, and by taking silent moments to connect to our inner self. Many people worldwide use these tools to shift their focus to the positive and lead more fulfilling everyday lives as a consequence. Some of the inspiration that I gathered from these tools will naturally flow into the discussion of country-related themes.

This book blends intercultural experiences with personal development theories, and if you are interested in these two wide-ranging topics, this book is for you. The book's ultimate aim is to increase curiosity and appreciation for other countries, cultures, and people. At the same time, I hope to provide inspiration—how to take little steps to make our lives happier, more balanced, and more fulfilled.

What's in This Book and How to Use It

Each chapter in this book is dedicated to one of the countries I lived in. I selected four themes for each country. It follows my life journey chronologically, starting in Germany and ending with my experiences in India, China, and Japan. The choice of topics is vast. They include positive mindsets, like the *jugaad* or *"I will figure something out"* mindset in India and the *yin and yang* concept in China. They discuss the importance of connection and meaningful relationships in our lives, such as the role of the family in Mexico and the role of social networks or supportive tribes in China and Japan. Some themes emphasize the importance of self-care moments and the ability to enjoy life. This spans from the French *savoir vivre* attitude to many Swiss people's ability to slow down and enjoy nature. And several themes explore the power of believing in something bigger than ourselves, be it spiritually, like in Mexico or India, or in terms of finding our life purpose, as with the Japanese *ikigai* concept.

My selection of themes is personal and subjective and by no means exhaustive. Each country offers many positive attributes and strengths. I chose to explore some of those that left a lasting impression on me and that continue to touch me. While I share about themes and behaviors of people in the countries where I lived, the book in no way aims to stereotype or offend people from any country in any way. It's impossible to make generalizations about the people of a whole country, and this is not the intention of the book. Instead, I describe some tendencies that stood out in my experience and that impressed me, and I believe they apply to at least some people of the particular country. While each country is beautifully unique, there are broader themes that run through all the countries. They are discussed in some more detail in the conclusion.

I hope this book can inspire you to see some aspects of the countries I talk about in a new or different light, and that some of the inspirations can serve you in your daily life, as well. Feel free to take whatever resonates with you and to leave the rest aside.

More than anything, this book intends to illustrate what we can learn or experience when we shift our mindset to focus on the positive attributes of a country and its people. The aim is not to see the world only through rose-colored glasses and to ignore important and challenging issues that need our attention. Instead, it aims to consciously focus on the positive take-aways: the positive things, people, and experiences, and the positive features that other countries and cultures can offer. I believe that travel and learning about other cultures and countries is a lifelong learning path. I am still far from always seeing the positive and from applying all the lessons I learned continually in my daily life, but it is a process. And I seek to continue to work with the values, attitudes, and mindsets that inspired me.

Ultimately, I believe that happiness, joy, balance, and the feeling of meaning and fulfillment come from within ourselves. Several techniques of the positive psychology movement can be beneficial in finding this space of deep contentment and inner peace. Yet, at the same time, we can learn a lot about achieving these states of mind by observing and exchanging with others. Given that we have such a rich diversity of cultures with varying customs, values, and beliefs in our world, it makes sense to open our eyes and make use of this richness and beauty!

GERMANY

Home, Sweet Home

> ❖ The Importance of Roots and Wings
>
> ❖ Learning from the Past and Finding Purpose
>
> ❖ The Upsides of Discipline, Positive Habits, and Perseverance
>
> ❖ Work Hard, Party Hard

We have no influence on where we are born in the world. Yet the region, the country, and the family we are born into will have a deep influence on our identities and lives. I was born in Germany in 1983. My parents came from a small village in Germany's Mosel Valley. My older brother was born in Trier, where my mother completed her university studies in psychology. I was born about two years later in Wuppertal, where my parents had moved due to my father's job with an international company.

Even though I spent most of my childhood years (with the exception of a few-months' stay in the U.S.) in Germany, I had from early on developed a curiosity and interest for other countries, cultures, and costumes. I love having my roots in Germany and to this day appreciate a lot of things in my home country. And at the same time, I love traveling, living in other countries and experiencing other ways of living and thinking. Hence, this first chapter on my very personal journey through the world starts in Germany and will talk about some lessons I learned in my home country.

The Importance of Roots and Wings

Two of the greatest gifts we can give
our children are roots and wings.

—Universal saying, attributed to multiple people[1]

This famous quote says that children need both roots and wings to be able to thrive in life. The saying implies that one of the greatest gifts that parents can give their children is creating a warm, loving home for them, where they feel safe and experience a natural sense of belonging, connection, unconditional love, and support that will eventually lead them to go out, explore, and lead the life they want to live. Having a strong sense of deep belonging and knowing that the family will stand behind them no matter what allows children to grow into autonomous, thoughtful adults who are willing to step out of their comfort zones and explore the world and discover their place in it. With the necessary amount of love and trust, children find it easier to later spread their wings and fly. And at the same time, it is likely that they will always return home voluntarily to reconnect.

While this saying is used globally, for me, it is strongly related to Germany, my home country, and to my family. My home had always been a pleasant mixture of different influences. While my father worked for a multinational company that required him to travel around the world quite frequently, my mother had set up her own psychology practice in our house, welcoming her patients there. My parents, my older brother, and I always had a very close bond, and I remember the many evenings and vacations when we discussed God and the world, usually with a good glass of Fuhrmann wine— given that large parts of my extended family are wine growers or otherwise involved in the wine business in Germany's Mosel Valley. Looking back at it now, I believe that my parents managed in a wonderful way to provide my brother and me with strong roots while at the same time awakening our curiosity to go out into the world and make our own way.

At some point after high school, I was living in Mexico doing my voluntary social service, and my brother moved to Chile for a university semester abroad. During that time, friends, and acquaintances often jokingly asked my parents why their children had migrated to the other side of the world. My parents would then often cite my grandmother, who used to say: *"Ships are safest in the harbor, but that is not what they were built for."*[2] Despite the geographical distance that was often between us when we lived in different countries or even continents, we felt an emotional closeness that no geographical distance could take from us. Thanks to new technology, we stay in very close touch, no matter where we live. Sometimes, we have virtual coffee or wine meet-ups, and it feels almost like sitting together in the same room.

Having Strong Roots

Like a tree that needs strong roots in order to grow, children need roots to feel safe and a sense of belonging so they can start growing to their unique potential. I always liked the image of a firmly rooted tree that rises to greet the sun, and I wish to provide this to our children. I will always be grateful for the safe and loving haven my parents provided to my brother and me throughout our lives. I loved to come home after kindergarten and school. My mom worked in the mornings and always welcomed my brother and me with lunch, then we would sit together and talk about our experiences. It became a natural ritual, and in retrospect, I notice that it helped me process experiences and feelings every day. In fact, our best conversations often happened when cleaning up the kitchen after lunch. My mom used to say *"Viele Hände, schnelles Ende,"* which translates roughly to *"If there are many hands, we finish quickly."* So, while doing the dishes together, we often had the most engaging discussions about news, fun things, or issues that troubled us. After my brother and I moved out, my parents always welcomed us with so much love when we returned home. Usually, we would start with a glass of champagne to celebrate our reunion and turn on some piano and saxophone music or Whitney Houston or Celine Dion, two of my father's favorite singers. Then we just took the time to sit together and hear about our current lives. I still appreciate these conversations so much. My father with his humorous, supportive style, always told us the newest jokes he discovered to make us laugh. He also loves world affairs, and we could discuss just about anything with him. And my mom, with her empathetic, loving style, would ask questions in a subtle way so I could easily share my thoughts, worries, and things going on in life.

I notice now how important these conversations were and how important it is for children to sit down with their parents and share what is going on in their minds. To create this kind of caring environment, it is necessary to spend some time together. How that is done can, of course, be very different for each family. But taking time out in the morning, at lunch time, in the evening, or on weekends to eat, sit together, and talk is so important to create these moments of connection and support. I always appreciated my parents' credo, which was: *"You can tell us everything, but you don't* have *to tell us anything.*" So, we felt inspired to share our stories or thoughts voluntarily. This approach is a very powerful one, which I would love to use with our children, as well. There might be moments when they don't feel like talking about something—and that's okay. Actually, even our three-year-old daughter tells me at times in the car when I pick her up from nursery: *"Ich möchte jetzt nicht erzählen, Mama."* (*"I don't want to speak now, mom."*) It usually happens when she feels tired or just doesn't feel like talking about the day. But often we start talking about something else, then quite naturally she shares how her day went and what she felt excited about. At times, we just turn on the music and sing or look out the window and comment on the landscape. I sometimes need to remind myself that it is okay if she is not in a talkative mood, but I still try to notice opportunities for conversation with her. Not only to hear about her day, but also because I just love to listen to her thoughts and theories about life as seen the world through the eyes of a three-year-old.

My parents also used to write down funny comments or theories that my brother and I came up with throughout the years. They kept them in a small booklet. They would pull it out from time to time, and it added a lot of humor and joy to our get-togethers. Often, we sat together in the evenings when we were growing up, reading through these comments and laughing whole-heartedly with the whole family or with visiting friends. They became running family jokes and sayings that to this day we occasionally quote. There can be a lot of wisdom in children's observations, and it's just wonderful to see the world from their perspective. So, recently, I have started writing down my daughter's remarks and theories that make me laugh or smile and compiled it into a little booklet at the end of the year. When I tell my husband or other people about it, our daughter often listens carefully, and I see how amused she is that we feel so much joy about her comments. We're not laughing at her, but rather it shows our appreciation for her thought processes. I have the feeling that many children like to be in the limelight for something funny they said. In *The Happiness Project*, Gretchen Rubin describes her intention to create "family treasures" in various forms. They can be pictures, photo collages, or, as she suggests, keeping a folder or a box for each family member in which one can easily store a nice drawing, a birthday invitation, a picture, or anything else from everyday life to keep as a nice memory for later years. In my opinion, this is a really nice idea, which can turn into a valuable treasure and helps nourish the roots that are so important.

Yet healthy families provide not only a secure environment for sharing, learning, and growing, but also build a sense of "we-ness" and belonging. For me, such a sense of "we-ness" often comes through a particular family language. Inside jokes that create some sort of intimacy or secret language that brings you closer together. My parents used to tell us anecdotes from their childhood and what people said in a certain moment, then quote these people when something similar happened in our lives. When my grandmother gave a certain name to our family dog based on the regional dialect one day, we just had to laugh. It sounded so sweet and funny that we often "quoted" her when talking about our dog. Or, when on our family trips, something funny would happen to us, we would often refer back to a certain phrase or word we used to describe a larger feeling or emotion. My husband and I use a lot of nicknames and made-up words. My husband is great at just inventing new words, and I have discovered the fun of it, as well. Since we use a mix of German and French at home, our family language is often a funny, messy mix of expressions, and, in a way, this feels very homey to me.

Spread Your Wings

I imagine that my love for traveling was partly encouraged by my father's love for it. He is a very active man who loves adventures and who was always keen to travel around the world, getting to know other countries and cultures. He's a "walking lexicon," as he knows so much about history, geopolitics, astronomy, and physics that he used to have an answer to any question I had during my school and university years. Working for an international company, he often traveled to the U.S., different European countries, China, India, Singapore, and Japan, and I remember how happy I always was when he came back from his business travels and had brought some small souvenirs from these countries for the family. While my parents loved to take us to Southern European countries for family vacations when we were small, at some point in our early teenage years, they decided it would be nice to show us some more parts of the world. So, they started organizing round-trips with lots of sightseeing activities to Nepal, India, China, Canada, and the U.S. for the whole family. Nowadays, I look back at these trips and experiences with gratitude. However, at that time, I sometimes envied my school friends who went on an easygoing vacation somewhere in the sun and came back to school relaxed and tanned, while I sometimes felt I needed vacation from our vacation. Yet, now I believe that these travels influenced my brother and me in that we both became interested in other countries and world politics. I listen much more carefully when hearing news about a country I lived in or traveled to, and I believe that the best foundation for lasting peace, international cooperation, and intercultural understanding is getting to know countries and people and their ways of living and thinking.

At the same time, I can say that I have felt and feel at home in many places in the world. In fact, I think that every country and city I lived in has left memorable traces in my heart, shaping me and leaving a lasting impression on my personality. The saying "Home is where your heart is" rings very true in this sense. And your heart can be split in between different places. While at times it can be difficult that you can't spend your daily life with all the wonderful friends you met across various countries, it is certainly a treasure to have friends around the world and to have felt at home in diverse parts of the world. And while I love keeping in touch with close friends that I made throughout my life journey, I also think that it's always important to have some people to hang out with in person. My father used to give me very good advice, which I continue to follow: *"Establish yourself comfortably where you live, no matter how long you live there. Even if it is for a few months, you should feel at home."* This advice from my dad, in combination with my mom's example of decorating homes in a cozy way, has helped me make myself comfortable in the most diverse parts of the world.

Spreading your wings, however, does not necessarily mean that you have to travel around the world. It is much more subtle. For me, spreading your wings refers to having the confidence to listen to your own unique dreams and to the inner voice that tells you what you want to do with your life. It can be anything that makes you feel passionate and alive. While writing this chapter, I reflected on all those persons who did not have the chance to have a secure, loving home that provided them with the roots I talked about. I do believe that such roots can help us to develop the confidence that our dreams and our aspirations matter and that we are worthy of being loved the way we are. Yet, at the same time, I believe that we can still learn to spread our wings—even if we faced hardships in our early lives. Some of the most inspiring people in this world went through a good number of hardships and came out even stronger for it. By trusting in our own inner force, we can surmount countless hindrances. Having a good support network—be it family, friends, or any other person or group of people who can help us to feel rooted and to start spreading our wings—is always of immense value. At the same time, the deepest form of belonging can be experienced when we are deeply rooted and grounded in ourselves—something we can keep working on our entire lives.

Having roots and a feeling of security and identity and at the same time wings that allow you to discover the world in your own way and at your own pace is a wonderful foundation for leading a happy, enriching, and fulfilled life. For those of us who are parents, it can be a nice exercise to think about concrete steps that we can take to help provide roots *and* wings for our children. We might ask, *what can I do so that they can spread their wings in the confident knowledge that deep inside they are rooted somewhere?* And for all of us, it can be deeply gratifying to not only have roots somewhere but to also help others feel rooted, so that we all feel confident choosing our paths and spreading our wings!

Learning from the Past and Finding Purpose

We Germans have a mixed reputation in the world. On the one hand, people describe us as efficient, hardworking, and punctual, while on the other hand, we inherited the description of being humorless, harsh, and direct, and possessing a language that sounds as if we were fighting all the time. The fact that our country initiated two World Wars also weighs quite heavily on us. But the German "economic miracle" and the fact that throughout the past seven decades Germany has made itself a name as a peaceful partner for many countries has helped lift some of the burden of its history.

I was often embarrassed as a child to drive with a German license plate on our car to our neighboring countries like the Netherlands or France. I thought that people must dislike us because of our nationality, and in some cases, I was probably right. And for a long time, I did not feel comfortable seeing German flags being waved around, mainly due to the nationalistic history that has marked my home country. During my time in high school, we learned in detail about Germany's history, the devastating World Wars, and the role that Germany played in them, particularly in World War II. We studied how anti-Semitism in the 20th century in several European countries found its sad peak when Hitler came to power in Germany and how, little by little, Jewish people were excluded from social life. We learned about the horrors of the persecution of the Jews and the concentration camps and the systematic ways they were managed, and we somehow tried to understand how normal human beings could be brainwashed into thinking they were superior to other human beings and had the right to extinguish them. I will always remember the sessions in our history class when Jewish survivors of the concentration camps came to visit us and talked about their experiences. Families had been torn apart; children had to watch their parents' murders and vice versa. And all of this in the name of keeping up a "superior race." I always wondered how people who had to live through all these humiliations and somehow survived managed to continue their life without falling into a deep sense of hatred and bitterness about their surroundings. And I felt impressed that some of those who had lived through these darkest hours came out particularly strong, with a heart ready to forgive and a will to make the best of life.

Victor Frankl, an Austrian neurologist and psychiatrist, was one of the Holocaust survivors who became particularly popular. He founded logotherapy, which focuses on the importance of discovering meaning in all its forms of existence as a reason to continue living. Some people have criticized Frankl's accounts of his experiences in the concentration camps for not representing the reality of most imprisoners correctly. Yet, his work was still very much appreciated in psychiatry and psychology circles around the world. It was translated into numerous languages and Frankl "became one of the key figures in existential therapy and a prominent source of inspiration for humanistic psychologists."[3]

This drive to say yes to life and to find a deeper meaning in one's existence, especially by someone who had to live through the horrors of the concentration camps and who lost his parents, his first wife and his brother during this time, has been inspiring for people around the world. People I met, from hotel owners in India to my yoga teacher in Switzerland, have told me that they felt inspired by his story. I recently read that Frankl sometimes asked his patients during the first logotherapy session: "Why do you not commit suicide?" And thinking about this question often revealed to people what their life purpose was. It could be personal (love for parents, a partner, children, or friends, or the willingness to experience a personal dream) or professional (a desire to finish a project or a career or work toward some broader goal) or a combination of both. While I found it quite a harsh question to ask during a first therapy session, with some reflection, I could see the value in it—since such questions can help us see what we live for in this world. A career coach I met asked another very inspiring question: "What do you want to be remembered for at the end of your life?" A very good question to help you reflect on what is truly important to you.

Coming back to Germany's history, I was impressed by the capability of some of the Holocaust survivors to move on and still make the most out of their lives, despite all their horrific experiences. For me as a German, I often felt guilty and helpless when learning about the horrors of this time. Yet, at the same time I felt that Germany was doing an important job in reprocessing history and the role that it played in it by teaching about the World Wars in much detail in school history classes. I hear sometimes that we are overdoing this historic review, and that nowadays generations have nothing to be blamed for anymore—that we should move on to the next chapter. And while I agree that contemporary generations should not be blamed for what happened in the 1930s and 1940s in Germany, I still feel that it is of immense importance to learn about our country's history and its flaws—in an attempt to understand how it

11

could come this far and to avoid something similar ever happening again.[i]

I found myself in a difficult position during this history revision process. On the one hand, I felt shocked by everything the Germans had done to the Jews and to other countries, and on the other hand, I loved my grandparents deeply even though I knew that they had been involved in the war in one way or another. I don't know the details of what my grandfathers were ordered to do when fighting in the war, but war is war, and the experiences must have been horrifying. I got to know only one grandfather personally; the other unfortunately died before I was born. I knew he struggled with nightmares from the war up to his death at 90 years old. He continued to emphasize that war was not good for anyone and that he would much rather have continued his life back home in the vineyards instead of going to war. When the Germans were defeated, my grandfather was a mere 19 years old, and he was kept in Russian imprisonment for four more years. While my grandfather initially never spoke about his war experiences, as he grew older, he started opening up and told my brother and me about some of his time as a prisoner of war. He talked about beatings, staring up the barrel of a gun, starving, and looking forward to eating a few potatoes at Christmas, but he always said he couldn't complain, because the Germans were the ones who had started the war. I admired his sense of reflection and endurance, and he will always be an example of someone who worked hard all his life and lovingly cared for his vineyard workers and his family.

What does all of this tell us about happiness and purpose, and what we can learn from Germany? I think that it is quite telling that some people from both sides of World War II managed to process their horrific experiences and find meaning in their lives. They spread

---

[i] Especially in today's world, where we have to observe increasing anti-Semitic movements again, I feel that digging into history and seeing the horrors that such sentiments can bring is of utmost importance.

love and harmony in their environments despite the brutalities they knew. This gives me hope that we human beings have deep inside us a fundamental goodness, which is worth nurturing. It can be so strong that it gives meaning to our lives and enables us to live a life full of purpose.

Despite the past of my home country, Germany stood up again after World War II, reconstructed itself with the support of the international community and some Western countries, which took it back into the democratic circle and peacefully reunited the divided East and West Germanies in 1990. I am personally still astonished and deeply grateful that this process took place peacefully. The quick economic reconstruction, often referred to as the "German economic miracle," which took place in the years following the war, keeps surprising people from the around world. It gave Germany the reputation of being a nation with lots of ambition, efficiency, and hard-working people. The will to learn from the past, to process it, and to persevere and improve are some traits that could be adopted when looking at Germany's history. On a more personal level, we can see that discovering our purpose and meaning in life, whatever form it might take, can not only help us surpass hardships but also develop a deeper sense of satisfaction and happiness in everyday life.

The Upsides of Discipline, Positive Habits, and Perseverance

In my mom's office, which sat between the room where she hosted her professional practice and the rest of the house, she had hung up a saying that struck me every time I entered the room. It read: "Discipline—at first it is difficult; afterward, it makes everything easier." I knew my mom lived by this saying. My mom is a lovely, beautiful, and whole-hearted person. She has the ability to listen and show such warm-hearted interest that people—even strangers—open up to her. I know many of my and my brother's friends loved coming to our place, not only to see us, but also because they enjoyed hanging out with my parents. My mom's sweet, empathic nature combined with my father's humorous, open-minded spirit, made people feel at ease in our home.

Discipline and Positive Habits

"Discipline" is one of the words often used to describe the typical German nature. It was one of the virtues—along with punctuality, diligence, and orderliness—that was propagated during the Prussian empire under Friedrich Wilhelm I. And it is entrenched in German society even now.[4] Many foreigners who visit or live in Germany have to get used to these sometimes seemingly rigid behaviors. When talking to foreigners who lived in Germany, I often had to smile when they told me that they were surprised that being punctual in Germany often means to arrive five or ten minutes early—even for casual encounters. In many cultures it is the norm to arrive a little later than the indicated time when it comes to more intimate meetings.

Both my parents are incredibly disciplined. While they enjoy spending time with family and friends and a good glass of wine in the evening, their motto is usually: *"Erst die Arbeit, dann das Vergnügen,"* which translates to *"Work first, play later."* I could see this discipline in all their daily actions. My mom always did whatever needed to be done before finally sitting down in front of the TV in the evening. This frequently led her to missing out on a movie or a show that she might have wanted to watch.

As for my father, some people might say that he is a workaholic—in a positive sense. Despite putting in long, sometimes stressful hours at work, he never complained about his job. For many years he made long commutes by car to prevent us from having to change countries to move closer to his work in the Netherlands. Even though it took him one or two hours to get to work, he never complained about leaving early in the morning and returning home rather late. After having dinner together and discussing our day, he would continue answering emails until late in the evening. He did this for more than 40 years. Even after officially retiring, he has kept working for several companies on a consultancy basis. He continues to enjoy it, and it shows the work and attitude of commitment engrained in him.

He is also a person who always has the bigger picture in mind. When I was in high school, at the start of each school year, he would ask my brother and me about our goals. They could be school-related, personal, or include such things as getting a driver's license. My parents would then help us identify the steps that we needed to take to achieve our goals. Looking back, I am very happy about this support. We were usually quite proud when, at the end of the year, we looked back on our goal sheets and could check some of them off. Despite these goal-setting exercises, my parents avoided exerting pressure on us in terms of grades or hobbies. They never wanted my brother or me to come home afraid because of a bad grade at school. So they told us that if we ever failed an exam, we would go and have ice cream to deal with the disappointment. They also never obligated me to sit down for long hours to practice piano. They explained that playing piano should be something fun and relaxing for me, not an extra chore. This kind of attitude helped us enjoy what we did or had to do. So, while both of my parents were themselves very disciplined, they were never severe or rigid in their behavior.

As for characteristic Prussian virtues, I often did not feel typically German. Punctuality was never one of my strengths and I have followed several time-management courses to improve myself. In my group of friends, I always had the reputation of being the one who would arrive a little late. Often, they would indicate an earlier

15

time—for example half an hour before the actual meeting time—to make sure that I made it on time. My international friends also remarked that I did not seem to be truly German in my behaviors. And I never particularly liked the above-mentioned saying about discipline that I saw every time I entered my mom's office. For me it had a strict and rigid connotation, and I never really liked the word *discipline* for some reason. I admired disciplined people since they got done what needed to get done. But I also admired people who could relax in the middle of chaos and take a break, even if they had not finished everything on their to-do list yet. I observed this attitude more often during my time in Mexico. Personally, I often leaned toward the latter approach, which frequently led to last-minute efforts to meet a deadline. But somehow, I felt that I just needed the freedom to see when my natural "flow" would set in.

I have learned over time that having more structure and discipline in my daily routine can make life much less stressful. For long-term projects like completing a Ph.D. or writing a book, it is indispensable to plan ahead and stick to a certain schedule. Otherwise, you might not finish. And many studies show that small, continuous steps are often the ones that move us forward with our endeavors. But, even knowing this, it's easier said than done. I recently became aware that I could still learn a lot in this regard, when I took stock of some of my common at-home behaviors. My husband has the habit of unpacking his suitcases as soon as he gets home from vacation or a business trip. He is disciplined like my mother and father in this way, and it might be one reason they get along so well. In contrast, my suitcase can sit half open in our bedroom for days or even weeks. And I am very proud if, after a week or two, I manage to unpack it completely. But after our last trip, I forced myself to unpack my suitcase within two days after arriving home. This small step meant huge progress for me.

In *The Happiness Project*, Gretchen Rubin proposes a similar long-term technique. She advises us to clean up for 10 minutes every morning or evening to avoid reverting to a state of chaos at home. Her book *Outer Order, Inner Calm* has great advice about how to create more orderliness in your home. This in turn can help to clear up space in your mind. Discipline can make daily life easier. For example, making a grocery list and sticking to it is a way we can avoid buying the tempting sweets or products we would like to stop eating. It makes it much easier to not give into temptation later on at home. Even more important than self-discipline is an environment for creating new, better habits that we want to stick to. James Clear explains this in detail in his eye-opening book *Atomic Habits*. He claims that people who appear very disciplined are usually those who don't put themselves in the way of temptation. They create positive habits and an environment in which less discipline is needed to stay on track. Since repetition is what makes a habit become automatic, it's important to repeatedly work on things that are important to us. The philosopher Will Durant said: "We are what we repeatedly do. Excellence, then, is not an act, but a habit."[5] I also like to remind myself of a phrase by the American leadership expert John C. Maxwell: "You will never change your life until you change something that you do daily. The secret of success is found in your daily routine."[6] With this in mind, "discipline" has a much more positive connotation.

The saying that welcomed me every time I entered my mom's office makes much more sense to me now and no longer yields my initial reluctance. Even though it requires some extra effort and will-power to be disciplined, it can make the rest of life much easier. It is up to each person to decide which kind of things he or she wants to be disciplined about. It can relate to anything that is important to us: sports, healthy cooking, a passion project, or such daily tasks as putting out the clothes for the next day to avoid losing precious time in the morning. I personally like the idea of having a bigger vision for one's life—a bigger picture of what we would like to achieve and how we would like to be. Then, I like to define small steps that can get me there. It is something that many personal development coaches propose. And something that my parents tried to teach my brother and me from early on, when we sat down together to establish our yearly dream and action plans.

Perseverance

Another term often mentioned when talking about the German nature is perseverance. Again, perseverance is not an attribute found exclusively in Germany, and it depicts much more of a personal trait than a cultural one. Yet, it is one of the typical Prussian virtues that has had an influence on the German culture. And it is something my husband regularly points out when talking about his German wife. He often laughs at my—in his words—"stubborn" ability to finish what I had intended to do in one way or another.

I know of occasions when I was perseverant and of occasions when I was not. In retrospect, I can say that I am much happier about the situations when I was able to stay resilient. For example, when I arrived in Mexico and started doubting that my decision to live there for a year and a half had been a good one, my parents suggested that I at least try it out for a few months. I gave myself from July to Christmas to see if I would like it. When Christmas came, I appreciated life in Mexico so much that I didn't think again about cutting my stay short. Instead, I thought about prolonging it! I had a similar experience in Maastricht during the first semester of my Bachelor's program, when I felt a lot of pressure and struggled to keep up with the enormous study load. After a couple of months, I considered calling it off. Yet, again, I pushed myself to try it for at least one semester. After this first hard semester, I had gotten used to the rhythm and even enjoyed learning at this fast pace. But,

I've also experienced how it feels when I was not very perseverant. After completing my Ph.D., I wanted to publish a couple of short articles out of the lengthy Ph.D. thesis I had written. However, I submitted my article drafts to only a couple of journals. When it didn't work out with them on the first try, I gave up and put them aside. Certainly, there were many reasons for my decision. We had just moved to Japan; I had given birth to our first daughter and suffered from complications; and I wanted to focus on our baby and on learning more about the Japanese language and culture. Yet, the underlying feeling that I hadn't tried hard enough to make it work stayed with me for quite a long time. It is important to know that you do have the option to call something off if it really doesn't work for you. But it feels much better to call something off when you know that you really tried hard to make it work.

I recently came across the concept of "The 20 Mile March." It implies that the quickest and least exhausting way to reach your goal is to keep moving forward with little steps on a continual basis. For example, a hike across the U.S.: it's much more efficient to march 20 miles a day on a continuous basis, rain or shine, than to exhaust yourself on some days and not advance at all on other ones.[7] It is perseverance on a daily basis that helps to steadily move us toward our dreams and goals.

And while persistence and a certain degree of discipline or well-established habits can be very useful to realize our ambitions, I believe that at the same time it is important to not put ourselves too much under pressure. Life is life, and unexpected things happen all the time that can throw us off the path for a while. Yet, while we may take things slower or put them aside temporarily, it really is about coming back to our goals or visions again afterward. Robyn Conley Downs developed a great method for this, which she describes in her book *The Feel Good Effect*. Her "Two Out of Three Rule" can help whenever you slip up or make a mistake or misstep in terms of your desired routine. For example, if you missed one workout, make sure that you show up for the coming two. If you procrastinated one morning on an important task, make sure that for the coming two work periods you keep focused. It's about doing what you set out to do on more days than you don't. This rule can help us to release ourselves from feeling overwhelmed or not good enough when we've failed once. What counts is the persistence to come back to whatever goal or ambition we set out to do.

For longer-term projects, it's a very personal choice to decide how hard you need to try to feel good about yourself, no matter whether or not you finish it or you decide to call it off in the end. There is a famous saying that says, "Perseverance leads to success." When looking at big movie stars, famous authors, and renowned scientists, one thing seems to be true for all: they didn't get where they are by giving up after the first rejection or even after the hundredth rejection. They knew where they wanted to go and they found ways to get there. If Option A didn't work out, they would look for a Plan B. Rachel Hollis, a famous motivational speaker, podcaster, and author, encourages her readers in her book *Girl, Wash Your Face* that hearing a *no* is not a reason to stop following your dreams. I often remind myself of one of her claims: "If you can't get through the front door, try the side window. If the window is locked, maybe you slide down the chimney. No doesn't mean that you stop; it simply means that you change course in order to make it to your destination."[8]

I admire people who have such strong determination. It requires you to hold down your inner critical voices of self-doubt and overcome the humiliating feeling of rejection. Rejection shouldn't be taken personally but seen as another lesson or a motivation to try even harder. The same is true for failures. Failures are lessons that bring us closer to where we want to be, if we are able to learn from them and use them for motivation.

As the concepts of discipline and perseverance are sometimes attributed to the typical German nature, I decided to include them in this chapter. But I believe they have more to do with personal traits than with cultural heritage. Even though it can at times be hard to develop and stick to these virtues, they can have extremely beneficial effects on our lives. So why not reflect on some areas in your life in which a positive new habit or a resilient, perseverant attitude could help you advance toward your goals and, little by little, build that dream life you have in your mind?

Work Hard, Party Hard

Antoine looked at me with a glance that expressed that he couldn't believe what he had gotten into. The bride and the groom had just stepped up on their chairs and started dancing to the rhythm of the music and to the applause of the wedding guests. The room transformed into a cheerful crowd of clapping people.

In May 2010, we went to Germany to celebrate the wedding of one of my best and closest childhood friends. We were sitting at the bride and groom's table next to the bride's mother. Even before the dinner started, my friend's mom took one of the schnapps bottles off the table, poured a glass for my husband, Antoine, and toasted with him, saying that it would be a wonderful evening. Antoine first looked at me in astonishment but then started laughing and joined in. Before dessert was served, the atmosphere had come to a point where not only was everyone swaying in their places, but many people had climbed onto their chairs to dance to the DJ's sounds. Antoine could not believe his eyes. This was far from a rigid, formal wedding that he might have expected in Germany. Soon all of us were happily dancing on the chairs. He later told me that he never believed that Germans were able to party so well. And now, often times when he listens to German *Schlager* music, he laughs and starts dancing and singing to the funny lyrics.[ii]

Despite the Prussian virtues, which might give the impression that Germans are disciplined workaholics, one should not underestimate how well Germans know how to party. There is a famous saying in Germany, which goes: *"Wer feste arbeitet, darf auch Feste feiern,"* which can be roughly translated to "He who works hard is also allowed to party hard." Indeed, the German word *Feierabend*, which refers to after-work hours, consists of the words *feiern* (celebrate) and *Abend* (evening). It expresses that once the work is finished, evenings are there to celebrate or at least to wind down somehow.

Germany is well-known for its famous Oktoberfest, which usually takes place in late September and early October in Munich, in Bavaria. Even though I have not yet visited the Oktoberfest in Munich—it's on my bucket list—I have attended versions of Oktoberfest in other countries. Some of my most memorable experiences stem from the times when we joined iterations of Oktoberfest in China and Japan. In Beijing, we were invited by the German embassy to an Oktoberfest. It was a wonderful experience observing how enthusiastically the Chinese people participated in this celebration. In Tokyo, Antoine and I came upon an Oktoberfest at one of Tokyo's shores by coincidence. And it was so much fun! Hundreds of Japanese people had gathered in front of the stage where a German *Schlager* band was singing typical *Schlager* songs. People were clapping, laughing, and toasting each other with beer. And I was extremely happy about the little booths selling sausages, the famous pretzels, and other typical German treats. It felt like a cliché, but I enjoyed the evening to the fullest. It was a great

---

[ii] Schlager music is a type of pop music in many European countries, often with happy or sentimental lyrics and upbeat instrumental accompaniment that animates people to dance or sing along.

experience seeing people from the other side of the world really enjoying this traditional German festival so much.

Yet, Germany is not only known for the variety of beers it has to offer, but also for its wine regions, particularly the one in the German Mosel Valley. When you enter the state of Rhineland-Palatinate, you find areas where one village after another is filled with wine taverns offering tastings and where vineyards surround you as far as the eye can see. My parents were both born in the same little village in the Mosel Valley. And both families were involved in the wine business and in vineyard work. Even though my parents moved away from their village during their university years, the wine culture remained very present in our family. It was quite common for us to have a glass of Fuhrmann wine with dinner or while philosophizing after dinner late in the evenings. Often my father would conclude our evening conversations with a humorous smile and the words: "Now, that we have solved all the problems in the world, we can go to bed." I don't mean to praise the effects of wine too much here, as you can have as much fun without drinking any alcohol. Yet, our evenings philosophizing about God and the world with a glass of wine in our hands form a very tangible part of my happy memories.

Even as a child, I loved attending the wine festivals which took place once a year in that Mosel village. People would be elected and dress up as Bacchus and wine queens and parade by the villages on wagons. At the end of the procession, everyone would meet at the village's fairground and celebrate together. Also, during celebrations with our extended family, people would dance and sway to the music while sitting down, arms linked with the people to the left and to the right. Germans even created a word for this swaying, *schunkeln*, which has no real English translation.

During such moments, it seems difficult to imagine that those swaying people are usually known for their sense of punctuality, discipline, and orderliness. But I think that this is the beauty of it all: each country has such diversity to offer in terms of customs, habits, and attitudes. In the end, it is about finding the right balance, as with everything in life. My grandfather used to say to his children when they had been out celebrating until late and needed to get up early to help in the vineyard: *"Wer feiern kann, kann auch arbeiten,"* which translates to "One who is able to celebrate, is able to work, as well." Yet, this is also true the other way around. He or she who works—and I mean all kinds of work here, be it in an office, in other work environments, or at home with the children—also has the right to celebrate and to let go. And this letting go or celebrating can take many forms, depending very much on what feels good to you at the moment. At one point in time, it could be gathering with friends to eat, drink, or party until late. At another time it could just be taking time for whatever makes you feel happy and relaxed. Life and success coaches have emphasized this time and time again. In order to be successful with one's projects and goals, it is important to celebrate the little milestones on the way and to consciously take time for what makes you feel good. This is very important in order to recharge your batteries and to be effective and motivated at work again. So, let's remember, from time to time, the saying: "To work hard, to party hard, and then to work hard again!"

Beautiful Lessons Learned from Germany

* **Provide roots and a feeling of unconditional love and acceptance to your children, your family, and your friends.** It is one of the most beautiful presents we can give. Deep roots of connection and the confidence to be loved unconditionally allows people to spread their wings and explore the beauties of this world!

* **Be open to learn from the past,** as learning from the past can be our most powerful teacher for proactively influencing our future for the positive.

* **Focus on what is meaningful in your life and what gives you purpose.** It can help to live through hardships and enjoy a deeper sense of satisfaction and happiness in everyday life.

* **Try to create positive habits and a perseverant attitude for dreams and ambitions that are important to you.** Installing positive habits can make it much easier to be disciplined about them. And perseverance in endeavors that are important to us will help us achieve our dreams and ambitions.

* **Work hard and party hard.** In order to fully show up for our personal and professional goals and commitments, it is important to take time to wind down, relax, and celebrate what we have already achieved. These moments of relaxation and celebration will charge our batteries to go back to work motivated and energized.

USA

Think Big and Dream Big

❖ **The Belief in Freedom, Dreams,
and Opportunities**

❖ **The Power of Assertiveness**

❖ **Friendly Daily Interactions**

❖ **Team Spirit, Encouragement,
and the Power of "Not Yet"**

W e were standing in the airport hall and my parents looked at me. "Will you be all right, dear?" I looked at them enthusiastically and said, "Yes, I think it will be great, even though I'll miss you very much." And then I gave them a deep hug, kissed them goodbye, and turned around to go to the security check and the gate.

At 16, I embarked on my first adventure all by myself abroad. Some years before I had visited the West Coast of the States together with my family. But this was the first time I'd be moving abroad by myself. Together with one of my closest childhood friends, we had heard about the option to apply for a high-school semester in the U.S. We were so excited about it that we immediately started looking for ways to do something like this as well.

A few months earlier, I had met a girl in school who had lived in various countries around the world. Her parents were diplomats, and I was deeply impressed by her natural ease switching between German, English, and French. I reflected on how nice it would be to live abroad, have new experiences, and learn other languages. And then there were of course all my U.S. idols! I grew up in the 1980s and 1990s in Germany and had been a fan of several U.S. television series since my early teen years. One of them was *Beverly Hills 90210*. I looked forward to every Saturday when the series would run. It depicted the everyday life of a group of friends at a high school in Beverly Hills, California. I loved the characters and imagined how cool high-school life in the U.S. must be. My brother and I also loved to watch American action series like *Knight Rider* or *The A-Team*, which portrayed various hero characters. I imagined the U.S. to be a place full of adventures and smart, interesting people.

To apply for the exchange program abroad, I had to prepare an application package. I remember devoting a lot of time to preparing a detailed photo collage of my entire family and myself in order to present myself to my future host family. When I learned that I had been accepted into the exchange program, I almost exploded with excitement. The next five or six months I would be living with a host family who had two teenage girls around my age in a suburb of Portland, Oregon. I couldn't believe my luck. So, there I was, 16 and ready to take up the adventure to explore the country of unlimited opportunities.

The Belief in Freedom, Dreams, and Opportunities

One of the first things I noticed when arriving in the U.S. was that everything seemed larger and bigger in comparison to what I knew from Europe: the roads, the highways, the cars, and even the house telephone, the shampoo bottles, and the vacuum cleaner at my host family's place.[i] I experienced that feeling of vastness, space, and a sense of liberty and freedom already during the road trip to the U.S. West Coast with my family a few years earlier. Sometimes we were driving for hours on wide roads surrounded by the most amazing natural landscapes one could think of. This time, in Oregon, I again enjoyed observing the large roads and the many city lights on my way to school. And once again, I experienced this feeling of spaciousness, excitement, and freedom.

I am not sure where this feeling came from. Maybe it has something to do with the fact that the United States with its 9.73 million km^2 is the fourth largest country in the world by area.[i] There is a lot of space, and knowing that you can drive for days without passing any country border can provide a sense of freedom and vastness. But there was more to it than the mere geographical dimensions. There was an omnipresent sense of liberty and big thinking in the minds of many people I met, as well. The U.S. with its history as a nation of immigrants has for centuries been portrayed as the country of unlimited opportunities. Of course, reality often plays out differently. Important ongoing discrimination debates show that background, race, and gender often continue to play an important role in terms of opportunities. At the same time, the country was

---

[i] When I moved back home to Germany, everything seemed in contrast so little and narrow that I sometimes felt like having stepped into Alice's wonderland.

for a long time known for being a true melting pot.[ii] Immigrants with Asian, African, and European descent all intermingled in this vast country. Some people argue that an assimilation has taken place among the various cultural influences. Others point out that aspects of different cultural backgrounds always remain distinct. Regardless of this, I find it impressive how people from all over the world have come together in the United States and formed this nation, which embodies freedom and opportunities for many. Believing that the sky is the limit is a mindset that keeps being exported through movies, songs, and political speeches coming from the U.S.

What amazes me about American friends and acquaintances that I have met throughout my life is the positive attitude that many display. A challenging situation is often times described as "an opportunity for growth." And criticisms would frequently be expressed kindly, using phrases like, "There's some room for improvement." I feel that such an attitude toward making the best out of situations can be extremely helpful in everyday life. And it is much more motivational than harsh or negative forms of criticism. A positive attitude can make it much easier to stir behavior into a proactive, positive direction. Such a "can-do" attitude is also represented in the "rags-to-riches" stories that many of us associate with the U.S. The underlying assumption that anyone working hard enough can create a successful life is part of this. While such stories may be clichés, I like the underlying idea behind them: to have a dream and to go for it and give it your all in order to reach it. This is not to say that every American person is doing exactly this—even though it would be nice if they did. But rather to say that many of those people who have become influential on a global stage repeated this motto and have made their dreams become a reality. Martin Luther King, Jr., used to say, "If you can't fly, then run. If you can't run, then walk.

[ii] Or, in Jimmy Carter's words, "a beautiful mosaic:" "We have become not a melting pot, but a beautiful mosaic. Different people, different beliefs, different yearnings, different hopes, different dreams."

If you can't walk, then crawl, but whatever you do, you have to keep moving forward."

The will to keep moving forward seems to form part of any personal success story, be it Oprah Winfrey, who started her famous talk show after she noticed that she did not feel at ease in her role as a reporter; Ellen DeGeneres, who kept pushing forward despite the hardships that she experienced when she came out; or Lady Gaga, who repeated insistently after the movie success of *A Star is Born* that everyone should believe and work hard for his or her own dreams. Quite certainly, any movie or pop star who has made it to the global stage has kept moving forward, despite obstacles and hindrances along the way. While this is not something specific to U.S. society, for me, the U.S. had always represented a pioneer role in terms of opportunities and embodying self-realization.

Studies have shown that it's the little daily steps and habits that help people to achieve their dreams. It is wonderful to have dreams and it is great to dream big. Yet a dream remains a dream until you start acting on it. The famous Walt Disney, who has influenced generations with movies, used to say: "The way to get started is to quit talking and begin doing." This is simple but very practical advice. Once you start to analyze what it takes to achieve or live your dream, you can break down the necessary steps into small, doable bites and start moving toward this dream of yours. For a person wanting to write a book, it can consist of writing a few hundred words a day. For someone wanting to set up their own business, it can be to do market research or to create a website. What is crucial is to create a road plan of how to get from A to B and to make the steps on the way manageable and tangible, so that they can actually be done.

Closely related to thinking and dreaming big is the idea of letting go of limiting beliefs. So many inspirational quotes relay the same message over and over again. Limits are mainly created by our own limiting beliefs. Often, we are our own biggest critics and the main hindrance to our dreams coming true. It might not even be our conscious beliefs but our subconscious mind telling us that we won't be able to do or become something or that we are not worthy of something. But at the same time, there exist powerful tools to help rewire our brain little by little to change these limiting beliefs for the positive. Our attitude to things can play a crucial part in this process. As one saying goes: "We can't change what happens to us in life, but we have the biggest power of all: our attitude about everything." And I think that this is an immensely powerful thought. Of course, agreeing to such a saying is much easier than really implementing it in everyday life. And I speak of experience when saying this as I can still improve myself very much in this regard. Yet, becoming aware that it is in our power to choose our thoughts and our attitudes toward life circumstances is the first step. Changing our thoughts and attitudes for the better is a second step. And with this, little by little, we can let go of limiting beliefs and work toward our envisioned dream lives.

The Power of Assertiveness

Another trait that I observed time and again in the U.S. was the power of assertiveness. I will always remember the political science teacher in the high school I attended. We were supposed to write an essay about the pros and cons of medically assisted suicide and make our own opinion about it. In my previous education, I had learned the structure of thesis, antithesis, synthesis, and conclusion. In Germany, I would usually start my essays with a general introduction to the topic, then discuss the issue in much detail before coming to a cautiously formulated conclusion. Even if I was in favor of one position, I would usually not completely disregard the other one. In the U.S., I had to adapt my writing style. Our political science teacher made it quite clear from the beginning when saying: "I want to know from the first sentence in your essay whether you are in favor of the policy or not. If I can't see that from the first sentence, no matter how good your arguments, you failed." For me this was quite stressful. I was not used to this kind of assertiveness and clarity, yet I understood that here I had to adapt my style and I did.

On one hand, taking up such a clear position can seem like promoting a black-and-white attitude toward issues. On the other hand, I also believe that clearly taking a position and standing up for it allows people to move forward. I continue to believe that it is good and important to be well-informed about the different pros and cons when making any decision. However, at some point, it is also important to take the first step in one direction in order to move forward. This can be observed in the realm of politics. The U.S. is, for example, generally much quicker in making decisions and acting on them than its European partners. In a way, this is not surprising. It takes time for the European Union with its 27 member states to agree on a position before being able to take action in conjunction. Yet, sometimes this makes the EU appear to be a bystander, rather than a union that proactively takes action in world affairs.

On a more personal level, it is not much different. If one takes too long to make a decision, a lot of precious time and energy is spent on the decision-making process itself. If fear of making a decision leads to not making any decision at all, this can create the paralyzing feeling of being a passive, impotent bystander, not the one sitting in the driver's seat of one's own life. If, in contrast, a decision is made, it is possible to proactively move on and work toward the defined goal. Of course, it is advisable to use the best possible knowledge and the natural gut feeling when making any decision. But even if the decision leads to some sort of failure, it can be regarded as "failing forward" and as a lesson learned that can pave the way for the future. Winston Churchill said, "Success consists of going from failure to failure without loss of enthusiasm." This is quite a nice saying to keep in mind when something is not going exactly the way we wish it to go.

In terms of assertiveness and standing up for one's position, I was impressed by the account of the American philanthropist Melinda Gates, who runs the famous Bill and Melinda Gates Foundation with her husband. In her book *The Moment of Lift*, she describes very honestly how it took her a long time to finally take up a public role in the foundation's work and to publicly advocate for family-planning services. She says that she found herself in internal conflict. She knew that family planning is a politically charged topic and that she might run into difficult public discussions when advocating for this topic. However, at the same time, she had learned throughout the years at the foundation how much family-planning services could help: for women's empowerment and also for the prevention of many tragic child and mother deaths. So, despite being uncomfortable openly addressing such a hot topic, she finally made the choice to do so anyway. Her deep conviction of its importance made her take this step. For me, this story was very inspiring. We might face difficulties or uncomfortable situations when standing up for a position or when advocating for a topic that is important to us. And it may take some time until we feel mentally ready for it. Nevertheless, I admire those people who stand up for their beliefs and convictions in a respectful manner. And who are as assertive as my political science teacher back in U.S. high school asked us to be.

Friendly Daily Interactions

"Sweetie, can I help you with anything?" When I heard these words from the lady in the shop, I first wondered if she was talking to me. "Sweetie" was for me an expression reserved for your partner, very close friends,

or family members. I looked around, but there was no one but me. She repeated: "Do you need any help with choosing, dear?"

It was not the last time that I was addressed with names such as *sweetie, dear,* or *honey* by people I barely knew in shops, at school events, or at people's homes. First, I was not sure how to react to it or what to think of it. In Germany, we are often more cautious with such words and sometimes tend to label the quick use of these words as superficial. But in a way I enjoyed being addressed that nicely several times a day. And I felt flattered by it. Of course, you should not assume that being called this way automatically means that you are, in fact, emotionally close to the person speaking. Yet somehow it made daily interactions much kinder and happier. In a study on this subject, Sandstrom and Dunn (2013) analyze the relationship between weak ties (i.e., acquaintances) and well-being. The authors conducted several experiments and found that "people with more weak-tie relationships reported being happier."[2] They also found that having genuine social interaction with people you meet in everyday life—like with a cashier at Starbucks—led people to have a more positive mood than if they only focused on an efficient interaction. The important role that close ties with family members and friends play for people's well-being has been well documented. It is interesting, however, to notice that the interaction with loose acquaintances or "weak ties" can lighten up our days, as well.

For me personally, I have noticed that I enjoy daily friendly interactions with people I only know superficially. I start feeling at home somewhere much more easily when I know the people in the next-door supermarket, bakery, or pharmacy. I also enjoy the quick exchanges with other mothers or the educators at the kindergarten my daughter attends when picking her up. And even friendly interactions with people I might only meet once in my life, like a seat neighbor in the plane or a cashier at an airport, can positively influence my mood.

I once saw a social media video where one person starts her day in a bad mood, then passes on this mood to some random person on her way to work. This person consequently gets upset and passes it on to another person at the next occasion. This goes on and on, and it shows how this cycle of negativity can spin across many people easily when they let themselves be influenced by it. At the end of the video, the woman who started off this cycle notices the bad influence that her mood had, not only on herself, but also on many additional people as the bad mood was transferred from person to person. She then decides to consciously make a change and start her day with friendly interactions with other people. They, in turn, pay forward this kindness to the next people they encounter as well.

This kind of experience might have happened to you, too. Maybe you have a bad day, and negative events, encounters, or news keep piling up. It may seem as if the universe has turned against you on such a day. I sometimes have these days when—as you say in German—I get up with the wrong foot. And as a consequence, everything seems difficult and becomes more and more difficult throughout the day. On such days, I just feel like going back to bed, hiding under the sheets, and waiting for the next day to come. And certainly, we can't always have wonderful days. As one saying goes, "For there to be light, there must be darkness." We can't feel enthusiastic and happy all the time; it is human to also have other feelings. Yet, I have noticed that despite having a bad day or a bad mood, it is sometimes possible to consciously put an end to these emotions. By accepting them, acknowledging them and then letting them pass by. I'm working on this myself when I feel upset because of something or someone. I try telling myself then that it is fine to feel this way. But then I try to consciously choose to leave this negative feeling behind and to move on in order not to destroy the rest of my day. If I'm angry with someone, it sometimes helps me to have a compassionate thought for this person. Often a person who acts rude or unfair is struggling with something in his or her life at that moment. I know it from experience that when I'm not in a good emotional or mental state, it shows in my behavior with others. It's good to realize that rude behavior from someone else is often not about you but about the person from who it comes from. It's not worth giving it too much attention or power over your mood or your day.

There are times when I manage to think like that and times when I don't. Sometimes when our family mornings start in a strange mood, my husband and I look at each other and realize that we started on the wrong foot. And in some cases, we manage to take it with humor and say that we want to press the reset button and start our day again in a nicer atmosphere. It is definitely something we keep working on. Recently I bought the book *Emotional Advantage* by Randy Taran, who started a very inspiring project called Project Happiness. It explains that it is normal and human to have pleasant and not-so-pleasant emotions. And the negative emotions are important, as they might show or teach us something important that we need to change or work on. While emotions come and go, it is up to us how we react to them. I know that I can still learn quite a bit in terms of my emotional management. My husband often describes me as a volcano that is calm for a long time and then just explodes. My mom used to say that this is the sting of the scorpion, my astrological sign. She told me that she considers me to be generally a very patient person, but if something goes too far for me, my stinger comes out. So, I can definitely keep learning about managing my emotions.

Coming back to everyday interactions with acquaintances, it can make a huge difference if people treat each other with kindness. And if they address each other with a nice greeting or a word of encouragement. It is very much related to the idea of "paying it forward." This implies that you pay the support or kindness you received from someone forward to another person. Let's be honest. If the lady in the shop is in a bad mood and makes no effort to be helpful, this can have a short or long-term influence on your mood as well. Nevertheless, it is possible to break this cycle of negativity by shaking off the feeling of frustration, anger, or disappointment once leaving the shop. And the same is true in reverse. If people treat you nicely while grocery shopping or buying your train ticket, these daily interactions become much more pleasant. And this can have a positive impact on your mood, which can then be forwarded to the next person you encounter along the way.

In the U.S., I really enjoyed the friendly tone that prevails when meeting people in the public realm. It is fairly easy to talk to someone, have a little side conversation or just a good laugh. And then everyone goes their own way again. Nelson Mandela used to say: "Take it upon yourself, where you live, to make people around you joyful and full of hope." This can apply to family and friends, but also to strangers one meets on a random basis. That being said, it should not be underestimated how important deep friendships and relationships are. They are the ones that ultimately take root and become the place for important deeper, more intimate discussions and exchanges. One challenge for a newcomer in the U.S. might be thinking that, because someone was very friendly to you, it means that he or she will be a friend who you can rely on in the future. As everywhere, friendships take time to grow and the mere presence of kind interactions does not change this. Yet, once expectations are clear, it can be very pleasant to have friendly interactions and a word of kindness with strangers and acquaintances in everyday life.

Team Spirit, Encouragement, and the Power of "Not Yet"

"Good try, Judith. Good try!" I ran back over the basketball court and clapped hands with my teammates when passing them. Many smiled at

me, and we exchanged a couple of nice words before setting up for the next round of running and scoring.

One thing I really enjoyed during my time in the U.S. was the team spirit and the spirit of encouragement. After a couple of months into my semester in the States, I joined the girls' basketball team at school. While I had played basketball a couple of times during sports classes in Germany, I was by no means great at it. In contrast to most of my teammates who would effortlessly make most of the baskets in our warm-up rounds, I was happy when I made a basket every now and then. Yet, I will never forget how nice it felt to be cheered on by them anyway. Each time I made an effort, even if the ball landed somewhere far off the actual goal, some of the girls behind me would shout out, "Good try!" Or, "You got this girl! Next time!" Similarly, we would praise each other whenever something worked out well. I loved this form of encouragement. It is very uplifting when people around you cheer you on, no matter how things are going at the moment. It makes you want to try again, to do it better, and to achieve your goal. So, I kept training to sink the ball in the basket in my host family's yard during afternoons until I felt more comfortable making baskets.

While encouragement among peers is something universal, it seemed particularly pronounced to me during my time in the U.S. There was something about this easygoing, positive attitude among many people that motivated me and kept me going. And it's something that I have found over and over again when meeting some of my American friends later on in life. There is a sweet tendency in many to encourage you, to provide an uplifting comment, and to make you want to reach for your goals. The cheerleader tradition, cheering on sports teams and encouraging the wider public to do so as well, comes originally from the U.S. It was first observed at a game back in 1898.[3] This cheering on of people, be it in sports or in other areas of life, is something I greatly enjoyed about the U.S.

During my time at a U.S. high school, I noticed the importance given to sports tournaments. Often, they become a big social event, with friends and families joining to watch a game. On the days when we had a basketball game against another team, we dressed up (usually with a nice skirt and a blouse) to show our fellow high-school students that something special was happening in the afternoon. There would be a cheerful atmosphere in the study halls and after classes finished the sports arena would turn into a festive reception hall. You could smell popcorn and cookies, and people would start arriving to watch the game. At first, I felt a little intimidated by this, as I was afraid that I would embarrass myself in front of everyone if I made a wrong move during the game. But then I noticed the supportive cheering of the crowd when something turned out well for our team. The crowd cheered encouragement even when things were not going in our favor. In the end, it seemed that the social gathering aspect of these games was as important as the actual game and the final scores. I started to appreciate the approach to combining sports with having fun and seeing it as a social gathering among family and friends. Indeed, some observers have claimed that American sports are very audience- and spectator-centered. In contrast, many European sports seem more player- and participant-centered. There is no better or worse approach. The audience-centered approach in the U.S. is just another sign of the important role that cheerleading and encouragement play in the country.

A Chicago high school offered another very inspirational approach to encouragement. It became famous for using the concept of "not yet" in its grading system. Instead of telling students that they failed a class and note down an F for a fail, the teacher would grade it as "not yet." This simple change of wording can have a tremendous impact on the way students perceive themselves and their abilities. The term "not yet" indicates that you are on a learning curve and that there is the opportunity to improve. It fosters a growth mindset and the understanding that you can develop the necessary abilities.

It is only a matter of time and effort until you reach the goal. In contrast, *failed* can have a negative impact on your self-esteem and the belief in your capabilities. Professor Carol Dweck from Stanford University explains the power of "not yet" in detail in an inspiring TED talk called "The Power of Believing that You Can Improve." She and her colleagues have done a lot of research on how to develop a growth mindset, rather than a fixed mindset. People with a growth mindset who are faced with challenges see them as an opportunity to grow. They know that with effort, strategy, focus, perseverance, and improvement, they will be able to reach their goals. Carol Dweck also advises parents and teachers to praise wisely. Instead of praising a talent or the intelligence of your child or a student, she suggests to praise the process they are going through to get somewhere. Focus is hence placed on the effort or the perseverance they are putting into something. According to her research this form of praise results in much better and more sustainable results.[4]

And that is exactly what I felt when playing in the basketball team in the U.S. and during many other interactions with American friends or colleagues. The effort as such was praised. Even if the desired result was not yet achieved, the mere effort of trying and showing motivation and the will to improve was praised. For the process of writing this book, I joined two author support groups. Both of them are mainly composed of Americans. And they are doing a wonderful job in praising every little step that others do on their way to writing and publishing their books. The commitment, the effort, and the growth mindset are much more valuable in this regard than a static IQ or a fixed talent.

I find this approach very inspiring. And I would love to transmit the belief that abilities can be learned and that obstacles can be tackled with the right mindset to my daughters, as well. It is something I keep working on myself to be able to be a good role model to them. So, when I start thinking that I am not able to do something, I try telling myself: *"Judith, you aren't able*—yet.*"* This intrinsically implies that, some day, I will be able to if I decide to go for it and invest myself in it. This beautiful lesson from the Chicago high school could serve as an inspiration for other schools across the globe.

Beautiful Lessons Learned from the U.S.

✻ **Dream big, think big, and don't let hindrances or failures stop you from moving forward.** Failures are necessary steps and part of the way to success.

✻ **Learn to be assertive in things that are important to you and your values.** Make conscious decisions and become the author of your own life instead of a passive bystander. It can make you feel more confident, in control, and ultimately happy.

✻ **Enjoy the little daily interactions that are part of your everyday chores.** Exchanging a few kind words with strangers or acquaintances can lift your mood and make these transactions more enjoyable. Kindness and positivity are contagious!

✻ **Surround yourself with positive people** who encourage you and try to be a positive supporter of others, as well.

✻ **Start seeing challenges as opportunities for growth and try to build a growth mindset** with the deep belief that abilities can be developed. If we desire something and work hard enough for it, it is possible to achieve just about anything. If you think you can't do something, tell yourself that you can't do it *yet*, but that you are well on your way to getting there.

MEXICO

Mi Casa es Tu Casa

❖ Hospitality, Food, and "Convivios"

❖ Strong Family Bonds

❖ The Presence of Faith in Everyday Life

❖ Happy Music, Happy Mood

At 19, I had the opportunity to move to Mexico. I was in my last high-school year in Germany, preparing to finish my *Abitur*, the university entrance qualification in Germany. Deep inside, I felt that I wanted to try a different life experience before starting university and plunging into books again. At that time, Germany required military duty for most boys my age. But many young adults chose to do a social service year instead, either in Germany or abroad. My brother had opted for a service year in Bristol, England. His work consisted of caring for a very sweet boy with physical and mental disabilities. I was impressed by the maturity that my brother gained during that time. He improved his mastery of daily tasks like washing, ironing, and cooking. But even more amazing was the degree of dedication and love with which he cared for the little boy. He loved organizing excursions with him and attended to all of his needs. I think that the social service year that many men decided to do was not only wonderful for the community they served, but supported their own personal growth, as well.

Inspired by my brother's experience, I thought that it would be an enriching experience to do something similar. Initially, I thought that I would love to do a voluntary social service year in a kindergarten or something similar in France. France had always attracted my interest. I wanted to learn the French language and get to know the country and culture better. Then one of my closest friends told me about her plan to spend her year in Mexico where her uncle lived and served as a priest. She had to undergo an evaluation and selection weekend in Münster, Germany, and asked me if I wanted to join her. Out of curiosity, I agreed, even though I never thought that I would like to pursue this option for myself, as well. The weekend was great. We did many exercises, role-play games, watched videos, and heard stories from young people who had already completed a service year there. It was a program based on a friendship between two Christian dioceses, one in Mexico and one in Germany.

I was chosen, along with my close friend, to move to one of the Mexican parishes for 17 months. I remember feeling surprised, and the decision to spend the year in France or in Mexico was a difficult one. Logistically, France was much easier. But I felt the experience in Mexico was a once-in-a-lifetime opportunity. I had never visited there, and I imagined it to be very different. I decided that I could still do something in France later on and should take this unique opportunity. My parents were initially not completely convinced of my choice. My father knew I disliked spiders and told me several times that I might encounter massive ones in Mexico. He reminded me that it was not such a safe country. Yet, they both knew my friend's uncle in Mexico and had visited him there shortly before and enjoyed the trip very much. So, after some back and forth, they accepted my choice and supported me whole-heartedly.

My Mexican experience was a very enriching, sometimes challenging, but greatly inspiring one, which deeply influenced my life. I am still in touch with many families I encountered in 2003 and 2004, and, thanks to social media, we connect on a regular basis.

Hospitality, Food, and "*Convivios*"

"Mi casa es tu casa," literally translates to *"my house is your house."* You'll hear this phrase often when visiting Mexico or other Central or South American countries. It implies that you are always welcome to pass by and that you should feel at home when visiting someone. It's a wonderful sign of hospitality and open-heartedness.

What I loved about Mexico was that people were very hospitable, friendly, and warm-hearted. Generally, I had the impression that people there smiled a lot more than people on the streets in Germany. And the spontaneous creativity that people often displayed really impressed me. I often think of one particular anecdote. In the parish where I lived that year, I met a wonderful lady, Doña Vicky. She took care of the cooking, cleaning, and washing in the parochial house and became like a Mexican mother for me. Her two lovely daughters became like sisters, and we still call each other *hermanitas* to this day. I loved helping her in the kitchen, and I enjoyed our daily long conversations. One day she prepared lunch for the priests and the other people working in the parish. As usual, she went to the market in the early morning to buy fresh ingredients, and she prepared a delicious Mexican meal for lunch. We were just about to finish setting the table when the kitchen door opened and six family members of one of the priests walked in: his parents, two brothers, and their wives—lovely people who were always welcome guests. They mentioned that they were just passing through our village and wanted to stop to say hello. After some welcoming words, Doña Vicky asked them if they wanted to join us for lunch.

They happily accepted. I stood in the kitchen—stunned. I was very happy to see everyone, yet I wondered how Doña Vicky would manage to spontaneously serve food to six more people. So, I just observed how she took leftovers from the day before and warmed them up, cooked some more rice, and made more tacos. She calmly managed to enlarge lunch with extra bits and pieces. A few minutes later, everyone sat and ate happily in the dining room. I admired not only the Mexican food, with its large variety of incredibly delicious dishes, but also the hospitality and open-heartedness with which people were welcomed.

The importance of get-togethers, or so-called *convivios* became obvious in my daily life. Almost every week, I was invited to some sort of *convivio*. It could be at a family's house or outside of church after mass. If there was a special event in the Christian calendar or if one of the priests had an anniversary or birthday or if there were official visitors in the parish, mass would often be followed by a *convivio*. Usually, people who worked for the parish would set up the tables and chairs and inform the community about the get-together. Everyone would bring a dish to share from home. These were some of the best meals I ever had in my life. Tables were filled with an incredible variety of delicious, often home-made foods. People shared their dishes and walked around happily talking with everyone. Often traditional Mexican music was played, which further animated the joyful ambiance.

This form of potluck dinner, where attendees bring a dish to share to a meal, is not restricted to the Mexican context. It is a method used by religious and community groups that simplifies planning and distributes the costs among participants. Originally the word *pot-luck* appeared in the work of Thomas Nashe in the 16th century. He used it to describe "food provided for an unexpected or uninvited guest; the luck of the pot." The modern meaning of the word, referring to a "communal meal, where guests bring their own food," originated most likely in the 1930s during The Depression.[1] Later in my life, and particularly during my years at university, my friends and I often organized potluck dinners and really enjoyed them. But my first acquaintance with this form of getting together in huge masses, celebrating, and eating together, was in Mexico.

Convivios on a smaller scale took place at people's homes on a regular basis. I often visited one family in the evenings, since one of the daughters and I had become close friends. My friend's house was already quite crowded. Her parents, her brother and his wife, and her sister and her husband and their little son, all lived under one roof. And regularly, many members of the extended family would show up in the evenings without notice. Often, my friend, her sister, her sister-in-law, and I would sit in the kitchen, discussing life while eating a taco or an enchilada. During such evenings, it was completely normal for my friend's cousins, uncles, and aunts to show up, join the discussion and the dinner. It never seemed to be a problem to provide another taco with *frijoles* and salsa to the guests. They were always welcome. There was not one time during the one year and a half that I spent in Mexico when I was not welcomed with open arms by the family when I passed by in the evening. And I usually came unannounced, since I did not have a cell phone yet. The same welcoming attitude was displayed by all the family members. And I am speaking about huge families. My friend's mother and my friend's father both had nine siblings each. This did not mean that people would not go on with things that needed to get done. If there was laundry to do or cleaning or ironing to finish, my friend's family would continue doing it, while talking to their visitors. I was amazed by this hospitality, warmth, and love. And I also felt it in many other families' places during my time in Mexico. I was grateful that my parents back home in Germany displayed such a sense of warmth and hospitality, too. Our house always had an open door for family, friends, neighbors and acquaintances. And yet, I was impressed that in Mexico such behavior seemed to be the general manner. The hospitality, generosity, and warmth that so many people in Mexico expressed brought the country and its people very close to my heart. Up to this day, this welcoming attitude remains present with me. I often receive messages from Mexican friends and families who write that they will always welcome us with open arms in Mexico. This wonderful way of hospitality is deeply engrained in the culture.

Strong Family Bonds

I noticed that strong family bonds played a crucial role in people's lives. The support of the extended family still seemed to play a much bigger role in Mexico than in Germany. It was quite common to have multigenerational households with grandparents, parents, children, and grandchildren living under one roof—or at least so close that they would see each other on a daily basis. This is, of course, not a generalization that can be made for Mexico as a whole. Another reality of the country is that many people migrate to the U.S., with families torn apart as a consequence. In addition, my observations are based on my experiences of life in the small town where I lived. Realities are often completely different in the larger metropolises. Nevertheless, the extended family, including aunts, uncles, and cousins, seemed to play a very important role. They act as a social support net that could step in if there were any problems. Since state-provided social security services are still less common than in many European countries, it is only natural that people rely more on their family members. In case of a challenging situation, it was common to turn to the extended family for help and support. When I returned to Mexico in 2010 to carry out research for my Master's thesis, I experienced this support system personally again. I had intended to do some research in the Northern city of Monterrey. My close friend's family was quick to locate a distant cousin of someone living in the city and informed him about my travel plans. Even though he didn't know me at all, he organized housing for my friend and I and welcomed us as if we were his own children. It was yet another moment when I thought that there is a lot to learn from the hospitality of the Mexican people.

As for the upbringing of children, I found it very nice that many of the teenagers and young adults that I got to know treated their cousins as if they were brothers and sisters. Aunts and uncles were consulted for all kinds of issues. Strong family bonds were omnipresent. And it felt like people, in particular young parents, were less isolated than in European or North American society. It was quite normal that an aunt, cousin, or the grandparents would take care of a child several times a week. Being a mother of two little girls myself at the moment, I feel that this is quite different for many of us here in Europe now. Our case might be special, since my parents live in a different country. We see each other very regularly on FaceTime and they go out of their way to visit and support us whenever possible, no matter where in the world we are living. But they cannot just hop over for a coffee or to help out for a couple of hours in case of need. Since we moved from Japan to Switzerland, it is however possible to see my in-laws much more often. And our daughters have developed a sibling-like relationship with their cousins who live nearby. This has made me think of the nice relationships with the extended family that I cherished so much in Mexico. As the African proverb goes: "It takes a village to raise a child." I often feel that young mothers in the Western world are too isolated and left alone with their new mother role. It is all the more important to find or create their own village or support system. The natural presence of such a village, as often observed in Mexico, was very valuable in my view. Yet, at the same time, it can also lead to irritating situations if several people are involved in the upbringing of your child. Everyone has an opinion on how to best treat or educate a child. A lot of tolerance and communication is necessary to avoid major conflicts. And some nuclear families in Mexico might have been yearning for some more privacy for themselves from time to time. In the end, it comes down to finding a good balance. But in terms of strong family bonds, hospitality, and family support, Mexico continues to be an inspiring example.

The Presence of Faith in Everyday Life

Another source of happiness and fulfillment for many people I encountered in Mexico was their faith. Mexico is home to the world's second largest Catholic population (after Brazil). In Mexico, 81 percent of the adult population identify as Catholics and 90 percent say that they were raised in the Catholic faith.[2,3] What impressed me in Mexico was how faith and the belief in God were integrated very naturally into people's everyday lives.

Back in Germany, my mom introduced me to the concept of a loving God, existing somewhere around us and taking care of and protecting everyone who believes in him. I liked this idea of God, as a symbol of love and support, very much. Even though I was not very active in church-related matters in Germany, it always felt very comforting to me to have someone to talk to and to believe in something bigger. There was a nice mixture of beliefs and opinions about religion in our home. My mom was raised Catholic. Her father was an organ player in a church in a little village in Germany's Mosel valley. Her mother had a beautiful voice and sang in the church choir and was at the same time sacristan. So, Sundays were often the busiest days for her family. One of my mother's brothers inherited his father's talent to play the organ and does up to this day. My mom inherited the beautiful voice of her mother. When the two of us attended a mass together, people would turn around and look at her when they heard her singing in her nice, clear voice. My father's parents were also deeply Catholic and regularly attended church as long as they physically could. Praying was always part of our lunch routine at their place. And while my father was raised in the Catholic faith, he has always been a critical thinker. He questions a lot of institutions, especially dogmatic ones. He holds a humorous stance toward the church, not rejecting it, as such, but he allows himself to make jokes about certain aspects and not take things too seriously. I think that I was very much influenced by these two approaches to religion and in my case, Catholicism.

When I decided to spend a year and a half in Mexico working on social projects in a parish, I was not sure what awaited me. But soon it became clear that the way of living faith in Mexico seemed quite different to everything I had known so far. The expression which struck me most was: *"Primero Dios,"* which can be translated to "God first" or "God permitting/If God wishes so." People would use this sentence for almost anything. When I said goodbye to someone I planned to see the next day, people often responded, *"Hasta mañana, primero Dios."* It signified that God willing, we would meet tomorrow again. Yet it was not completely in our hands if it would be happening or not. Similarly, if I would say, "Let's meet here at the bus stop tomorrow morning at seven to take the bus to Mexico City," my friend would answer, "Yes, see you here tomorrow at seven, *primero Dios.*" The German part of me was a bit confused by this behavior in the beginning. For me it was clear that if we made an appointment for seven o'clock, this was a commitment. It was an appointment between the two of us, and I didn't really understand what God had to do with it. I wondered if this phrase was used as an excuse if you were running late or didn't show up at all. With time, I learned, however, that the expression signified something different, something deeply engrained in people's minds. That there was a higher power—God—who would always come first and who would always have the final decisive power. I noticed that with time I started to like and embrace this idea. Another common phrase was: *"Lo pongo en las manos de Dios,"* translating to "I put it into God's hands." This was especially the case if someone was facing a major transition or challenge. People would say: "I will do my best to solve this and go through this. But not everything is in my hands, and at some point, when I can't do more, I put it into God's hands." Somehow this belief that things happen for a purpose, seemed to make people's lives much easier, accepting, and serene. Related to this phrase was the saying: *"Dios sabe lo que hace."* ("God knows what he does.") It seemed that especially in challenging situations, like after the death of a loved one, an accident, or another life-changing event, people would often use this phrase. It showed trust in the fact that God knows what he is doing and why. And that if he thought that you could go through this trial, you would be able to do so. Even if he called someone to his side (in the case of someone dying), he would also know why.

I initially struggled a bit with this interpretation of God. I asked myself why a loving God who knew what he was doing would allow murders and tragic accidents to happen if he could have avoided them in the first place. Since I had direct contact with a lot of priests on-site, I would often engage in discussions about this. The most satisfying answer that I would get was that there were also bad things and feelings on Earth. But that these were not something God had created but something man-made. With the love that God represents, there comes also freedom. Freedom for human beings to decide how we want to live and design our lives on Earth. God would not intervene all the time on Earth, in man-made problems or natural disasters. But if something bad or tragic happened, he would always be there to receive his believers in his arms and give us love and comfort to go through this. I really liked this idea and explanation, and I noticed that it gave me comfort, a footing, and a feeling of serenity in everyday life. I think that as a 19-year-old living in Mexico, I was the least afraid ever in my life of dying or the death of a loved one. I had the deep belief and feeling that things would turn out fine for everyone in the end. It was a wonderful, peaceful feeling.

With time, I started to appreciate this natural going together of faith and everyday life in Mexico. The natural way of including God and his way or wishes in many daily moments made the faith very vivid and approachable. Sooner than later, I would also say *primero Dios* in all kinds of situations. And when I moved back to Germany, I noticed that I often wanted to use that expression but could not find any equivalent for it in German. Even though I later noticed that a similar German expression exists *("So Gott will.")*, it is not used as commonly as in Mexico. Similarly, people in Mexico would often say *"Que Dios te bendiga,"* or "May God bless you," and also this phrase felt very comforting. Up to this day, my friends and I continue to say it in almost every message we write each other.

Yet, there was something else that impressed me about faith and the church in Mexico, and that was the joyful attitude among the people working for or attending church. In Germany, I had several times come across priests who seemed so serious that I could not believe that they were declaring the good news of the Bible and of a living Jesus. I remember that during the evening Easter mass, one of the priests in our town would often say with a very serious, almost sad, voice: "That was the good news, and now Happy Easter to everyone." My father and I would sometimes joke that the way he said it sounded as if the world was about to perish the next day. This one experience can of course not be generalized to all the motivated and enthusiastic priests in Germany who inspire their communities on a constant basis. I just noticed a special atmosphere of joy and lightness during the Mexican masses. It could be related to the mentality. Often times people would smile, laugh, and clap if a happy or enthusiastic announcement was made. It could also be related to the music. Many of the Spanish church songs were very melodic and spread a sense of joyful hope. When listening to such songs accompanied by light-hearted guitar sounds, I often felt like dancing or moving happily to the music. It somehow felt less dramatic than in German masses that are often accompanied by organ music. Even though I love organs and I think that they can sound absolutely beautiful, they often carry a bit of a dramatic, heavy character. In Mexico, I was part of a choir led by young adults and sometimes I felt like being part of a trendy pop band, rather than a church choir. Many song interpretations expressed an intrinsic happiness. The most beautiful version of the Lord's prayer (*Padre Nuestro*) I ever heard was the song version of it in Mexico. I felt alive, and my heart would start to jump when listening or singing along. And it was very motivating to participate in masses with hundreds or even thousands of enthusiastic people, young and old alike.

I also enjoyed the approachability of the priests. Since I spent time with them on a daily basis, I realized that they also enjoyed lots of experiences and things I might never have thought of. For example, one of the priests who lived in the parochial house had been a very good soccer player who had even been asked to join a famous soccer team. He had decided that his vocation was to become a priest. Yet his interest in soccer had never ceased and I found him often in his free time watching or attending soccer games. The other priest was a big fan of Regional Mexican music. Often, I woke up in the morning to happy sounds of this music filling the entire house. He also had quite an adventurous driving style. Sometimes I did not know if I should laugh or jump out of the car when we sat down and he would make the sign of the cross before speeding away over bumpy streets. It was also common to attend family parties or gatherings together. And I will never forget the images of dancing priests joining in for tequila shots during such occasions. This joyful behavior made the priests very authentic. It was something that I deeply appreciated during my time in Mexico.

Despite these wonderful approaches to faith that I got to know in Mexico, I had not completely lost the critical stance that I had acquired from my father. I kept wondering about the missionary nature of the Catholic church. And about all the people who were brought up in different cultures and religions. So, one evening while enjoying a tequila with one of the Bishop's closest helpers during a social gathering, I asked him a question that had been occupying me: what did he think about the billions of people living in other parts of the world who weren't Christian? Did he really believe that they would—as it was sometimes preached by some people in the church—all be lost souls? Just because they were born and grew up in a different cultural setting with a different religious or non-religious upbringing? I couldn't really believe this. And to my surprise, this man told me that he didn't really believe it either. We had a wonderful discussion about our impression that something higher and more powerful than us human beings existed. I expressed my view that this power could probably have different names and that you could approach or worship it in various ways. In our eyes, it made no sense to fight in the name of God or any other name given to this power, since this could not have been in the intention of the originator of everything. That someone in such a high position in the Catholic Church engaged with me on such fundamental questions felt very reassuring and comforting to me.

It was also in Mexico, six years later when I returned to conduct research on a health-related issue for my Master's thesis, that I came across the book *The Secret*. Written by the Australian television writer, producer, and author Rhonda Byrne, it has become a universal bestseller with millions of copies sold in more than 40 languages. The main message of the book is that you can achieve and become anything in life if you put your wishes out into the universe. It explains in detail the Law of Attraction and how you can use it for your own well-being. I was so mesmerized by the book and the revelations in it that I recommended it to several friends and to my mom. Much later in my life, I was struggling with some situations and almost lost hope that things could change for the better. During a phone conversation, my mom reminded me of this book: *"Judith, remember the message of that book that you recommended to me once? I think that it's time that you start living by it again."* She had been using *The Secret* ever since reading it. She had quite successfully attracted and fulfilled lots of her dreams and wishes. The Law of Attraction is a spiritual approach to attracting good things and people to your life. And it has helped countless people around the world transform their lives for the better. For me, the sentiments of spirituality and especially faith and hope will always be closely linked to the time I spent in Mexico. The daily presence of faith and hope in a loving God—as I experienced in Mexico—seemed to help people live a grounded, calm, and serene life. The importance that hope plays in our daily lives cannot be underestimated. Hope shifts our awareness to the positive and to pragmatic, solution-oriented behavior. We might have different approaches to faith and hope, yet I deeply believe that hope and faith can help us live our lives in a happier and more fulfilling way. And Mexico can be an inspiring example of how to include faith and spirituality naturally in our everyday lives.

Happy Music, Happy Mood

"Me muero por suplicarte, que no te vayas mi vida
Me muero por escucharte...decir las cosas que nunca digas..."[i]

I was sitting on the bed in my room in the parish in Mexico, listening to the song *"Me muero por conocerte"* by Alex Ubago for a countless time, trying to understand the lyrics. I was intrigued by this particular song, which sounded so wonderfully romantic and melancholy to my ears. So, I listened to it over and over again with a dictionary in one hand, trying to understand what the song was about.

I think I fell in love with Spanish music from the first moment I arrived in Mexico. Since I did not know much more to say than *"Hola, como estas"* when I arrived in Mexico, I had a lot to learn. The first weeks and months were often quite exhausting. It took a lot of energy to make sense of what people were telling me. And even more, trying to express myself in this completely new language. For me, one of the most fun and motivating ways to learn a language is by listening to music in the language. When I listen to a song I like, no matter the language, I often feel the urge to understand and learn the words. And I love singing along to them once I've learned them. I have had this experience with English, Spanish, French, Italian, Dutch, and even Chinese and Japanese songs. In Mexico, I would often listen to songs I liked for entire evenings, reading through the lines and learning what the words meant until I knew them by heart. In my opinion, Spanish is a wonderful language for music. It can be very romantic, passionate, melancholy, happy, or energizing. And while music plays an important role in countries around the world, for me the presence of music in Mexico was somehow extra

---

[i] In English: "I'm dying to beg you not to leave me, my love. I'm dying to hear you say the things that you never say..."

striking. It was an important part of everyday life and, especially, special occasions. I remember enjoying the rides in the little vans traveling from village to village when the drivers would put on some happy Mexican music. Often, I felt like dancing right away when stepping out of the van. At family parties, music and dancing usually played a very important role. For special occasions, like anniversaries, wedding proposals, or expressions of love, sometimes *mariachis* would be hired. *Mariachis* are a group of musicians who play a very particular genre of regional Mexican music on stringed instruments. The regional costumes they wear are often adapted from *charro* (cowboy) outfits. In 2011, the Mexican *mariachi* culture was recognized as an Intangible Cultural Heritage by UNESCO. Mexican and Spanish music in general has accompanied me ever since I lived in Mexico. As soon as I hear salsa beats or one of the traditional Mexican songs such as *"Mexico lindo y queriiiido,"* my heart starts to jump. Usually, I can't stop myself from moving around and singing along—which has a direct positive impact on my mood.

Music is a wonderful way to express feelings or to lift your mood. I play piano and one day, my organ-playing uncle offered me a piano songbook in which he had written: "Music is the only language in which you can't lie."[4] I like that saying very much, as it emphasizes the beautiful role that music can play in our lives. Studies have shown that music can have very positive effects on our health. Researchers from the famous medical journal *The Lancet* pointed out that "people who listened to music before, during, or after surgery experienced less pain and anxiety compared to patients who did not listen to music."[5] Music listeners were even in need of less pain medication. Similarly, in music therapy, there are programs that help to manage stress, enhance memory, and alleviate pain. They manage to "tap into [the] processes of comfort, relief, and enjoyment."[6] Music can also be a wonderful tool to improve mood, self-esteem, and quality of life every day. One study released in the *Journal of Positive*

Psychology found that "people who listened to upbeat music could improve their mood and boost their happiness in just two weeks."[7] So it seems that the nature of music plays an important role when it comes to regulating our moods. Upbeat music has been proven to have a positive impact in this regard. So the next time you have a bad day, it could be worth a try to turn on some upbeat music and see if it has a positive effect on your mood. And on good days, it is in any case a good idea to turn on some music and to sing or dance along!

Beautiful Lessons Learned from Mexico

❋ **Be hospitable and creative.** If there is food for one, there is food for another one. Spontaneous visits and get-togethers can sometimes be the nicest ones.

❋ **Take time to listen to people who come to you.** Of course, you also have to follow your schedule and priorities. But don't forget to live the moment and be open to listening if someone needs you.

❋ **Get together with friends and family on a regular basis.** This creates happy moments and exchange and gives energy for the tasks ahead afterward.

❋ **Have faith in a higher power that is supportive and present in good and in bad times.** Be it God, the Universe, some spiritual power, or whatever is most appropriate to you.

❋ **Send your wishes out to the universe!**

❋ **Enjoy listening to music!** Listening to happy, upbeat music can have a very positive impact on your mood. And you can even start learning new languages by listening to music.

Chapter 4

THE NETHERLANDS

Don't Worry, Be Happy

> ❖ *A Window to the World*
>
> ❖ *Colors, Candor, and the Art of Not Taking Things Too Personally*
>
> ❖ *Simplify Your Daily Life, Take It Easy and Be "Gezellig"*
>
> ❖ *Move Your Body*

When I was seven, my father took a job in Hengelo, the Netherlands, and we moved from my birth city, Wuppertal, up North to Germany's Münsterland, to a town close to the Dutch border. It allowed my father to commute across the border each day while my mom continued working as psychologist in Germany. In the beginning, I did not want to move and felt upset about leaving my home and my friends behind. Yet, I quickly started to enjoy our new environment. The German Münsterland is known for its comparatively flat landscapes where bicycling is very popular. Soon, my brother and I were allowed to bike to school with our own little bikes. My brother also negotiated with my parents to get a dog after moving, so that we would have a nice companion on our new journey. He has always been a good negotiator from a very early age. So, we started this new chapter in a little town just across the border from the Netherlands.

A Window to the World

After our move, we often drove across the border to our Dutch neighbors' markets for shopping and good meals in local restaurants. I noticed that many of the houses we passed had no curtains. They displayed large, wide windows, and if you wanted, you could observe people inside eating together or watching television. This was quite a contrast to most German houses. My mom's close Dutch friend explained that having no curtains did not mean that everyone would be peeking into the houses. On the contrary, people would usually behave quite discretely. This openness was less for others to look inside but for the people living in the house to be able to look outside and enjoy the view. Another theory holds that it is another way of expressing honesty and transparency, which are both highly valued in Dutch society. Having open or no curtains or blinds shows that the behavior at home is like that in the public sphere. You have nothing to hide.[1]

When I returned to the Netherlands later to pursue my Bachelor's degree, I observed great open-mindedness as well. The Netherlands has an extensive history of trade activities. The sea surrounds the country in the North and in the West, which makes it a strategic place for receiving goods shipped to Europe. The city of Rotterdam has the largest and busiest cargo port in Europe. Those historic trading activities and the constant contact with the outer world has very likely influenced the Dutch culture and people's mindsets as well. Dutch people have a reputation of being very open, transparent and direct. This doesn't only hold true for their quite relaxed laws on soft drug use and prostitution. It also holds true for the generally open-minded and cosmopolitan attitudes.

I love that most people can speak or understand various languages; I feel this contributes to the mindset. It makes it easy for the Dutch to get in touch and communicate with people from around the world. The Education First English Proficiency Index has repeatedly ranked the Netherlands in first place in the past years. This means that it is the country with the most proficient English speakers in the world, outside of the Anglosphere.[2] Many Dutch people also have a good grasp of German and understand and speak it well. In the Netherlands, movies and series are usually not dubbed but broadcast in their original language, with Dutch subtitles. It is likely that this contributes a lot to the language abilities of many Dutch people. Exceptions are made for children's series when children are not able to read yet. This is different for Germany, for example, where usually all movies and TV series are synchronized to the German language. Such small differences in terms of television broadcasting can make a huge difference later on. The benefits of watching movies and television in a foreign language are huge. We notice this with our three-year-old daughter who we're raising bilingually in German and French. Recently, we allowed her to watch some English cartoon series. My husband and I are impressed by how much English she has learned in a few weeks' time. She started singing and counting in English. And when she plays with the figurines from this particular series, she only speaks in English. Sometimes I tell myself that I should watch some more foreign news or movies in order to keep improving my language skills as well.

I used to joke that as a consequence of many Dutch people speaking German and English so well, my own Dutch language skills remain fairly limited. I lived in Maastricht, in the Southern part of the Netherlands, for almost three years while pursuing my Bachelor's degree in European Studies but didn't make a lot of progress. Some of my German friends learned to speak Dutch well during this time. But for the majority of my German classmates, it was not easy to learn Dutch. We attended courses at university in English and at the time I struggled to keep up with all the reading and writing in English. Since in my Bachelor cohort the majority of students were German, most of my university classmates used English or German as the language for our conversations. This made me sometimes feel like I was living on a little German island in the Netherlands. I still tried to get a basic grasp of the language by taking a couple of courses and trying out some small talk in Dutch when going shopping. But my efforts often halted when my Dutch counterpart would kindly ask after a couple of words if I came from Germany. When I confirmed it, usually they would respond in very decent German. And I felt ashamed for my very basic Dutch and often switched to German or English as a consequence. I think that today I would do it differently and insist on practicing the language of the country. Here in Switzerland, it still happens that people answer me in English, even though I speak to them in fluent French. They might hear my accent and try to be forthcoming by switching to English. And for certain, more complex, discussions, I indeed like to switch to English. But for transactions in everyday life, I keep responding in French until they understand that I prefer to speak the local language.

While some Dutch people I have met are very humble about their language abilities, others are very confident. This is probably more of a personal trait than a Dutch one but I noticed it, in particular, during my exchanges with Dutch friends and acquaintances. On a recent trip to South Africa, a lovely couple around my parents' age sat next to me in the plane. We exchanged small talk in English and they asked where I was from. When they learned that I come from Germany, the lady said, "Oh, I speak some German as well, but it is very poor since I haven't used it in years." She then went on to converse with me for almost an hour in perfect German. I was stunned. This lady who had learned German years ago at school and through watching television, spoke in such a natural way, as if German was her second language. And although I had lived in the Netherlands for almost three years, I could only stumble over a couple of sentences in Dutch. It again showed me the ease many Dutch people have conversing with people from around the world. On the other side of the spectrum a good Dutch friend at university had not learned much German. But this did not prevent him from playing around with sentences and words as if he had. He often said to me, "Judith, the secret to learning a language is to just speak it. Say what you can, add a couple of words in another language if you don't know something and make mistakes. It doesn't matter. What matters is that you practice and learn by doing." I admired his confidence. And I can probably still learn a lot from this confident attitude. This attitude seems to be engrained in many people in the Netherlands. Which brings me to the next subchapter.

Colors, Candor, and the Art of Not Taking Things Too Personally

"Of course, you can wear these brown shoes with your black jeans. They fit perfectly. I would even say that you should get the red ones. They are even more fancy." The lady in the shop gave me an encouraging smile while I scrutinized the shoes I had just tried on.

It might sound a little conservative, but for many years I only bought black autumn and winter shoes. I thought the classic black style fit best with my blue and black pants. But as I stood in a small shoe shop in a Dutch town close to my hometown in Germany, I discovered some brown shoes that I liked a lot. There were even some dark red leather shoes that had caught my attention. My mom was with me, as we had embarked on a ladies shopping tour, and she kept eyeing the shoes as well. "It's true, Judith. They look very good on you." And while I still wondered if they would fit with most of my wardrobe at home, I could not refrain from looking at the sales lady who was wearing a colorful dress and colorful tights with her red boots. She looked beautiful. I would never have dared to wear such a combination, but she looked great—confident and full of energy.

This was one of my early lessons about the confident and self-reliant behavior of many of the Dutch people. Throughout my time in the Netherlands, I frequently saw women in very colorful and playful outfits—and I loved it. There was a nice energy that radiated from them. They seemed to wear a natural confidence regarding clothing, following the motto: "Wear whatever you feel like wearing." One of my close Dutch friends who works in the sports business, explained that colorful shirts and shoes can even serve as motivators for people to do sports. Over the years, I have become a bit more confident in my clothing choices. I often buy colorful sweaters since I feel they make me look and feel less tired. I wear them especially when I feel tired after a sleepless night when our little ones woke up a lot. Sometimes I find myself switching from a grey sweater to a bright red or green one since this raises my energy level. Recently I bought a bright yellow dress with a blue-and-white flower pattern for the baptism of our youngest daughter. At first, I hesitated about my choice. But then I thought about what I had learned from our Dutch neighbors. And while my father lovingly called me a "colorful hummingbird" when he saw me, I also received several compliments on the outfit. And most importantly, the dress was very comfortable and light—perfect for a warm summer day. The lesson that stood out to me was to listen to myself and to only buy clothes that I enjoy wearing. I still sometimes buy clothes which might look perfect on others, but just don't feel very comfortable on me. And these are usually the clothes that keep taking space in my wardrobe without ever being used. However, sometimes I want to buy something that I love, but which is rather unusual. During such situations, I recall my experiences in the Netherlands and give myself a push to be more confident when making my choices.

My parents also experienced this Dutch influence in their house in Germany. One of my mom's closest friends is a Dutch interior designer. Ever since she has had a say in my parents' refurnishing decisions, I have noticed that my parents have made a lot of bold choices. A blue leather couch replaced the brown one. A bright red carpet took the place of its dark red predecessor. Yellow armchairs took over where the old brown armchair had been. The dining room was redecorated in a variety of green colors. Certainly, the use of colors depends a lot on the personality of a person. And it does not have to be all about color. There are people who prefer to keep it more classic. The lesson that I want to point out here is the attitude that I often encountered in the Netherlands: Be yourself and dress up and decorate your home in whatever way pleases you.

These observations align with another trait that I observed time and time again in many Dutch people I met. They carry a seemingly self-confident nature. While it is impossible to generalize about a whole country, I can say that most of the Dutch I met displayed a special air of confidence. It came through in their way of speaking, thinking, and addressing others. They often showed a very open and honest interest in others, and you would usually receive very open and honest comments as well. My father, who has worked for a Dutch company for almost 40 years, used to joke: "Oh, Dutch people can tell you: 'You're an idiot, but please don't take it personally.'" Of course, this comment is excessive, but some truth lies in it, as well. I've found that the Dutch usually tell me quite bluntly what they think, without meaning to offend.

I think that there is something beautiful to learn from such an honest, direct approach: Don't take things too personally. I tend to take things quite personally, be it a comment, a gaze, or a critique. Sometimes, I find myself thinking about it for hours or even days after. Yet, I tell myself that I should stop taking comments so personally and instead try to take them with a sense of humor. Often, people do not mean to offend with their comments, even if they are blunt. But if you don't feel confident or well in that moment, you might interpret them as negative. Of course, there are times when people say things to offend or hurt. In such situations, it can help telling yourself that these comments say more about them than about you. My mother, a psychologist, used to tell me when I was a child, "If someone insults you, just take it as a projection of this person. It is more about him or her than about you." She even encouraged me to say, "I take this as a projection," and return it back to the person. At times it might be necessary to seek a conversation when something has hurt you, especially if it came from someone close or important to you. Other times it is good to let these comments bounce off. When talking to another mom about common conflicts that can arise in everyday life, she once gave me the following tip: "Think of yourself as being an astronaut. You are in your astronaut suit and everything mean or provocative bounces off it, while you continue to go where you want to go." I love this idea and try to remind myself of it when encountering challenging comments or situations in daily life. You can even treat unpleasant encounters with strangers this way. Or show compassion for the person being rude by just letting the comment bounce off you. My mother used to tell us that my brother had already mastered the skill of not taking things too personally at a young age. In the rare moments when my mom got upset about a comment or some treatment by someone, my brother would say: "Don't take it personally, Mom. It's not your problem." That very healthy attitude from a little boy is one that he has continued using throughout his life. And I think that in terms of positive bluntness and the art of not taking things too personally, we can learn a lot from our friends in the Netherlands!

Simplify Your Daily Life, Take It Easy and Be *"Gezellig"*

Another attitude that I noticed in my Dutch friends and acquaintances was a tendency to not take things too seriously and to simplify life whenever possible. During my university years, I observed that many of my Dutch classmates did not stress out as much as their German counterparts when it came to exams and grades. Many were also ambitious, but usually, it was as important to take part in the latest activities of one of the many famous student associations (*studentenverenigingen*) as to study for the next test or exam. Many Dutch employers view extracurricular activities and the skills learned from them as equally important as grades. I also joined a couple of associations and enjoyed the activities and evenings and events spent together very much. Sometimes, I had the impression, though, that some of the Dutch students were a little unnerved by their German fellows who were often perceived as overly competitive and ambitious. What I enjoyed when observing many of my Dutch colleagues was their ability to not take things too seriously and to enjoy life in the midst of filled study plans.

I came across that "take it easy" attitude again and again when meeting other Dutch friends around the world. Recently, I read an article about Dutch moms and why they are supposedly the happiest moms. Without taking the title of the article too literally, I spotted some arguments that reflect some of the attributes that I observed as well. For example, the author claims that Dutch moms know how to outsource. This can mean to involve others, for example grandparents, in childcare activities, without feeling guilty about it. According to the article, many Dutch moms are good at finding a family rhythm with the children that is convenient for everybody, including the mother. So many mothers today still try to take care of everything and everyone on their own. This is, of course, completely fine if the mothers blossom while doing so. But, if they get into a state where they only feel exhausted and lose themselves in the process, it is no longer healthy. I know from personal experience and from many of my mom friends that this can happen easily. And so, it is very encouraging to realize that outsourcing some aspects of family life is nothing to feel guilty about. It can, instead, be an important aspect, so that everyone in the family can blossom. It is widely known that if mothers thrive, they can take much better care of their children and their family as well. The author also observes that in the Netherlands, children are given a lot of freedom, so that they can develop into independent individuals. She argues that parents don't attach themselves so much to their children's failures or successes. Instead of seeing children as a reflection of themselves, they treat them as "autonomous beings with individual characters, strengths, and weaknesses."[3] It seems that this treatment is appreciated by the children themselves, as well. In a 2013 report by UNICEF, the Netherlands was number one in a comparative study on children's well-being in 29 rich countries. Since then, Dutch children have often been labelled "the happiest kids" in the world.[4] There is a quote by Kahlil Gibran, which I often saw on postcards when I was small, that goes: "You may give [children] your love, but not your thoughts, for they have their own thoughts." I was always intrigued by this saying. The idea is to not put all your baggage on your children, but to let them be self-worthy, independent individuals. This is a beautiful thing for parents to strive for, in my view.

In regard to family life, I noticed that many of my Dutch acquaintances followed a well thought-through routine to make daily life easier and less stressful. It is, for example, quite rare to see little children in the streets after around six o'clock in the evening, since this is the time most Dutch families have dinner and get the children ready for bed. Also, friends' invitations can be well-structured. I learned in the Netherlands that it is okay to indicate exact invitation times. Invitations to aperitifs often include the beginning and the ending time (say, from 6:00 p.m. to 8:00 p.m.). My parents are often invited to time-defined cocktail hours in Amsterdam. At first, I felt surprised about such clear indications. But then again, it takes pressure off the host and also gives freedom to guests to plan for a meal or a trip to the theatre afterward. Of course, there are cultures where such an invitation would be unthinkable. I also don't want to imply that it's the best form of invitation for all occasions. But, it is nice to know that this option exists and that it's fine to make that choice if it suits you best.

The Dutch can teach us that things don't have to be complicated to be nice. For example, it isn't an issue at all to invite someone for coffee and just offer a cup of coffee and a cookie with it. It is not always necessary to prepare a home-baked cake or something time-consuming. What matters is to have a good moment together and to be *gezellig*. *Gezellig* is a very important word in the Dutch language. It refers to an ambiance, a place, or an event that radiates a cozy, comfortable, relaxed, and often homey atmosphere. If something is *gezellig*, it is easy, informal, unconstrained, or convivial. Having a glass of wine with someone can be *gezellig*. Or taking out a folding chair and sitting for a while in the sun can be *gezellig*. It just involves a very easygoing attitude.

From my observations in the Netherlands, I found that there often seemed to be a nice balance between structuring your day and following schedules on the one hand—and taking it easy on the other. I think that many of the observed behaviors fit well into the category of "simplify your life." And I think that we can take some inspirations on how to do this from many people in the Netherlands!

Move Your Body

"You can't seriously be saying that coming here to university by bike is a sport for you, Judith." One of my Dutch classmates at Maastricht University looked at me with big eyes and started laughing. *"Yes, it is kind of,"* I responded. *And trying to make my point clear, I added, "I mean, I bike down here every day for 20 minutes and then back home for 20 minutes. It actually involves a good deal of effort."* My classmate didn't even try to hide his astonishment about my position. *"Come on, Judith. This kind of biking is not a sport. It is a means of transportation."*

He was not the only one who regarded biking to school or to work as a completely normal means of transportation. Studies in 2016 showed that the Dutch, a population of about 17 million, own approximately 22.5 million bicycles. This means that, on average, there are 1.3 bicycles per person—more than in any other country in the world.[5] Estimates show that almost a quarter of the Dutch cycle every day and that the average Dutch person cycles 1,000 kilometers a year in 250 to 300 cycling trips.[6] These are quite impressive numbers. For many people, like my former university classmate, cycling is the most natural way of getting from point A to point B. Often it is not regarded as a sport but as a simple means of transportation.

The word *Netherlands* means "low-lying country," and large parts of the country lie below sea level. Yet lots of these areas were reclaimed with careful water management techniques. The country is not only lying very low, but the landscapes are generally also very flat. This makes it an ideal place for biking. Anyone who has been to some of the larger cities like Amsterdam or Utrecht might be surprised by the enormous numbers of cyclists in the streets. The huge bicycle parking areas, with hundreds or thousands of bicycle racks are also remarkable. Studies have shown that using cycling and e-biking as a means of urban transportation has the potential to cut energy use and CO_2 emissions by up to 10 percent by 2050. According to these estimates, it could also save societies trillions of dollars.[7] Brian Cookson, former president of the International Cycling Union, emphasized, "Cycling is a crucial means of transport for millions of people around the world...if more governments followed good examples like the Netherlands or Denmark to make their cities better for cycling, we'd see huge benefits from lower carbon emissions, hugely reduced costs in transport infrastructure and potentially safer, healthier places."[8]

Cycling is a very natural and integral part of everyday life in the Netherlands. As mentioned before, also in bordering Münsterland, Germany, cycling is part of daily life for many people. Since we moved close to the Dutch border when I was a child, cycling became a way of life for me too. During my teen years, biking brought a great sense of freedom and independence to my friends and me. We visited each other by bike, cycled to activities or even met at bars and went to parties with this means of transportation. It was especially useful before we got driver's licenses. Public transportation was not yet very common in the small town where I lived, and by taking a bike, we were not as dependent on our parents to take us to places.

So, while I was used to bicycling since my early childhood years, the biking intensified during my university time in Maastricht. During those years, I lived with three other girls in a shared apartment where we cycled a few kilometers every day to get to the city center or go to the university. And while cycling had been a means of transportation for me for a long time, I still considered it a sport, as well. At least it was something that added movement to my daily life. Movement that I missed if I took the car to go everywhere. So besides being a means of transportation and having a positive impact on the environment, cycling was also good for health reasons. It is actually recommended to do 20 minutes of moderately intense movement, like walking, biking, or running, every day.[9] Taking a bike for short trips to the post office or the bakery can meet this recommendation easily.

Certainly, not every country is equally equipped for biking trips. The Netherlands or the flat Münsterland area are ideal since you don't have to struggle to get up hills. Also, the biking infrastructure plays an important role as biking lanes make trips less stressful, safer, and more enjoyable. During our years in Beijing, my husband and I used to cycle a lot as well. We were impressed by how well-developed the cycling lanes were in the part of Beijing where we lived, the Chaoyang district. I enjoyed biking as a way to avoid having to deal with taxi drivers who couldn't understand what I tried to say in Chinese, and it gave me some feeling of independence. In Tokyo, on the contrary, we did not use our bicycles a lot. One reason was that we had to cross hilly areas to get to where my husband worked. Another one was that the public transportation system (buses, metros, etc.) was so well-established and easy to use that we made great use of it. In Tokyo, we also moved around much more between different city districts than we had done in Beijing. The mere distances kept us tied to public transport over biking while living there. So, using a bike as a natural mode of transportation—as in the Netherlands—can be equally convenient in other countries if the biking infrastructure is well developed and if this mode of transportation fits regional and personal circumstances.

When we moved back to Switzerland in 2017, I thought about buying a bike, yet I did not act on my plan until spring 2019. Our second daughter was just a few months old, and my husband and I had become used to using our cars for almost every outing. We live in a small village with very little means of public transportation. So, using the car for everyday needs outside the village has become the norm. But one day, we thought it would be wonderful to discover the region and the beautiful nature around here through a different lens. After some consideration, we bought two e-bikes and a carrier with two child seats for our daughters. We have done many bike excursions with the girls, and we enjoy them very much. You get a different feel for the landscape and the nature when traveling by bike. I love smelling the grass or the flowers or biking through small forest lanes. My husband became so motivated that he tries to do several bike trips each week. He really misses it when he doesn't have the time to go. He bought the mountain bike version of the e-bike and regularly drives up the mountain range close to our home and sends me beautiful sunset pictures when arriving at the top. He also started biking to his work in Geneva several times a week. He says that his quality of life has increased a lot since he avoids the hour-long traffic jams in the mornings and evenings, and instead gets his workout in a beautiful setting twice a day. So, while cycling can certainly be used as a means of transportation, it can serve as a workout tool as well. It's a nice example of the powerful concept of "habit pairing." "Habit pairing" implies that you combine something you love doing with something you should be doing. In this case, you could pair your duty to go to work with your love for biking or being out in nature. Such pairing activities can be very handy when trying to create good new habits.[i]

The mindset to include sporting activities naturally into our everyday lives was also exemplified by a close Dutch mama friend I met in Tokyo. We were both pregnant at the same time. One day, when discussing the projects we had planned for our time in Japan, she told me that she intended to set up her own business in Tokyo. It would be a local branch of a larger company in the Netherlands, called Mom in Balance. Mom in Balance is a total-body workout program for mothers-to-be, mothers who recently delivered, and mothers looking for a good work-life balance. The trainings would take place outdoors all year long. The Dutch founder, Esther van Diepen, had the idea of creating the program after living in New

---

[i] The television show *CBS This Morning* released a story on the concept of habit pairing based on Gretchen Rubin's *Happier* podcast. It suggested pairing watching television with being on a treadmill or doing laundry while listening to your favorite music or podcast. These pairing exercises can be great for establishing positive new habits.

York, where she had observed many soon-to-be moms working out in New York City's parks. She decided to create a comprehensive outdoor work out for moms, allowing them to exercise and meet other like-minded mothers at the same time. She first introduced the program in the Netherlands, and now Mom in Balance is present in various countries across the world. My friend who started the local branch in Tokyo often told me how important it is for mothers to take time for themselves. We need not only to stay fit and healthy, but also need to regain balance and energy for our busy everyday home lives. She emphasized the positive effect that training outdoors had on the mind. And come rain or shine, she would be motivated to deliver the workouts in a good mood. The saying "There is no such thing as bad weather, only bad clothes" held very true in this case.

Yet, no matter what our natural passion or preference is sports-wise, what counts is that we show up for it. Some people have the discipline to do their weekly or daily sports program by themselves. Others are "pairing" their exercise, for example, by listening to podcasts while jogging. And yet others need accountability partners in order to show up. I love yoga, pilates, and dancing or exercising to happy music. And I have noticed that for me some sort of accountability mechanism is very good. When I sign up for a weekly yoga or dance class, odds are high that I will also attend it. I love to practice together with others. Accountability can help particularly in those moments when you don't feel motivated. When recently, it was raining and dark outside in the evening, I was not very motivated to leave the house for my weekly dance class. My parents were visiting and I would have much rather continued sitting with them and having a glass of wine. My father said, "This is why we make appointments, Judith. To show up and do what we are committed to doing." It reminded me of his inherent self-discipline that I mentioned earlier. He told me that we could have a glass of wine after my exercise. And with this in mind, I went, and upon entering the gym with the happy music, I was more than glad that

I had done so. I still believe that there are times when we should be flexible and allow ourselves to change our plans. Yet, generally, accountability mechanisms prove to be very helpful in achieving our dreams and goals. No matter what kind of physical activity we enjoy doing—whether it is a sport, a means of transportation (when biking or walking somewhere), or a step like taking the stairs instead of the elevator, we can certainly learn something from the inclination of many people in the Netherlands and consider physical activity a normal part of everyday life!

Beautiful Lessons Learned from the Netherlands

* **Keep an open attitude to other people and countries.** If you want to learn a new language, watching movies and the news in different languages can prove to be very beneficial.

* **Bring some color into your life.** They can vitalize you and boost your energy levels.

* **Be confident and do and wear what makes you happy.** Believe in yourself and go for what makes your heart sing. It does not matter what others might think as long as it makes you happy.

* **Do not take the comments or behaviors of others too personally.** Often it is more about them than about you, and it is not worth spending your energy on the negative comments or behavior of others.

* **Think about how you can simplify some of your daily routines** and don't feel shy to get support when necessary.

* **Don't stress yourself too much for little things.** Take it easy, and take time to be *gezellig*.

* **Build some physical exercise into your daily routine** in a natural way.

Chapter 5

FRANCE

Savoir Vivre

> ❖ *Food and "Savoir Vivre"*
>
> ❖ *Philosophy and Values*
>
> ❖ *Romance, Charm, and Elegance*
>
> ❖ *Sunlight in Provence and Personal Wellness Islands*

When thinking about France, the first things that often come to mind are the Eiffel tower and the romantic sound of the French language. I associate France with that charming, elegant, and somehow mysterious flair that seems to surround many of its places and people.

From an early age, I developed an interest in France and always thought that one day I would like to live there. One of my earliest and closest childhood friends was half German and half French, and this probably contributed to my fascination for the country. When playing at her house, I heard her mother speak to her in French. I loved the sound of the language, even though I didn't understand it at that time. Later on, we traveled to France's Bordeaux region for summer vacation with my family. I enjoyed these trips, and I felt fascinated by the Atlantic Ocean. My brother and I loved jumping and playing in the big waves. Also, the trips to Southern France filled my senses with color and scents. During our trips to the French supermarkets, we would buy fresh melons and delicious cheese. Even then, I liked the French way of life. In my mind, France will always be linked to images of fresh baguettes, fresh salads, cheese, and a bottle of wine.

During my Bachelor studies in Maastricht, we were encouraged to do a semester abroad. I immediately knew that I wanted to go to France. My top choices included Aix-en-Provence, Paris, and Grenoble, and I felt very excited to learn that I had been selected to study at Aix-en-Provence. So, in summer 2007, I left for one semester abroad in the country of cheese, wine, and *savoir vivre*.

Food and *"Savoir Vivre"*

We were sitting on the balcony of the apartment in Aix-en-Provence, and the father of my host family looked at me with a funny look: "Judith, do you need any help with the fish?" I looked up slightly embarrassed. The plate in front of me resembled a little disaster zone. I had tried to fillet several little fish but it hadn't worked in the most sophisticated way. After a short moment of reflection, I happily accepted his offer.

Later, when talking to my brother about eating habits and how to eat certain foods elegantly—especially tricky foods like fish that has to be filleted or certain finger foods —he said he was quite happy to have learned how to correctly fillet a fish. He found it especially useful for the times he visited his in-laws in France. Our parents had shown us how to do it. But I was not very good at it yet, and it became apparent during that particular evening at my French host family's place. Several French dishes are not easy to eat elegantly without some practice. If you watched the movie *Pretty Woman* and remember the scene when Julia Roberts tried to adhere to dinner etiquette while eating *escargots* (little snails), you have an idea of what I mean.

Food and dinner etiquette play important roles in many French households. In 2010, UNESCO included "France's multicourse gastronomic meal, with its rites and its presentation" on its list of "world intangible heritage." This label "seeks to protect cultural practices in the same way as UNESCO protects sites of cultural value and great natural beauty."[1] Pairing wine with the dishes, table dressing, and the precise placing of cutlery, water, and wine glasses form part of the dining rite that was awarded this distinction.

It's no secret that getting together to eat and drink well and to spend quality time together plays a very important role for many people and families in France. With my host families in Montpellier and in Aix-en-Provence during my French language studies, I enjoyed sitting together, eating, and discussing God and the world. Probably I enjoyed it so much because it reflected habits from my own upbringing. And even if I was still struggling to get my sentences together in French at that time, I enjoyed the conversations and listening to the others during these lively and cheerful moments. A recent study by the Organisation for Economic Co-operation and Development (OECD) shows that the French spend generally more time eating than people in other OECD countries. On average, they spend two hours and eleven minutes per day on eating and drinking. That is 40 minutes longer than the OECD average and more than twice as long as the average time spent in the U.S. France is closely followed by other Mediterranean countries like Italy, Greece, and Spain.[2]

France follows a certain serving order during a several-course menu. Meals usually start with a soup or salad before the main course. Cheese, a sweet dessert, and a *digestif* or a *tisane* (herbal tea) would sometimes round off the feast. The French propose an incredible myriad of delicacies, often topped off by a particular mix of French herbs, like *herbes de Provence,* an herb blend from the South of France that often includes thyme, rosemary, oregano, bay leaf, and basil. And there are lots of cuisine techniques. It is said that people in Northern France prefer to cook with butter, in Southern France with oil, and in the middle of the country, they use both. French meals can be quite heavy and hearty. Just think of croissants, *entrecôte* with Café de Paris butter, or the famous *tartiflette* cheese meal from Savoy. It is all the more surprising that the average French person is far from obese. Scientists have found that this "French paradox" can be explained by the fact that people in France eat smaller portions on average. Portions served in France can seem minuscule compared to those served in the U.S.[3] And since we tend to eat what we have in front of us, smaller portions can make a huge difference over time. Others argue that the low obesity rates can be explained by the amount of time the French take to sit down and enjoy each bite, instead of shoveling down their food.[4] This gives the brain more time to process and to signal a state of satisfaction.

When thinking about the traditional importance of the order of dishes, I recall an anecdote that my father shared. As a young man, he and one of his best friends traveled to France on one of their first trips outside Germany. Beside the linguistic hurdles they encountered when trying to apply their basic high-school French, he laughs about one of his first visits to a little French restaurant. They ordered from the menu and received a small salad. In German homes, it was quite common to eat the salad as a side dish to the main dish, so they waited for the main course to arrive soon after. And they waited. And waited. And waited. No main course came. After about half an hour of waiting, they looked at each other desperately. And as they were very hungry, they decided to eat the salad. As soon as they finished, the waitress passed by relieved. Finally, they had finished their starter—the salad—and she could serve the main course. It was a lesson about how food rituals vary from culture to culture, one my father never forgot and that continues to make us laugh to this day.

Of course, a multicourse eating ritual is not the reality for every meal in every French household. Yet there is a tendency to get together with family and loved ones to enjoy food, drinks, and conversation. France's former ambassador to UNESCO, Catherine Colonna, said, "The French love getting together to eat and drink well and enjoy good times in such a manner. It is part of our tradition—a quite active tradition."[5] Having a couple of glasses of wine while dining is also common. I love to think back to a lunch with one of my French professors and a couple of other university colleagues in Paris. In the bistro where we lunched, many people enjoyed a glass of red wine before heading back to work. In that cozy, relaxed atmosphere, we decided to have a little carafe of wine before returning to work, too. Also, people indulge in a newspaper or a book while enjoying a coffee or cappuccino in one of the many bistros in any French city. It might be these little daily pleasures, like taking the time to read a book while having a cappuccino or enjoying a glass of wine during lunch hour, that inspired the French term *savoir vivre*, which means "knowing how to live and enjoy life in a particular manner."

Philosophy and Values

The amount of time the average French person devotes to sitting down to eat and drink is not only related to the pure act of eating and drinking slowly. Sitting down for a meal also involves taking

85

the time for good conversation and spending quality time together. The advantages of having family meals together have been widely reported.[6,7] Studies show that common family meals not only help strengthen family bonds, they also help inspire and boost social and language skills in children. Families who eat at home also save money, as eating home-cooked meals is often much cheaper than eating out. Also, the food choices when eating together are often much healthier. One study even found that children who ate five to seven times per week with their family reported much better school grades than those who ate three times or less with the family per week. And it has been reported that children who enjoyed regular family meals were less likely to develop symptoms of depression or drug abuse.[8] Of course, there are cases where common family meals don't prevent a form of drug abuse or depression. And this shall by no means pass judgment on families that have to deal with such challenging events in life. Yet, family meals can help bring emotional support when difficulties arise for the family members. Getting together allows families to exchange, to stay connected, and to feel that there is a safe, common space at home. Sharing struggles can be a way to help find solutions. And celebrating good news together makes it much more fun.

During my childhood, my parents put a lot of emphasis on sitting down together for dinner with the whole family. Since my father could not make it home for lunch and only arrived relatively late at night, we used to have dinner quite late. As a consequence, my brother and I often went to bed later than many of our schoolmates. Yet, for my parents it was important to have some quality time together as a family in the evenings. We shared news about our respective days and often the evenings ended in lots of laughter and deep philosophical discussions. I really enjoyed these evenings. It was a moment for all of us to come together and connect.

Now, in my own little family, I notice how difficult it can be logistically to arrange for such evenings together. My husband travels frequently for work and sometimes comes home relatively late.[i] And I am often quite worn out by the end of the day when I pick up our older daughter from the nursery. But I still try to plan on eating together. While writing this, our younger daughter was about 10 months old, and her dinner consisted of a bowl of baby food. Often, I was busy feeding her and would only start eating once she was done. But it is wonderful to observe the interaction between her and her older sister. She loves observing her big sister and laughs or tries to get her attention with some sort of noise. Then our older daughter shares some of her wonderful three-year-old theories about life, which are so sweet to listen to. It is especially nice if my husband is home and joins these little family conversations. If, during the week we did not have a lot of time to sit down at the dinner table together, we would usually try to have some quality family time together during the weekends. We might start cooking late afternoon and sit, eat, and talk together for hours—something we all enjoy very much.

When learning about French traditions around eating and conversation, I was intrigued when learning how much emphasis is put on the subject of philosophy in French high schools.[9] It is part of the French *baccalauréat*, the French high-school completion requirement, and students have to pass the philosophy exam before being able to move on to higher education. While in many European countries, students learn about philosophical thoughts and theories, in France, students are required to put the concepts and theories they learned into practice.[10] Studying philosophy is compulsory and takes up a core role in France's secondary education. The number of hours of philosophy courses varies according to the focus the students

---

[i] This was the situation while writing this chapter, before the COVID-19 pandemic hit the world and travel became very restricted. Since then, my husband has not been traveling, which has changed our family eating routine for the better.

choose. But everyone is exposed to a few hours of philosophy courses per week. In the annual exam, students have to answer to questions like "Can a scientific truth be dangerous?" "Is it one's own responsibility to find happiness?" "Is truth preferable to peace?" Or, "Can one be right in spite of the facts?"[11,12] I was quite impressed when reading the type of questions students in secondary school in France are dealing with, and I really liked it. Such questions oblige students to think critically about questions that might concern them or others in society. And it encourages them to apply philosophical thought to conversation.

Philosophy as a subject was introduced in one of the first ever exams when the baccalaureate was launched in France in 1809. Originally, philosophy became a mandatory subject in order to create model citizens, citizens who could think critically and freely form their opinions.[13,14] Montesquieu emphasized the importance of citizens with critical thinking abilities for the newly proclaimed republic to work. The Age of Enlightenment—or the "centuries of philosophy"— as the 17th and 18th centuries are sometimes called, certainly played an important role in making philosophical discussions an integral part of the school curriculum in France. The intention was to engage people in philosophical discussions that everyone could understand or relate to. These included discussions on happiness, justice, and work. For a society as diverse as the French one, it was considered of utmost importance to develop a space where people could discuss, agree, and disagree. Attention was put on doing that in a respectful way and showing tolerance for other opinions. Simon Perrier, head of an association of French philosophy teachers, describes the ultimate goal of studying philosophy as: "The aim is to teach students to reflect on what they learn every day at home and in school. They learn how to approach issues thoughtfully by being introduced to philosophical texts."[15] Hence, space for engaging in personal reflection is provided for children from an early age. Pierre-Henri Tavoillot, head of the philosophy department at Université Paris-Sorbonne, observes that "many ordinary French people develop a love for intellectual and literary pursuits that continues later in life."[16] Philosophical meetings of high quality can be found "even in the smallest villages across France."[17]

Personally, I very much like that students are introduced to such philosophical questions at quite a young age. To think about such questions makes you reflect deeply about personal and societal values. Prioritizing these very values can be very helpful for decision-making and personal behavior later on in life. I'm part of a women's support network, and we regularly talk about personal growth practices and how to find and follow our own personal paths that make us happy. One session dealt with our personal values and asked us to not only identify them but also to prioritize a few of them. Such reflections can make it much easier to decide certain issues in everyday life. In one of her TED talks, bestselling author Brené Brown mentions that one of her core values is courage. So every day she tells herself that she wants to choose courage over comfort. And this attitude leads her behavior and decision-making throughout the day. As parents, it can be helpful to think about some of the core values that are important to us and to practice these in order to serve as good role models for our children. There is not one common blueprint for values. Everyone is different and can have different things they value most. But it is worth thinking about some personal core values. I have noticed that three of my core values are open-mindedness, empathy, and authenticity. For me, it is important to be open to different ways of thinking, living, or whatever it may be. Since I am interested in intercultural learning and appreciation, open-mindedness is crucial. Empathy is, in my opinion, important in order to be able to put yourself in someone else's shoes. This makes it much easier to express loving kindness for them and their behaviors. Authenticity can make relationships much more meaningful. By expressing your views, beliefs, joys, and struggles in a genuine way, it becomes much easier to connect with others on a deeper level. I enjoy engaging in deep discussions with people. And if people are authentic—and, as a consequence, also vulnerable—I find it much easier to connect with them. As I write about three of my core values, there is still a long way to go to adhere to them consistently in my everyday life. My husband would probably argue that sometimes I am not open-minded at all when I have a strong opinion on how something should be done at home. And he would probably be quite right. We can always continue to work to live our core values.

During my time in France—and also later on, when meeting with friends and acquaintances from France—I often noticed an inherent interest in engaging in deep, reflective discussions about world affairs, politics, or life in general. I am often surprised and impressed by arguments and reflective lines of thought that come up. Maybe this love for lively discussion and philosophizing is linked to the early exposure to philosophical questions in France. And maybe it is something that can inspire us to think about some questions to which no easy answers exist.

Romance, Charm, and Elegance

*"Elegance is when the inside is as
beautiful as the outside."*

—Coco Chanel

For many people, France and the French language are intrinsically linked to notions of romance, charm, and elegance. During my university years, I started to enjoy watching French movies. Among them was the classic *Amélie* and *Paris, Je T'aime*. I was drawn into the romantic, charming, and sometimes very melancholy atmosphere of these movies. I watched *Paris, Je T'aime* countless times. It consists of several short vignettes that take place in different *arrondissements* in Paris. Each one reveals insights into very different lives and surroundings, but they all somehow link to the idea of love in its various forms. There was something mysterious about these movies that reflected what I felt when I visited France. They held a special, charming, and sometimes melancholy atmosphere.

The French language is considered by many to be the most romantic language in the world. And French women are known for having a very natural charm. Jamie Cat Callan, author of *Parisian Charm School*, exclaims: "We live in un-charming times, and if we bring a little more charm into the world, we will all be living in a better place." Charm, according to her, consists of an "irresistible combination of elegance, confidence, and mystery."[18] It is something we all can cultivate in our own lives. Felicia Czochanski summarizes several of Cat Callan's lessons on using charm while dating. One of them consists of not putting too much pressure on yourself or on others. Instead of going out for an official one-on-one date, it seems quite typical in France to first have informal dates and encounters at dinner parties. Another casual way of dating is to meet for active dates, like a walk outside. Being in nature and wandering around can take off some of the pressure when getting to know somebody. [19]

I think back to a date with my husband when we had just gotten to know each other. We met at a friend's birthday party and continued talking and, later on, dancing when we moved from club to club after the party. Shortly after, we met to have a coffee, and we wandered through Geneva toward the coffee place together. I had just arrived in Geneva and did not yet know the city very well. I really enjoyed Antoine's explanations about the city when we crossed the river and passed shopping areas and strolled through the old city. It was very easygoing. Simply walking around together can relieve a lot of pressure and nervousness you might feel on a first one-on-one date.

I feel spending time in nature still does wonders for our relationship, even now. We used to jog or bike together from time to time. Often these were the moments when we started the best conversations about things going on in our lives. I noticed that having these moments in nature together often helped us address an issue we were struggling with in our relationship. Or it helped us to just update each other on some important thoughts and considerations about things going on in our lives. Now, with the addition of our two little daughters, we rarely have the opportunity to do sports outings together. But recently we started doing bicycle trips with the whole family—with our little ones sitting in a trailer in the back. This has given us the opportunity to engage in these kinds of conversations in nature again. Of course, it is also possible to have very good talks over a one-on-one dinner in the evening. The French expression *tête à tête* means having a private, face-to-face conversation, usually in an intimate setting. Yet enjoying some intimate togetherness from time to time in nature can also lead to wonderful moments of connection in a casual, scenic atmosphere.

During my time in France, the elegance and allure that many of the French women naturally emit impressed me. I liked the way their clothes and accessories often naturally balanced chic and casual style. They also exuded a certain confidence. Some articles claim that French women just don't overdo it and accept themselves as they are. This doesn't mean that you can't emphasize your favorite aspects of your appearance. But emphasis is often on staying naturally elegant. And less is usually considered more. If you stand behind your flaws and strengths alike, you wear a natural confidence that can make you very attractive.[20] I think Coco Chanel expressed the charming beauty secret of many French women very nicely when she said: "Beauty begins the moment you decide to be yourself." So maybe the most charming thing we can do is to work on feeling comfortable in our own skin and equally appreciating the imperfections and the strengths we all have. Imperfections—inside and out—make us human and natural. Once we start appreciating them, we might be one step closer to seeing the myriad of beautiful aspects in ourselves and others alike.

Sunlight in Provence and Personal Wellness Islands

"Bonjours les amis. Bienvenus à Aix-en-Provence. Ce n'est pas Aix en 'vacances'. Et ce n'est pas 'sexe' en Provence. C'est Aix-en-Provence," *the good-looking man in front of us said with a smile on his face. The other exchange students and I had to laugh. This was our first introduction to the course "Civilisation Française" at the university in Aix-en-Provence. Our teacher had just explained jokingly that instead of being in Provence for vacation or for having sex, we had come to Aix-en-Provence to study.*

Despite these initial specifications, I often had the impression of being on vacation during my time as an Erasmus student in Aix. There was something so charming about the city, and I really enjoyed the morning walks to university with my housemate. We passed through the narrow labyrinthine streets lined with buildings in light ochre colors like you see in many Mediterranean areas. The colors alone made me feel like I was on vacation. People strolled around the streets walking their many dogs everywhere. But what I liked most was the special sunlight in the region. When leaving the city for an excursion with friends or when going to the airport to pick someone up, I'd drive by the beautiful hills that always seemed to be submerged in the special golden sunlight of Provence.

I now understand why so many painters and artists came to Provence. The sunlight with all its variations, reflecting on fields of lavender, sunflowers, and raps is beyond beautiful. Paul Cézanne, one of the most famous artists of Aix-en-Provence, is one example of artists who painted the same subject countless times in varying color variations. He is known to have painted one of his favorite subjects, the Sainte-Victoire mountain, more than 60 times. The special sunlight in Provence drenched the same subject in all different color variations and probably played a very important role in its popularity with artists. Vincent van Gogh also traveled to Provence and painted 350 works of art during the two years that he spent in Arles and Saint-Remy-de-Provence. Some of his paintings from there became his most famous oeuvres.[21] Van Gogh was so impressed by the "yellow sun" in Provence and by the beautiful clear colors that he wanted to create an *"atelier of the future"* for artists. His vision was to assemble artists in Provence as he felt that it was a beautiful, inspiring place to work on creative arts. The intense blue sky, the dark green cypresses, the olive trees, the flowering fruit trees, or the violet lavender fields inspired him. The clear colors in the landscapes quickened his imagination. Some say the ice-cold mistral wind, a northwesterly wind in Southern France that can blow for days, might be one reason why nature's play of color is so beautiful. Once the wind has ceased, the landscapes are left in the most clear, amazing color variations.[22] Similarly the famous *calenques* (mountain bays) in the Marseille and Cassis areas are of stunning beauty. The water coming from the sea and flowing through the fjord-like bays have the most amazing color variations of blue and turquoise. When wandering around there, I felt awed by the amazing beauty of nature.

The sunlight in Provence and the charm of the region brought me to recognize that it can be very powerful to look for places where we feel at peace and where we can get into a flow state. It can be beneficial for work, for an artistic project or simply for self-reflection or relaxation. Vincent van Gogh and many other artists went to Provence, attracted by the setting and atmosphere in this beautiful region. It seemed to help them get into a perfect state of mind or flow to work on their art. Of course, we can't all move to Provence or to our favorite vacation destination, but it is possible to look for little wellness islands in our surroundings in everyday life. It can be a nice café, a special place in nature close to home or a room at home where we feel lighthearted and comfortable. For me personally, my workroom located under the roof in our house is that place. We painted it in light cream and white colors and lined it with bookshelves full of inspiring books. We added souvenirs from our travels to Asia, Africa and Latin America, too. Every time I look at the lotus-leaf soap in the adjacent bathroom, I feel calmed since it reminds me of a spa. And when I see the little fans in their beautiful boxes covered with Chinese writing, I am reminded of the charming area in Beijing where we bought them. I love going up there when I have to concentrate on work and for writing this book. It is my favorite place to sit and be. On clear days, we have the chance to see Mont Blanc from the window and sun floods the room.

Such "wellness islands" in everyday life can be transformative, and you might even have more than one. In Japan, I loved to sit on our balcony and observe the skyline of Tokyo. In China, I had several cafés I frequented while working on my Ph.D. thesis. These kinds of places can not only be very helpful and inspiring for one's self, but it can also be wonderful to explore these wellness oases with your partner or friends. It might be a park, a restaurant, or a bar that makes you feel at home and in your element. In China, we often met at the same bar with a group of friends on Thursday evenings. Simply arriving at the bar put us in a comfortable, homey mood.

So, while it can be a beautiful experience to visit Provence to experience its special atmosphere, I think that we can find something similar to the sun of Provence in our daily lives when we look. We just need to make sure that from time to time we take the initiative to find and visit the places where we feel good and comfortable to focus, to reenergize, or just to relax and unwind.

Beautiful Lessons Learned from France

☀ **Take a moment to sit down and enjoy eating and drinking.** It is much healthier and more enjoyable to eat consciously and to savor every bite.

☀ **Make time for family meals and meals with friends.** Nice discussions when sitting together are wonderful for bonding and like food for the soul.

☀ **Reflect on some philosophical questions.** They might reveal some of your core values and knowing one's core values can make daily life decisions much easier and more consistent.

☀ **Add some charm to your daily interactions.** Charm can be like a sunray in everyday life and can make our world a little more beautiful.

☀ **Pay as much attention to feeling good from the inside as to feeling good from the outside.** These are the secrets of Coco Channel for beauty and elegance.

☀ **Bring a Provence atmosphere to your home by establishing "wellness islands" in your everyday life.** Regularly visit these places to relax, recharge, or get into a flow state of mind.

Chapter 6

SWITZERLAND

Relax and Enjoy

❖ *The Love for Nature*

❖ *Develop a "Can Do" Mentality
Through Outdoor Activities*

❖ *Coziness, Taking It Easy, and the "Apéro" Concept*

❖ *Innovation, Collaboration, and
a Stage for World Affairs*

I n 2008, I moved to the beautiful country of Switzerland. I was about to finish my Bachelor's degree in European Studies in Maastricht, and I felt motivated to keep studying and specializing. After the Erasmus semester in France, I felt the desire to continue learning French as I was fascinated by the language. However, I did not feel confident enough to pursue a Master's degree in French. I was all the more excited when I discovered that a graduate institute in Geneva offered a bilingual Master's degree in English and French in Development Studies. My travels and experiences living abroad had opened my interest in learning more about other countries and their political, economic, and social developments. The possibility to study societal dynamics and human development policies in depth intrigued me. So, I was over the moon when I received confirmation of my acceptance to the Master's program. Even though I had not visited Geneva before, I felt intuitively that it was the right place to go next. I could never have dreamed that I was about to meet my future husband a couple of weeks later or that Switzerland would become the adopted home country for me and our daughters.

The Love for Nature

In all things of nature there is
something of the marvelous.

—Aristotle

When thinking of Switzerland, the images of the majestic, beautiful landscapes that you encounter in the various parts of the country immediately come to mind. As a child, I often watched the famous *Heidi* movies, which portrayed a little girl living with her grandfather in the Swiss Alps. I loved the movies, the nature, and the innocence that they depicted.

Even now, I still often feel like I'm living in a fairytale when I see the spectacular landscape surrounding us here in Switzerland. I love the route we take when visiting my in-laws. On the highway, the views are so spectacular that you have to be disciplined to concentrate on the street instead of the view. Similarly, when I drive to our three-year-old's nursery, I am mesmerized by the beauty of the scenery. We drive through vast fields with flowers, horses, and cows; through vineyards; and from time to time, we catch glimpses of the lake and the majestic Alps and Mont Blanc in the distance. The different color variations of the sky always paint the view in a changing, stunning perspective. In these moments, when taking in the beauty of the surroundings, I sense a deep feeling of serene happiness and tranquility. Recently, I started going for occasional jogs, and I could not get enough of the magnificent views. So, I kept jogging the same path to enjoy some of the same views over and over again.

During my Master's Studies in Geneva in 2008, the institute where I studied was located five minutes from the famous Lac Léman (Lake Geneva), the second-largest lake in Central Europe. It's situated between Switzerland and France. Every now and then, I would stroll around the lake pathway after classes or during lunch break. And each time, I felt like I was on vacation. I loved breathing in the fresh air while standing at the water's edge and looking at the incredible panorama of the Alps in the background. Cities that are connected with water through rivers, lakes, or the sea, share an exceptional atmosphere. And strolling on waterfronts can have a deeply calming and refreshing effect. The landscapes in Switzerland are quite frankly amazing. From the Alps with their great majesty, to the Bernese Oberland with its famous Eiger, Mönch, and Jungfrau mountains, or the iconic forests, and stunning pristine lakes. Some lakes have intense turquoise colors due to the glacial particles that make the lake color appear blue-green. Also, the Lavaux region at the coastline of the Lac Léman is of exceptional beauty with its vast terraced vineyards illuminating the view on the lac and the mountains in the background.

Switzerland represents a paradise for nature activities all year long, and people love being in nature. In summer, you can enjoy picnics at the lake, swim, or go hiking. In winter, you are never far from the mountains for a day of skiing, sledding, or snowshoeing. And also in spring and autumn, you can find a myriad of things to do outdoors. For me, coming from Northern Germany, taking a ski vacation had always meant a drive of 10 or 12 hours to reach the ski resort we visited in Austria. Here in Switzerland, you can drive somewhere in the morning, enjoy a day of skiing and return home the same evening. The beautiful scenery and the well-developed tourism may explain why people in Switzerland enjoy spending time in nature so much. But the love for nature and for spending time in it is not exclusive to Switzerland. And the benefits of spending time in nature hold true for all of us, no matter where we live.

Many studies prove the positive effects that nature has on our well-being. Richard Louv, author of *Last Child in the Woods*, writes about a nature-deficit disorder that is not "an anomaly in the brain" but "the loss of connection of humans to their natural environment."[1] He says that a close connection with nature helps improve our physical, mental, and spiritual well-being as it makes us feel alive from the inside. Research has shown that nature can have a positive impact on our hearts, nervous systems, and even on our eyesight. Also, the stress hormone, cortisol, is lowered by being outdoors and other problems like hypertension can be avoided or reduced by spending time in nature. Nature can additionally help in emotional regulation, in improving memory function, in building attention and focus, and in enhancing problem-solving and creative skills. Studies have also found that nature walks helped people suffering from depression to regain energy and a will to recover. And research continues to examine if regular walks or trips into the wilderness could help patients who are fighting with a terminal disease.[2]

In our world now, with an increased use of technology, social media, and a trend toward urbanization, staying close to nature can seem difficult at times. Experts encourage us to find ways to incorporate nature, for both children and adults alike, into our everyday lives. When reflecting on the research about the importance of nature for children and adults, I had to think back to my childhood. Even though I was born in a large city, my family and I were lucky enough to have a big garden. I spent much of my childhood in the garden with my brother and a little group of friends. We would climb up trees, build tree houses, play hide and seek, and make fruit salad with the fruits we found on the various trees. When we moved up north to a small town in Germany, this new environment increased our connection to nature even more. My brother and I biked to our primary school on our own bikes, and we spent whole afternoons playing with our close school and neighborhood friends outside in the cornfields, in the forest, and in our gardens. We collected flowers and played "flower sellers." We went to the little river running through the town and sat on the tree branches overhanging it, and discussed our joys and worries. Or we created little houses with twigs and leaves we found outside. We always found new inspiration for play. As Richard Louv describes in his book, it felt so natural to spend time outside then that we thought that it would be the same for all our lives and for our children one day, as well.

But, if I am very honest with myself, I have to say that I lost some of this nature connection during my teen and adult years. While reading *Last Child in the Woods*, I realized how important it is—especially in our times of constant media intake and access to technology—to consciously work on keeping or recreating this nature connection myself and also for our children. Sometimes I still cannot believe how quickly times have changed over the last two decades with the Internet revolution.

When I heard about "surfing the Internet" when I was a young high-school kid, I imagined someone with a surfboard in his arms. Slowly, I became used to writing emails, and nowadays, it seems difficult to imagine how we used to live before the Internet made its way into our homes. It is so convenient and brings a myriad of opportunities; it is in continuous development with artificial intelligence in only its infancy. I am personally very grateful that it is so easy to stay in touch with friends and family across the world, thanks to the Internet. But at the same time, as many of us already know, it also has its downsides. The constant availability and the never-ending flow of messages, requests, notifications, and news affects our minds. It requires a lot of thoughtful consideration, planning, and discipline to not let the electronic devices take over our daily rhythms. Study after study is showing how important it is for the body and the mind to be able to switch off from time to time. It's essential to find moments of mindful calmness without being interrupted by any technical device. An outing in nature can be one of the best things to do. If you are like me and you've lost some of your connection to nature, it could be worth consciously considering how to include nature more in your everyday life. It might come in the form of a weekly stroll, a bike tour, or just organizing a picnic from time to time in a nice place nearby. Studies have shown that nature outings can be great ways for family bonding as well.

Recently, my husband mentioned that it was necessary to cut some of the tree branches and flowers in our garden to prepare the plants for the coming winter. It was autumn, and there were many leaves on the ground. While my husband was busy cutting the trees, our three-year-old daughter and I took on the job of collecting the leaves and branches. It was such a satisfying activity. I felt very close to the trees and flowers and to nature in general. After two hours of garden work, we were all exhausted but happy at the same time. And I loved seeing how much fun our daughter had in helping us. That day I decided I would make an effort to include some more nature activities in our everyday lives again, even small ones to begin with.

Many schools and even nurseries are incorporating nature activities in their schedules now. A few weeks ago, our three-year-old told us proudly that they had been going out to plant spinach with one group of her nursery. I later saw pictures of her and her close friend, watering the seeds with a watering can. And they have been returning and are very keen to observe their spinach leaves growing. Research has indeed shown that gardening has very positive effects on both body and mental health. Many people living in the so-called blue zones, where people are famed for their longevity, share one common hobby: gardening well into their 80s and 90s. It provides a moment of mindful calmness that can come close to meditative practice. At the same time, it engages people regularly in moderate physical exercise. Through this activity, people are also exposed to the sun or at least to natural light, which boosts vitamin D levels and their moods at the same time.[3,4]

Another beautiful side of being in nature and connecting with it is how you start to feel part of something bigger. On a recent trip with my husband to Namibia, we were blown away by the expansive, virgin, and very diverse landscapes we encountered. We saw a variety of desert landscapes, from dunes to red stone steppes, that took our breath away. We sat by a fire in the evenings and watched the countless stars twinkling above us. The experience revived a feeling in me that I had lost for a while: that we are all part of something bigger and of a circle of life. We observed wild animals and their erratic behaviors and reflected on how nature works. These amazing experiences left us with a comforting calm and insight about the essence of life. Of course, one does not need to fly to Namibia or live in Switzerland to connect with nature. It can be equally nice to bike through the neighborhood or to take a walk in a park, a field, or a forest nearby. Nature can revitalize us. And nurturing our love for nature can be very fulfilling, no matter where in the world we live!

Develop a "Can-Do" Mentality Through Outdoor Activities

Switzerland is a perfect place for all kinds of outdoor activities and hiking adventures. My husband and I often organized hiking weekends with our families or friends. While I don't consider myself to be the natural hiking lover who wants to go hiking all year long, I really enjoyed each trip. There was something very satisfying about walking for hours through nature, and I often had the impression that I grew calmer with each step. Swiss nature lends itself to many types of outdoor activities. One activity that I discovered in Switzerland was canyoning. Canyoning is an adventure sport that involves climbing, jumping, swimming, and gliding while navigating your way through canyons and waterfalls. I will never forget my very first canyoning experience. After a year of dating, Antoine had mentioned that he would love to do a canyoning tour for his birthday. I was very motivated when he said this, as I thought that canyoning was canoeing—and I loved canoeing. So, I happily agreed. It was only days later that I understood the difference between the two.

On the day of the activity, my heart started sinking when we reached the canyon with our two guides and a small group of people. The guides showed how we were supposed to rope down the canyon to reach the river that we were going to descend. We were equipped with a helmet and our neoprene suits, and we were told not to forget to push our feet against the canyon when letting ourselves down—to avoid crushing our faces against the canyon. My heart was racing. But once I started going down, it was not as scary as I had thought. When I reached the riverbed, I could not believe that I had descended a canyon wall all by myself. The next couple of hours were full of adventurous activities. We jumped from rocks, slid over little waterfalls, and passed with ropes over canyon walls before letting ourselves drop down into the river ponds. Each activity pushed up my adrenalin level, and I had to take my courage in both hands countless times. Yet, each time I managed to slide or jump down somewhere, I felt not only relieved but also happy and proud of having achieved it. It was like the feeling I often experienced when hiking up a mountain. At some point, I would feel exhausted and would want to give up and return. Yet, nothing could be more rewarding than pushing through and reaching the top, or—in the canyoning case—the final destination.

Research has shown that our will to achieve our goals is present from our very early years. Even very small children want to achieve their goals, not just any way, but on their own. For parents, it might be difficult at times to see their little ones stumble, fall down, and hit themselves over and over again. For babies and small children, however, no fall or bruise will make them stop getting back up to continue exploring the world. The explanation for that can be found in brain research. To make an effort and then have success releases dopamine, which in turn generates a real feeling of exaltation. The body rewards itself, and it starts already as a baby. This can also explain the sense of satisfaction that we have after a good workout or after achieving something we were working toward.[5]

The founder of the Swiss organization where my husband works knows how rewarding and stimulating the achievement of milestones can be for people. In 2010, he encouraged his employees to take part in a glacier climbing tour. The goal was to ascend the Breithorn glacier in the snow-capped Zermatt area, located more than 4,000 meters high. My husband and I decided to participate. We did not walk up the 4,000 meters. We first made a large part of the journey in an aerial cable car and then walked up the last part ourselves. It was a wonderful experience. We were equipped with all the necessary equipment for a glacier trek and participated in preparatory training. While the climb was quite a physical exercise, we were rewarded with spectacular views when we reached the top. We had the most stunning panorama in the perfect sunshine, and we enjoyed a picnic at the peak. This is when you realize that the effort, the sweating, the pain, and the perseverance paid off. And this is something so true for many things in life. For any major project we engage in, we often need to invest a lot of effort, resilience, and perseverance.

Take Thomas Edison, one of the greatest inventors in history. In his effort to devise a new type of storage battery, Edison had made over nine thousand experiments. When one of Edison's associates asked with sympathy if it wasn't a shame that this tremendous amount of work had not gotten him any results, Edison apparently responded with a smile: "Results! Why man, I have gotten a lot of results. I know several thousand things that won't work."[6] This relentless attitude to keep trying and going paid off in numerous groundbreaking inventions with which he blessed our world.

Coming back to my husband's boss: he knew about the type of satisfaction and sense of achievement that a glacier-climbing experience could have for his employees. And he certainly wanted them to integrate this drive for achievement and the accompanying satisfaction in their work and personal lives as well. In my view, an excellent way to engage your employees and invest in their personal growth.

Coziness, Taking it Easy, and the "*Apéro*" Concept

"Look for the bare necessities,
The simple bare necessities,
Forget about your worries and your strife..."

—Baloo, *The Jungle Book*

In the movie *The Jungle Book*, Mowgli and his bear friend Baloo walk around the jungle, and Baloo starts singing the famous song about being happy with the bare necessities. In German, the translation of this song is a bit different, and it goes: *"Probier's mal mit Gemütlichkeit, mit Ruhe und Gemütlichkeit, jagst du den Alltag und die Sorgen weg."* The word *Gemütlichkeit* is difficult to translate into English, yet it comes close to the notion of coziness and comfort. For me, the concepts of coziness and comfort are closely related to my image of Switzerland. I was positively surprised by the ability of many of my Swiss acquaintances, friends and especially my in-laws to simply enjoy the moment, take it easy and make themselves comfortable. And that is why this song often pops up in my mind when thinking of Switzerland. It implies that when you take it easy and care for your bare necessities—whatever they may be at the moment—you can forget your worries and your everyday stress for a while.

One of the many features that I appreciate about my Swiss husband is his ability to enjoy the moment and see the positive side in little things. He has the wonderful ability to make you look forward to something and then to enjoy that moment thoroughly when it comes. For example, when he talks to me about a new recipe he is about to try, he describes in detail what it will taste like. Or he gets out the sun chairs in the morning before leaving for work and tells me to have a nap on one if I have the chance during the day. Or he buys a nice bottle of wine and describes to me in detail the different flavors. Or he describes a country he wants to visit with me. This thirst for life and for the pleasant experiences and adventures that life has to offer is something that I appreciate a lot and that is also very contagious. I can see where it comes from since his whole family is like this. I am amazed by the enthusiasm and the happiness that my mother-in-law shows for the little pleasures in life: warm sun rays when sitting on a terrace, a tasty cup of cappuccino, an afternoon spent together. When she visits us and I prepare a simple cereal breakfast in the morning, she happily exclaims each time that she loves the wonderful, cozy breakfasts at our place. And my father-in-law and my sister-in-law have the same unique ability to enjoy the moment.

Of course, I cannot generalize my experiences based on one particular Swiss family. But I have experienced this coziness and comfort feeling with many people that I have met across the country. Already the way of speaking seems much more relaxed than in many parts of Germany. In addition to the different official national languages in Switzerland (German, French, Italian, and Romansh), you can find a myriad of different dialects in the Swiss-German part of the country. Even though I am not always able to understand them completely, I really enjoy listening to them as they somehow reflect this flexible coziness attitude that stands out to me in the country. It is not only about the pleasant sounds but also about the speed with which people speak. In Germany, sometimes people speak at such a fast pace that you can get dizzy listening to them—and I am certainly no exception. My husband told me quite often when we started dating that I was speaking like a high-speed train when telling him a story in German. In Switzerland, and from what I observed particularly in the German-speaking part, people talk with much more calmness and tranquility. It can be quite a change for someone from Germany, but it often has a relaxing effect on me. Some studies found that people in the Bern canton in Switzerland speak the slowest in the whole country, with five syllables per second instead of six, compared to other cantons. This might not seem like a big difference in a second, but in a minute, it will account for four to five sentences less. Adrian Leeman, the linguist who conducted this study, explains this slower pace by the long vocals being used in this particular dialect.[7]

Another study by the English psychologist Robert Wiseman on the walking speed of the average pedestrian in 32 cities showed that people in Bern's city center walk quite slow in the international comparison. People in Singapore, in contrast, seem to be almost jogging through the city.[8] My point here is, however, not about the speed of speaking or walking in Switzerland. Instead, it is about the attitude toward life. It seemed quite often to me that people don't stress out as much in their everyday lives and they spend less time hustling around. This can have a very restorative and calming effect on your everyday life.

In addition, many people seem to enjoy the small moments. Many books and inspirational slogans tell us that we should enjoy the moment and live fully in the present. And yet, this often still seems a difficult thing to do for many of us. I am still trying to learn something from this positive attitude of my in-laws who understand how to savor little moments. I have started using a five-minute-journal application, which asks you at the end of each day to mention three amazing things that happened in your day. Even though I don't manage to do it every single day, I notice that my mood generally improves when I do it as I start to appreciate the little things in life, like a nice conversation with a friend or a good laugh with my daughters or my husband. These are some of the things that I may have started taking for granted without consciously appreciating and reflecting on them from time to time and feeling grateful. Many successful and happy people across the globe advise you to keep a gratitude journal to make life happier and to attract more and more good things, people and vibrations into your life. And there are many ways to do it. You may want to write down three things or people to be grateful for every day. Others stretch it to writing down ten items every day to start looking at the tiny things in everyday life to be happy for. For example, the smile of a stranger or a sequence of green traffic lights when driving. Indeed, Canadian author, entrepreneur, podcaster, and public speaker Neil Pasricha is leading a movement focusing on the awesome little things in everyday life.

When Pasricha faced some severe difficulties in life, including a divorce and his best friend's suicide, he started writing down one awesome thing a day on a blog that he created. They were things like a cashier in the supermarket who opened up a new line when he was waiting at the check-out or getting all his clothes from the washing machine into the dryer without dropping anything. His blog became a huge success and scored over 100 million visits and Pasricha has since then published several bestselling books on the "awesomeness" in everyday life. They make me smile a lot since they point out little everyday things that are just awesome when they happen. And it is such a pleasure to see how easy it is to add some lightness and awesomeness to your life, by acknowledging such moments and by appreciating them. Now every time I manage to put the whole washing machine load into the dryer in one go, I have to think of other people who are happy when that happens—and it makes me happy, too.

Another example which shows the Swiss tendency to enjoy the moment and have a cozy time is the concept of organizing an *apéro*.[9] It is something that I quickly started to appreciate after moving to Switzerland. When invited to somebody's place in the evening, people frequently offer an *apéro*—a sort of cocktail hour—usually including alcoholic or non-alcoholic drinks and some finger food. The finger food can be anything from dried meat, cheeses, grapes, olives, tomatoes, or crackers to very sophisticated finger-food creations. The idea of having an *apéro* together is usually to spend some quality moments together, without creating too much fuss about the preparation. I have come to love this *apéro* culture, and we do these cocktails often. When Antoine and I cook during the weekends, we often start early in the afternoon with some sort of *apéro*. It is a very cozy moment when you sit down for a drink with some snacks before eating or even cooking the main meal. It is often one of my favorite moments, since it is so easygoing and flexible and puts you in a pleasant, relaxed mood before sitting down for dinner.

We try to always have some olives and tomatoes in the fridge to offer as an *apéro* whenever someone comes over. We also noticed that it is quite a common thing to do among neighbors. When we first moved to our little village close to Geneva and introduced ourselves to our next-door neighbors, they immediately asked if we'd like to stay for an *apéro*. So, we had a nice bottle of wine and some finger food together—an excellent way to get to know each other in an informal setting. This way of saying, "Let's have an *apéro*" relates very much to what bear Baloo told Mowgli in the jungle book: that with a sense of coziness and taking it easy, the day-to-day stresses melt away, and happiness will come your way!

Innovation, Collaboration, and a Stage for World Affairs

Despite the Swiss sense of taking it easy and taking it down a notch in many day-to-day interactions, they are also known for working in a very efficient and productive manner. Switzerland is not only known for its cheese, its chocolate, and its watches. For years, Switzerland ranked among the top five out of approximately 140 countries in the global competitiveness report published yearly by the World Economic Forum (WEF). Switzerland is also ranked continuously as one of the most innovative countries worldwide, earning the first place on the global innovation index in 2018. It is a mixture of internationally recognized research centers, strong technology know-how, and a qualified and productive workforce that makes Switzerland such an innovative country.[10]

In terms of innovative research, Switzerland was the country with most patent applications per million inhabitants in 2018—and not for the first time. With 956 patent applications per million inhabitants in 2018, Switzerland reached an all-time high and outdistanced the other European countries by far. The EU had an average of 139 applications per million in the same year.[11] The quality of the research in Switzerland also reflects in the percentage of citations in national scientific publications by researchers from other countries. Switzerland has indeed the "highest share of the most frequently cited scientific papers on a worldwide basis."[12] It is also the country with the highest proportion of doctoral-degree holders among the working-age population. This can be attributed to the substantial number of foreign Ph.D.s living in the country. It is also remarkable that 25 percent of students and more than 40 percent of researchers at Switzerland's higher educational institutions come from abroad. More than half of the teaching staff in the world-renowned institutes of technology in Zurich and Lausanne come from outside Switzerland. The high salaries help attract experts from all over the world; Swiss university staff members earn on average twice as much as they would earn in neighboring countries. This results in a "brain gain" to Switzerland's advantage. Another unique feature in Switzerland is the efficient collaboration and the information and technology exchange between universities and companies. Leading-edge companies choose Switzerland as a location due to the enormous possibilities for synergy with academic and research organizations. And public-private cooperation is a term that is encountered daily in Switzerland's research universe. [13,14]

You might have heard of the famous Swiss Solar Impulse project: a Swiss-led mission to fly a solar-powered plane around the world. It is one of the great examples of close cooperation between the academic world and the private sector. Efforts of industry partners and the Federal Institute of Technology in Lausanne (EPFL) were summoned to deal with the multitude of technical challenges involved in the endeavor. It was, however, not just some kind of "adventure" in which the two pilots, Bertrand Piccard and André Borschberg, engaged. It was a trial combined with the message that by using such technology, we could drastically reduce the world's energy consumption. This would be a leap forward toward saving natural resources and improving the quality of life. Also, the European Organization for Nuclear Research, known as CERN, is based in Switzerland. It's one of the world's largest and most respected centers for scientific research and countless pathbreaking innovations can be attributed to it. The World Wide Web (WWW) was, for example, invented by a British scientist, Tim Berners-Lee, at CERN in 1989. [15,16]

A country where innovative thought, creativity, and outside-the-box thinking is not only supported, but stimulated, is an attractive magnet for people with innovative ideas. The strong Swiss currency and the comparatively high salaries are also desirable incentives. Of course, not everything is only rosy. The University of Bern found in research in 2014 that one quarter of the Swiss workforce felt exhausted and worn out. Some 300,000 people or 6 percent of the working population was close to a total burn-out on a physical, emotional, and mental level.[17] When it comes to gender equality in the workplace—such as equal pay and supporting women's career choices, for example, with suitable childcare arrangements—there is a lot of room for improvement. Switzerland was, in fact, one of the last countries in Europe to introduce women's suffrage rights, as late as 1971.

There is something unique to this innovative, dynamic nature of working hard and making things work, often through forms of creative collaboration. During my Master's studies in Geneva, I learned about several public/private partnerships in the global health sector. I remember that I was impressed when learning about the innovative set-up model behind these organizations. They were based on a dynamic public/private cooperation model, allowing them to combine advantages of each sector and making them very efficient. In terms of innovative collaboration between the public and the private sector, there is a lot to be learned from Switzerland. Certainly, safeguards are necessary when these two sectors start cooperating. But tremendous opportunities can open up if walls are crossed and people start working together.

Switzerland has a worldwide reputation when it comes to collaboration and bringing different parties to the table. It has been hosting international organizations and conferences for more than 150 years. The foundation of the International Committee of the Red Cross (ICRC) back in 1863 was only the beginning of Switzerland's active involvement in humanitarian and diplomatic affairs. Geneva has especially made itself a name as a hub of global governance initiatives and is therefore often referred to as "International Geneva." Even though the city of Geneva is comparatively small—with 201,818 permanent core residents and 597,269 permanent residents in Geneva canton in 2019—it hosts 42 international institutions in the Lake Geneva region.[18,19] It also accommodates around 750 NGOs and the permanent representations of 177 member states, including Switzerland. This small, yet very cosmopolitan city, is home to 32,000 civil servants, diplomats, and civil society representatives and hosts more than 3,400 meetings annually with a total of 182,000 delegates from all around the world. There are also more than 4,700 annual visits of heads of state and government, ministers, and other dignitaries.[20]

While living in Geneva, I always felt the international, cosmopolitan atmosphere. From my first day in Geneva, I was impressed by the myriad of languages spoken around me. Whenever I entered a tram, I would hear people speaking French, English, Spanish, Portuguese, Italian, Arabic, and many other languages. And I loved this ambiance. It had something very multicultural about it, and I was impressed by how people from so many different countries were living peacefully together in such a small place. I also enjoyed the variety of food that you could find in the city. Cuisines from all over the world were represented, and I discovered delicious dishes from countries I hadn't even visited yet, opening doors for new culinary and cultural experiences. It is diversity and openness and the opportunity to learn from people with lots of different backgrounds that make Geneva and its surroundings so special. The executive chairman and founder of the World Economic Forum (WEF), the International Organization for Public-Private Cooperation headquartered in Geneva, recently stated in a documentary:

> *"If we did not feel the need to talk, the need for*
> *dialogue, we would live in a global dictatorship*
> *in which everyone had the same opinion. This*
> *means that to talk, and to let others talk too,*
> *is absolutely necessary for us to live together*
> *and for the social cohesion in our world."*

—Klaus Schwab, Executive Chairman and Founder of the WEF
in the Political Documentary *The Forum: Behind the Scences
of the World Economic Forum in Davos*, 2019/2020.[21]

While some people have criticized the WEF for being a club of elites and for providing controversial figures a powerful platform, it is also praised for bringing people and organizations together to discuss issues of global concern. People from different sectors (government, business, civil society, and academia), various political affiliations and even opposing parties in conflict situations. When I learned about the activities and the summits of the WEF, I was at times concerned about some of the practices of participating businesses or politicians, as well. Yet, I became increasingly convinced by the argument that you can change opinions through constructive dialogue. In the end, the heads of companies and countries are also human beings, with the ability to listen, learn, and change if they see the need to do so. So, by bringing them to the table to discuss political, economic but also social issues, new perspectives can be opened. And if several leaders in politics and business agree to do something—for example, in terms of protecting the environment or turning attention to a particular need in society at large—the consequences are enormous since they can set new paradigms and ethical standards in their respective realms.

I found Klaus Schwab's emphasis on the need for dialogue highly appropriate and relevant for today's world. If we didn't acknowledge the need to talk and exchange, we would live in a global dictatorship, one in which only one opinion would be accepted. However, if we want to avoid such a situation, there is a need to talk, to listen, and to see where we can find common ground. It seems to me that in today's world, we have been losing some of these capabilities. Often there is no will to understand where the other party is coming from and why they are acting the way they are. Once we understand this, it's much easier to find solutions and compromises that can work for everyone. Sometimes very innovative ideas can even be born if the different parties open up and pledge to work together.

Collaboration is equally important in the personal realm. The renowned Vietnamese Buddhist monk Thich Nhat Hanh emphasizes in his teachings on mindfulness the importance of staying in a respectful dialogue with your loved ones. Whenever we feel rage, anger, or disappointment, he advises us to first pause and think of walking and breathing attentively. He explains that shouting at or punishing our vis-à-vis with hurtful words will only be a negative boomerang for ourselves. Most likely, the other person, when hurt, will do something to hurt us back. This can quickly escalate into a major fight. It is a widespread habit to release our anger on the person who seems to be the source of our suffering. And while Thich Nhat Hanh says that it is important to let your loved one (be it your partner, child, a parent, or a good friend) know if he or she hurt you, he advises to let them know calmly. And to work on finding intelligent strategies to avoid the suffering that occurs to everyone if arguments or fights escalate.[22]

I know that I can still work a lot on better managing my emotions. Even though I know it doesn't help at all to raise my voice against my husband or my daughters, it still happens—especially on days when I feel tired, exhausted, or overwhelmed. On such days, a minor thing can suddenly escalate into a severe fight, and it takes lots of energy and good will from both sides to calm down afterward again. I hate these situations, and since I am very harmony-seeking, I usually try to reconcile as soon as possible. Yet still, I often tell myself that it would have been better just to remain quiet, to hold my tongue, or to count to 10 before answering a statement or behavior that upset me. It isn't easy to stay calm when emotions seem to overrun you, yet it is worth it to keep working on it. I noticed very often how much stronger we are, on a personal as well as on a professional level, when we cooperate and try to find good solutions that everyone can live with.

Recently, when my husband came home after a week-long business trip, he entered the living room and mentioned that he thought it was cluttered with way too many things, which made him feel uncomfortable. At first, I took his remark as a personal insult. I had tried to keep it as orderly as possible with two children under the age of four. Images of me cleaning up the kitchen and the living room several times a day popped up in my mind. I felt the urge to say that he had no right to say such a thing to his exhausted wife after being away for such a long time. However, after a moment of reflection, I understood that it really seemed to be a problem for him. People certainly have different tolerance levels for clutter. When looking around the room, I could see many toys laying around. And my papers and some dried flowers on our dining table probably did their job as well to make him feel uncomfortable. So, I proposed that we clean up the living room together after the girls were in bed, and he happily agreed. We did a great job as a team, going through all the toys and deciding which ones our daughters played with the most. We put the other ones in a cupboard in the basement. After that,

I arranged my paperwork and got rid of the drooping flowers. We looked through our travel souvenirs and discussed which ones we wanted to leave in the living room and which ones we wanted to put elsewhere in the house. And it ended up being a lovely experience with a great result: a living room that both of us appreciated much more again. It is just to show how cooperation in such situations can be much more constructive, helpful, and joyful than starting the blame game. And it is certainly one of my intentions to keep working on that.

This reminds me of Switzerland and its role as a platform for discussion of issues of global concern and as a bridge between sectors; I think that it represents an excellent example of the benefits that collaboration can bring. Creating good communication channels and a platform for dialogue is indispensable if we want to work toward an atmosphere of understanding, tolerance, and cooperation. And this holds true on a professional as well as on a personal level!

Beautiful Lessons Learned from Switzerland

✳ **Go out and enjoy the beauty that nature has to offer.** Nature can have a very restorative, refreshing, and calming effect on our busy minds.

✳ **Nature outings can also be great opportunities for family bonding.** And seeing the beauty of nature through the eyes of children can be extra magical.

✳ **Use outdoor sports or activities to develop a "can-do" mentality** that you can then apply to all areas of your life.

✳ **Slow down every now and then and take time to appreciate little things that make your heart sing daily.** Think of the dancing bear, Baloo, forgetting about the stresses of daily life.

✳ **Always have something in your fridge to be able to invite friends, neighbors, or family for an** *apéro.* These can be the most spontaneous and relaxing occasions for nice, informal exchanges.

✳ **Think of the great advantages that communication and dialogue can bring on a personal and on a professional level.** Listening and learning from each other can help to avoid misunderstandings and find common ground.

✳ **Believe in the outcomes that collaboration can bring.** Working together can bring out the best aspects from different people and organizations and lead to very innovative outcomes!

Chapter 7

INDIA

Incredible, Vibrant India

- ❖ Curiosity, Openness, and the Will to Learn

- ❖ Hospitality and a Taste of "Spicy India"

- ❖ Spirituality and Tolerance

- ❖ The Concept of "Jugaad:" Solving Problems with Creativity and Resourcefulness

"We live in a wonderful world that is full of beauty, charm, and adventure. There is no end to the adventures we can have if only we seek them with our eyes open."

—Jawaharlal Nehru

There is a lot of truth in this statement by Jawaharlal Nehru, India's first Prime Minister after India's Independence from British rule in 1947. There is a lot of beauty, charm, and adventure in this world—sometimes, we just need to open our eyes or change our attitude to see it.

I was only 14 years old when my parents, my older brother, and I left for a three-week round trip to India and Nepal. My father loves travel and adventures, so my parents set up a trip for the whole family to explore this part of the world. To say that I was not really prepared for this journey would be an understatement. While I remember having a serene impression of Nepal and its breathtaking nature, I was quite overwhelmed at seeing the harsh disparities between rich and poor when I arrived in Delhi. Luxurious hotels and private drivers went hand-in-hand with mutilated children begging on the streets. I remember experiencing sensory overload on all possible levels: the noise, the colors, the smells, and being touched regularly by people in the street; it just left me feeling exhausted and overwhelmed. While I found the country fascinating, I often didn't know how to deal with all these sometimes very contradictory impressions and experiences that we made.

One morning we left for a boat ride on the Ganges River, close to the spiritually renowned city Varanasi. The sun was rising and its reflections were beautiful on the water, but I noticed a strange smell. Our guide explained that people were burning the corpses of deceased family members at the riverside. I remember that I felt shocked when hearing this. Only later I realized the important role Varanasi and the Ganges River play as sacred sites for Hindus. Since the Ganges is considered a holy river, many cremation ceremonies take place daily on its river banks. Maybe the situation would not have been as shocking if I had known a little more about these practices before actually seeing them first hand. It probably did not help that shortly after our boat trip, a group of people suffering from leprosy surrounded us and begged for food and money. I felt sympathetic, puzzled, and helpless at the same time. I had no idea how to respond to the situation. These experiences were entirely out of my comfort zone. I left India bewildered. For weeks after, I kept wondering how a country could be home to so many rich and poor people at the same time. In contrast to this, Germany seemed like a very homogeneous country.

However, over the years, when learning more about India during my Master's and Ph.D. studies, I discovered the many facets that "Incredible India," as it is often called in tourism circles, has to offer. Even though poverty and disparities are challenges that continue to be addressed, there is also this other, very modern, competitive, and highly promising side of the country. Over the past decades, millions of people formerly living in poverty have joined India's growing middle class. An analysis from Bain and Company for the World Economic Forum in 2019 showed that between 2005 and 2018, the percentage of lower-middle–income households increased from 23 percent to 33 percent; and there was an increase in upper-middle–income households from 7 percent to 21 percent.[1] At the same time, the percentage of low-income households has continually fallen. The projection for the upcoming decade is promising. While India is already one of the largest economies in the world, analyses have shown that India's consumer market could become the third largest in the world by 2030. There is a lot of potential in the country: not only the relatively young population structure, but also the steady economic growth, the expanding and globalizing middle class, and the country's competitiveness in many sectors (for example, in the information technology sector or the emerging pharma markets for generics) is auspicious. So yes, there is still widespread poverty in the country, but at the same time, there are many promising trends that show the potential of the country as a whole.[2,3]

As for me, after my first encounter with this huge and diverse country in my early teenage years, I gave it another shot a decade and a half later, when I revisited India for my Ph.D. research. As life sometimes plays out, my Ph.D. topic dealt with a variety of Indian health-insurance schemes providing quality healthcare services for the most vulnerable parts of the population. Before embarking on my first field research in South India, I told myself that I needed to prepare a little better than for my first trip at the age of 14. Of course, I did a lot of research on healthcare-related issues. But this time, I also read numerous India guides with tips on how to deal with a variety of everyday situations foreigners were likely to encounter. And while these helped me a lot, I still faced situations where I felt overwhelmed. But I also managed to change my perspective and see and perceive the beautiful things that this vibrant, incredible country has to offer.

Curiosity, Openness, and the Will to Learn

"Madam, madam. What's your name? Where are you from? Are you married?"

I looked into the faces of the children standing in front of me. Maybe I should have seen this coming since I had heard these questions countless times from children and adults alike during my time in India. Yet, this time, I still felt a little surprised. I thought that we'd found a private little getaway where we could withdraw from the usual hustle in India's streets. I was in India for my third field research trip for my Ph.D. thesis, and Antoine came to visit over Christmas and New Year's. We had spent some very nice yet also intense days in the slum areas where I was conducting some research. After that, we traveled to a small resort in the state of Kerala to get some rest and to enjoy some togetherness. On that particular day, we took a walk from the resort toward the sea. Suddenly, a group of small children with big, beautiful, curious eyes looked at us. Antoine and I looked at each other and smiled hesitantly before we started to answer the questions from the little group in front of us. Being stared at and bombarded with countless questions happened to me continuously during my time in India. In the beginning, I didn't feel very comfortable with the sometimes quite penetrating stares, and I didn't know how to deal with it. Whether I was on the bus, walking in the streets, or entering one of the hospitals where I conducted interviews, I always felt several pairs of eyes on me.

There were days when the feeling of constantly being observed didn't bother me very much and I found it almost amusing. But there were also days when I just wished that I would not attract as much attention. One day, I went to a local copy shop to print out some surveys for my research. It took a while until it was my turn, and they told me to have a seat while they prepared my order. I was not in the best mood that day. I felt tired and quite warm due to the heat. It was all the more disturbing to me that people in the shop kept staring at me—and not discretely, but quite directly. When a lady sat next to me with her child and started staring at me from a close distance, I didn't know how to react. And when she started touching me and told her child to do so, too, I politely said, "Goodbye," and told the shop owner that I'd just take the copies he had finished and come back on a different day. On a different day, I might have engaged more with the woman and the child. In retrospect, I can even understand her behavior. She might not have seen many foreigners before, and she was likely just curious. But on that day, I needed some distance. I felt that everything was becoming too much for me, and I started to feel irritated. So, I allowed myself to stay in my private room for a day, chatting with family and friends from back home and recharging my batteries for the continuation of my research journey.

I don't believe that I have ever felt such opposing emotions in such a short period of time as in India. Sometimes I was amazed by the liveliness and the bustle in the streets. And sometimes, I just wanted to avoid it all and withdraw. There is a constant noise level on the roads and it takes some time to get used to it, especially if you come from Germany or Switzerland. The continuous honking of all kinds of vehicles contributes to the persistent background noise. I found it quite telling and amusing to read that Audi had developed louder and longer-lasting horns for the Indian market. The article explained that the amount of honking done on an average day in Mumbai was the equivalent to the total amount of honking done in Germany in a year. For that very reason, horns had to be adapted for the Indian market.[4]

While the incredible liveliness, the staring, and the contact approaches could sometimes feel overwhelming, it was at the same time very nice to experience the interest of people in learning about other people and cultures. Once you start seeing the questions not as intrusive inquisition but as a genuine interest to learn about something different, it becomes much easier to take them with humor and serenity. Of course, there are days when you don't feel like repeating the same answers for the umpteenth time. Travel guides advise travelers to give polite, short answers and move on. I even know people who invented some answers that would be more satisfying to the audience. Like, for example, "Yes, I'm married," instead of engaging in lengthy discussions about why you were not yet married. Some questions caught me by surprise, like: "How much money do you make? Do people have sex before marriage in Europe?" etc. I had to reflect on how to answer. Often, I tried to find an indirect way of responding to divert the conversation to a different topic. Many travel guides suggest to start asking questions yourself as the person in front of you will probably be happy to share about his or her life as well.

The reality of being observed continuously became even more clear during my research work. One day I visited a registration center for a health insurance program. I wanted to understand how the smart-card distribution for health-insurance schemes for low-income households functioned. I was in the middle of an interview with people working at the center when a group of reporters showed up. They had learned that a foreigner had come to their town to learn about their health-insurance system. They started taking pictures of me and asked me questions about my research, my home country, and why I was interested in learning about the program. Before I knew it, I found myself talking with them, and the next day an article with pictures of me appeared in the local newspaper. My role switched continuously from being the observer to being the observed during my time in India.

I drew many positive lessons from this experience. For example, many Indian people just seemed to love to communicate and to learn. I learned with time that asking questions was something done out of curiosity and interest and usually without any bad intention. People would use the opportunity to learn about a different country or belief system when they had the chance to do so. And what better opportunity is there than asking foreigners coming to your country about their home countries and belief systems. There is a genuine interest in learning and discussing. This also holds true for politics. It is hard to find an Indian person who does not have a political opinion, and I loved the passion with which people enjoyed discussing politics.

Generally, it's impressive to observe how democracy works in India, with a population of nearly 1.4 billion people. Estimates show that, within the next decade, India will overtake China population-wise and become the most populous country in the world.[5] With 28 states and 8 union territories, there is a lot of diversity in India in terms of languages, customs, religions, and political parties. Just imagine that the South Indian state of Tamil Nadu is home to approximately 82 million people.[6] And the most populated Indian state, Uttar Pradesh, had a population of roughly 238 million people in 2020.[7] Hence, each Indian state could be a country by itself. The unity of this vast country and the ability to keep it up in a democratic manner is, therefore, all the more fascinating. In the 2019 parliamentary elections in India, almost 900 million people were eligible to vote. It is no wonder that the actual election process stretches over several weeks. And it's mind-boggling to think of the logistics involved, especially since there must be a polling station within two kilometers of every habitation.[8]

India is also home to one-fifth of the world's youth. More than half of the overall population is 30 years old or younger and one quarter of the population is under the age of 14.[9,10] There have been countless studies on the role that India's youth will play in the coming decades. If inclusive education policies and adequate preparation for the labor market are pursued for India's youth, there is a huge potential for the country, given its great human resources.

What I would like to emphasize here, however, is the ability of many Indians to approach foreigners effortlessly. It is a great way to learn about different origins, belief systems, and customs. In a way, it is what I wish to do with this book: increase curiosity for and appreciation of other mindsets, customs, traditions, and beliefs. I sincerely believe that every country in this world has something beautiful to offer and that we can all learn and gain a lot from interacting with each other and taking away the positive lessons that resonate with us. It might be hard to argue that the intention behind every *"Madam, what's your name and where are you from"* is to learn about life lessons from other countries. Sometimes it is just pure curiosity or the will to practice the English phrases that were picked up somewhere or learned at school. Yet, the interest in people—and especially in those that have different origins or lifestyles—has something magical about it. Imagine if we used the opportunity to learn about different cultures and belief systems when meeting people from other countries.

However, I think often we don't want to seem intrusive or impolite and therefore refrain from asking questions. Or maybe we believe our questions seem stupid. When I was a child, there was a song in a children's television series that went something like, *"Wer, wie, was—wieso, weshalb, warum—wer nicht fragt bleibt dumm!"* Translated, more or less, it means, "Who, how, what, and why—who doesn't ask stays ignorant." I liked the song and its message very much. And I loved it that my parents always emphasized that we could ask anything. Indeed, it is much more intelligent to ask questions than not to ask questions if you don't know or understand something. Asking gives you the chance to grow intellectually and personally. However, I know personally that it's not always so easy in reality. During my university years, I was often shy to ask a question in class if I thought maybe it was a stupid question or that I could know the answer myself if I had done all the readings. I still have this fear or shyness at certain moments when being seated in an audience or with some prominent speaker. But I have also come to learn that people are usually delighted when they receive questions after their presentations. It shows that people listened to them and are interested in learning more. And quite often, people are also happy to talk about themselves. So even questions about personal opinions or advice are, in most cases, very welcome.

I am often amazed by the questions that our three-year-old poses. I can see her mind working and thinking when she reflects about something that troubled or interested her. I think most parents have gone through the phase of "why" questions of their toddlers or preschool and school children. Quite often, our daughter asks me about something, and as soon as I respond to it, she continues with endless *"Why?"* questions. It can be challenging at times, and sometimes I just don't have an answer for every question. But at the same time, it brings out new thoughts as well. You become interested in many things and details that you might not have thought about before, like for example, "Why can horses run faster than cows, even though they both have quite long legs?" Or "Why are helicopters louder than planes?" Of course, I am still relieved when, after a handful of answers, she replies with a kind "Okay." It means that I have addressed the topic to her satisfaction, and we can move on to something else. Mallika Chopra, daughter of the renowned spiritual leader Deepak Chopra and an incredible leader, author, and speaker in her own right, published a book titled *100 Questions from my Child*. In it, she addresses many questions that I have heard from our older daughter as well. I love reading about Mallika's attempts to answer those questions with consideration, and her attempts to include values like empathy and tolerance when responding. It shows how much the way you reply to a question influences the thinking of children.

I think that as we get older, we tend to lose the innocent, child-like curiosity that we used to have when we were smaller. We are afraid of looking stupid or of being too obtrusive. Of course, there are moments or situations when people do not want to answer questions, and we should respect that. But why not be a bit more open, curious, and eager to learn when meeting someone who seems interesting to us. We can learn so much by simply talking to people and getting to know their viewpoints on issues. I often love to talk to taxi drivers about the country I am visiting or living in. Questions about the country or the city or sometimes even about some political issue can trigger the most exciting and insightful conversations. When taking Ubers, it is similar. I have had very insightful conversations with people from the most diverse corners of the world. I always enjoyed catching glimpses of how it is to live in a country and to see the beautiful aspects as well as the challenges. Sometimes the drivers ended up showing me videos from back home to illustrate something they were talking about. Of course, you do not have to take every statement as the "ultimate truth" about a country; there is no one correct perspective. There are many different personal truths and viewpoints.

In today's world, where many countries are facing increasing clashes between opposing camps, it can only do us good to ask questions and to learn about others' viewpoints. We don't always have to agree, but it opens up a different perspective and potentially even offers the opportunity to find commonalities in heated, charged environments. At least we could continue learning how to stay respectful when communicating, even when opinions differ. Especially nowadays, when hate speech has become a new norm on Internet platforms. With the algorithms used by social media channels, it is easy to stay in one's bubble of opinions that get confirmed every time we read an article or see an ad. In research, this is referred to as confirmation bias. If we genuinely want to reach out to each other and try to overcome the deep cliffs that have formed in many societies, we need to be open to leave our bubble from time to time to engage with people with other opinions. This can start with day-to-day interactions with people who have a different background, be it country-wise, job-wise or in some other way. By asking some simple, curious, open-minded questions—as children and adults alike did many times during my various stays in India.

Hospitality and a Taste of "Spicy India"

"Please, have some more." "Only a little bit, please." "We cooked it especially for you." I was about to explode after three servings already. The food tasted delicious. Several bowls filled with meat and tasty vegetables in gravy sat in front of me, and my friend was about to serve me a fourth time. The only thing I could think of saying was that I loved

the food—and I really did!—but that I had quite a sensitive stomach and needed to stop eating before falling sick. With some regret, but also some comprehension in her eyes, my friend stopped serving me.

I was sitting on the floor with two of my closest research-assistant friends during my research in Tamil Nadu in Southern India. They were both social workers and had offered to help with my surveys and interviews in different slums in the city of Madurai. They were lovely and very supportive, and our friendship grew over the weeks that we had worked together. That day they invited me to my friend's hut in one of the slums. I didn't know that their surprise consisted of a wonderful homemade meal. It was in the middle of the afternoon, and I had already eaten lunch earlier that day. When they showed me with enthusiasm what they had cooked, I felt touched and surprised. I had not expected to have a major meal so soon after lunch. Yet, it smelled delicious, and it was such a nice gesture that I had to take a few servings. However, after several servings, I felt that I would explode if I continued eating. My stomach had started to hurt, and I did not know how to kindly explain that I was just, frankly, full.

I had read about the delicious food and the great sense of hospitality in India. And I had learned that sometimes the least offensive excuse when not being able to eat any more was just to say that you were having stomach problems. Many Indians know about the sometimes-sensitive stomachs of foreigners visiting their country. India, also known as the "home of spices," is famous for its variety of spices. It has the largest domestic market for spices in the world and is "the world's largest producer, consumer, and exporter of spices."[11] India's spice trading goes back thousands of years ago, and even today, India "accounts for half of the global trading in spices."[12] The country produces 75 of the 109 spice varieties listed by the International Organization for Standardization (ISO). I enjoyed enormously all the different tastes that Indian dishes have to offer. There are countless *masalas*—a mix of various ground spices—used in Indian cooking. And the variety of tastes in terms of dishes is incredible. Food and dishes vary among regions in India. In the North, a lot of wheat is used for *rotis, naan,* and *chapati*—flatbreads that usually accompany a meal. In the South, the food is much more rice-based. Rice flavor is used a lot in South Indian cuisine to produce *idlis* or *dosas*— steamed rice cakes and rice batters—that are usually served alongside food. Many dishes in South India are based on legumes and the food is generally lighter, often vegetarian, and usually much spicier than in the North. Yet, Indian cuisine is as diverse as the country itself. [13]

A study on cuisine trade asserts that Indian food is the fourth most popular food in the world, coming just after Italian, Japanese and Chinese cuisines in popularity. While people across the world appreciate Indian food, it is particularly popular in the United Kingdom, South Korea, Thailand, Japan, Germany, France, and the U.S. Joel Waldfogel, who conducted the research, claims that such a strong presence of a country's cuisine across the world represents a sort of "soft power." It helps spread Indian influence, and the cuisine trade represents a form of direct foreign investment "in which home country ideas are used to produce abroad with local inputs." [14]

In India, the custom is usually to eat food with your hands instead of using cutlery. I found myself quite often in embarrassing situations when I tried to shovel rice mixed with gravy into my mouth using only my right hand. The left hand is traditionally used to clean yourself after going to the toilet, so, it is often considered unclean and not to be used while eating. Trying to eat using only my right hand proved challenging. I was used to eating chicken wings or hamburgers with my hands, but I had never done it one-handed. And I certainly hadn't learned to eat rice, sauce, or many vegetables with one hand without creating a complete mess. Many of my Indian friends and acquaintances laughed out loud when watching me eat. Often, they offered me a spoon out of sympathy after having

watched most of my food landing back on my plate or on my shirt—
not in my mouth. Even though it was a tricky experience, I also
enjoyed eating with my fingers. It adds an extra sense while eating.
Instead of focusing just on the smell, taste, and appearance, in India,
the sense of touch and feeling the consistency of food is added. It
can offer a whole new experience to eating pleasure. Now, when my
husband and I order Indian food, we love using our hands, especially
when we have *naan* to dip into the different sauces. Enjoying our
meal this way is almost like being back in India, and it reminds us
of our time there.

Even more amazing than the delicious Indian food was the sense
of hospitality we encountered in India. There is a Sanskrit verse
from ancient Hindu scripture, *"Atithi Devo Bhava,"* which is often
translated as, 'The guest is equivalent to God."[15] An Indian friend
of mine explained that the verse expresses that guests are honored
and seen as a manifestation of God. And so, they are treated with
respect and warmth and are greeted with open arms. This attitude
is deeply ingrained in Hindu culture, and many people and families
in India seem to live by this saying. The way people from the most
diverse backgrounds welcomed me with open arms touched me
deeply. Daisy, a lovely lady and tour guide in Madurai, personified
hospitality. I met her during my first research trip. From the very
beginning when we barely knew each other, she and her whole family
did everything to make me feel at ease in Tamil Nadu. She showed
me around, ordered Indian clothes in my size for me, and invited
me countless times for dinner at her house. She also ensured that
wherever I went, I could reach her or her husband in case I should
face any problems. On one of my very first trips to India when my
mom visited, we were invited to the house of a man who was a friend
of one of my mother's friends in Germany. The man and his family
picked us up, prepared a wonderful meal for us, and we engaged in
long discussions about India, Germany, and my research project.
Such hospitable behavior, even toward very distant acquaintances,

impressed my mom and me deeply. Later on, an Indian friend of mine offered to put me up at his and his mom's place for my entire stay in Delhi. Also in the villages and slum areas I visited, I was amazed by the sense of hospitality of the people. Even people living in dire poverty offered my research assistants and me a cup of tea or soda or even asked us to stay for lunch.

Reflecting on the great sense of hospitality I encountered in India, in Mexico, and in other countries I visited, I wondered why in the Western culture (in Germany, Switzerland, and many European countries), it seems less common to just welcome people if they arrive unannounced. Maybe it is because everything is so planned out that if a person just shows up out of the blue, it does not fit into our schedule. I face the same challenges with my sometimes-overloaded schedule. And I don't think that there is any bad intention or a real lack of hospitality. It is, rather, a belief that I need to show up for what I committed to do, as it would be impolite not to. So, if someone rings the doorbell when you are about to leave for a meeting, you might have to explain that you do not have time at the moment—to honor the person who is waiting for you. This seems to function the other way around in many other cultures, where it might be considered very impolite to not attend to the spontaneous visitor and where it is much more accepted to cancel personal meetings last minute. I think it's hard to define one of the two ways as being the better, more empathetic one. They are just different, and the approach you adopt simply depends on the societal and cultural norms. But what I do think we can learn from countries like India is to treat our guests, once they are with us, with warmth, sympathy, and generosity. And I like to think of the saying: "If there is food for three, there is food for four, as well."

So, what can we take home about Indian food and hospitality? In terms of food, it could be to try out new spices or some of the Indian masala mixes from time to time. They can give a whole new experience to ingredients that we have been using over and over again. In terms of hospitality, I think that it is up to everyone, personally, to find out what resonates most. For some, having spontaneous visits is the most natural thing, and they really enjoy having a full house most of the time. For others, this is stressful, and a calmer retreat is needed. Yet, if we notice that someone needs some warmth or someone to listen to them, I think that it can be valuable to occasionally change our plans to help the person who might be in need of a cup of coffee or a good talk. In my family, we used to refer to the rescheduling of activities due to unforeseen events or visits as *Fuhrmann'sche Planungsflexibilität* or "flexibility à la Fuhrmann." This concept made us feel less guilty for what we didn't achieve—and happy and grateful for what we did. I personally think that what really counts more than anything when receiving guests is to make them feel welcome. And many people from India set shining examples of this welcoming attitude.

Spirituality and Tolerance

I had to refrain from laughing. The big elephant standing in front of us at the temple's entrance had just put his trunk on Antoine's head and left a wet little puddle. Antoine looked as astonished as me. But our Indian friend Daisy jumped in excitement: "This is a sign of good luck!" When, shortly after, a bird pooped on his shoulder, she couldn't believe it. "Wow, that's even double luck. You are such a lucky man."

I was often surprised in India about the excitement and the belief in luck, destiny, and different forms of karma. I remember that Antoine and I looked at each other and had to smile at some point. Even though he probably could not initially understand why it was considered lucky that he had been chosen by the animals for their supposedly good deeds and stood there half wet and with bird poo on his shirt. But Daisy smiled from ear to ear and reassured us about what a good sign this was before leading us inside the temple.

India, with all its diversity and wealth of ideas, never ceased to surprise me. I had gotten used to taking off my shoes when entering a temple or a holy space, though the first few times, I wondered if I would find my sandals again among the masses of shoes and sandals at the temple entrance. We were in Madurai, the cultural capital of the South Indian state Tamil Nadu, known for its impressive temples and called by some ancient scholars the Athens of the East.[16] I had come to the city several times for prolonged stays for my Ph.D. research on healthcare-service–related issues. Even if, at times, I had felt overwhelmed by the crowds, the smells, colors, etc., I really liked the city. It was colorful and had a friendly atmosphere, and I had encountered some wonderful people who helped me with my research. Antoine had come to visit me for a couple of weeks over the Christmas and New Year holidays. My friend Daisy, who worked as a tour guide and who helped me a lot with translations during my interviews, had been thrilled to introduce Antoine to the wealth of information on Hindu gods and beliefs when visiting the well-known Meenakshi temple in the city. When I visited Madurai a couple of years before with my mom, Daisy had also shown us around, leading us to various temples in the city. She explained some of the rituals that people would do to attract certain things to their lives. When she heard back then that I was in a relationship—but not yet married—she proposed that my mom and I walk around a particular statue a few times. She insisted this would help me get engaged and marry very soon. At that point in time, I just wanted to be polite, and, as I was interested in learning about different beliefs and traditions, I engaged in the exercise. Then, about two years later, I stood there, newly married to Antoine and I thought back to that episode. I cannot tell if our ritual that day had really been a decisive force in our getting married. But why not try out things that might somehow support you on your path?

I had the impression that many Indian people believed that trying out something spiritual was always a good option. As long as no harm was involved, it could only be for the better. Maybe this was also why I often found myself in rickshaws decorated around the driver's seat with images of Hindu gods, a Buddha statue, and Jesus on a crucifix, all lined up next to each other. I was at first quite astonished that people seemed to have no problem at all combining several different religious beliefs in their everyday lives. And in many ways, they seemed to believe in all of them. I am not sure if this was linked to the fact that several religions, such as Hinduism, Buddhism, Jainism, and Sikhism have their origin in India, or if it was because Hinduism is a polytheistic religion where millions of gods have their place, and a couple additional figures—like Jesus or Buddha—could only be a welcome addition. I remember that one of the girls who helped me a lot during my research in the slums kept telling me how important Jesus was in her life. At the same time, she took me to various Hindu rituals in temples, where she made sure that I correctly followed her in doing the right rituals at the right time. The author Karin Kaiser has traveled and lived in India for extended periods and wrote an excellent book about understanding the many facets of India. She explains that Hindus are generally very open and tolerant toward people of other faiths and people who hold no beliefs at all. There's no comprehension of the strict separation of religious persuasions, and it is completely natural to include several religions in everyday life.[17]

I appreciate this widespread religious and spiritual tolerance. The Indian Constitution includes the separation of religion and state, as well as freedom of religion. However, it can't be ignored that India also faces religious tensions, especially between some of the more extreme Hindu and Muslim groups. It has been argued that many of the significant disputes between Hindus and Muslims are less about religion, but are more politically orchestrated conflicts.[18] Yet, the vast majority of the population seems very tolerant in their views, welcoming other faiths and influences from other religions with open arms.

Spirituality is something that many people are looking for in our fast-paced world, filled with materialistic promises on every doorstep. Especially during challenging times, we might look for some sort of guidance that connects us with our deep, inner self and that helps us gain clarity and peace. Spirituality can be interpreted and experienced in many different ways, and there is no one right path for it. Yet, it often comes down to understanding the purpose of one's life and the relationship with everything and everyone. And often, there is an ingrained consciousness that something bigger than ourselves is at work. A spiritual practice can consist of a contemplative practice like meditation, prayer, journaling, practicing mindfulness, etc., or, in a religious framework, one might visit a church, a temple, a synagogue, or a mosque. It could be a personal relationship to a higher power that comforts us or a connection to nature or art—things that can also be deeply spiritual.[19]

Spirituality has the potential to improve physical, mental, and emotional well-being. Spiritual practice can help create a stronger immune system, lower the risk of depression, reduce stress, lower blood pressure, and help achieve better sleep—an essential aspect to rejuvenate and be well-rested and energized.[20] Chad E. Cooper, a renowned leadership and business coach, claims that spirituality can also help people to have higher self-esteem, be more optimistic, have positive relationships, and follow a strong purpose in life. In his article "The Importance of Spirituality Versus Religion for Living a Legendary Life," he observes that there are certain tensions that can arise when people believe their religion is the only correct spiritual way that exists on Earth. He emphasizes the need to follow a truly spiritual approach in which we accept that "we are all different, but are all part of the same human experience."[21] Instead of creating more separation of groups and creating disparity between identities such as race, age, sexual definition, and religious belief, we can focus on the commonalities that we all have. Believing in something bigger, higher, something that we can't fully explain, is spiritual and we may call it God, Goddess, Buddha, or any of numerous other titles. However, a "highly exclusive belief system can leave no room for anyone else's human experience and tends to be unbending to diversity and acceptance." Cooper continues to stress that a spiritual life is "all-inclusive and allows respect of all others to live their life on an equal basis."[22] If someone falls ill and asks his friends and relatives to pray for him, these prayers can be done by Christians, Muslims, Hindus, Buddhists, Jews, or people from any other religion. What counts is the good spiritual intent no matter in which form you worship. Spirituality does, in this sense, remove all the labels that tend to separate us.

I have often thought about questions relating to spirituality and religiousness. As I mentioned earlier, I was born in Germany, and both my parents are Catholic. For my mom, visiting church holds a significant meaning; to her, it feels like coming home. For my father, it has less importance. Yet, both of them reject strict dogmatic views and intolerant religious behavior. In fact, both of them are very interested in influences from other religions as well. My father is a big fan of the Dalai Lama and his teachings and has been to several of his conferences. My mom enjoys books and teachings on mindfulness by the Buddhist monk Thich Nath Hanh. I always appreciated their openness in spirit. When I faced doubts about whether I needed to focus on the influences of one religion exclusively, I was always reassured when they told me that I should not worry too much about the human-made religious restrictions. And that the higher power—whatever we may call it—would most certainly embrace a form of worship that would serve harmony, peace, and connectedness of people on earth. Of course, we are influenced in our beliefs by where we were born, how we were raised, which experiences we had, etc. And being lovingly introduced to religious rituals can be something that can give us a lot of hope and keep us grounded in life. But we can still be open to learn from others and discover what type of worship or spiritual practice works best for us. In my case, I am Christian and believe in a loving God. Yet I also enjoy reading teachings from Buddhist monks and Hindu swamis. And I find that the teachings have a lot in common when addressing essentials, such as expressing love and compassion for others and yourself. I was, in fact, very touched and inspired when learning about the deep friendship between the Dalai Lama and Archbishop Desmond Tutu. On the occasion of the Dalai Lama's 80th birthday, Desmond Tutu flew to Dharamsala to spend a week with the Dalai Lama discussing how to find joy in the face of suffering. Douglas Carlton Abrams, a renowned international author, joined these two spiritual icons during these conversations and provided excerpts of the conversation in a book titled *The Book of Joy: Lasting Happiness in a Changing World*. What I found deeply touching was that both men, though grounded in different religions, emphasized the importance of the same values and attitudes in their conversations, appreciating the other person and his religion as deeply as their own background. It was something that gave me hope that we can transcend differences in religious beliefs when focusing on what deeper values we all have in common.

Another spirituality aspect from India is included in yoga practice, which originated on the Indian subcontinent more than 5,000 years ago. I very much enjoy participating in yoga classes, as I find these sessions to be deeply nurturing for body and soul—especially if you find a teacher whose teaching style resonates with you. Yoga has been described as a "contemplative discipline, which integrates both mental and physical practices with the ultimate goal of attaining *paramatman* (pure consciousness)."[23] There has been a yoga boom in Western societies in recent decades, and today you can find yoga offered in almost every town. A research study by the Department of Psychology of the University of East London has shown, however, that there are spiritual differences between different yoga practices. The original intent of yoga was to be a spiritual exercise with a search for meaning via practices of self-awareness, self-discipline, and self-control, enhancing one's spiritual and personal growth. But as yoga has come to be a universal practice, societies have adapted the yoga forms. In Western cultures, you can also find yoga courses that focus more on fitness and flexibility. There is no problem with that, as such. The intentions of people attending yoga courses are different and so are the offers. The study mentioned above, however, found that people who had set themselves a spiritual intention when joining a yoga course reported having psychological benefits of an improved sense of well-being compared to those who focused solely on physical fitness. For mere fitness, other sports could be equivalent to this or even more appropriate.[24] But each person is unique, so each person has something different that feels natural to him or her for being spiritual. It might as well be a walk or a hike in nature or just some contemplative time at home. Focusing only on our physical and emotional well-being is, in most cases, not enough. At some point in our lives, we are likely to ask ourselves bigger questions that can only be answered with some sort of spiritual or mental practice.

The tolerance in terms of spirituality that I encountered in India impressed me, and it is something that I deeply appreciate. And I believe that tolerance and openness to different ways of thinking and living are crucial if we want to make our world a more harmonious, peaceful, and loving place.

The Concept of "*Jugaad:*" Solving Problems with Creativity and Resourcefulness

"Shall I turn the music up louder?" The rickshaw driver screamed while making eye contact with me in the rear-view mirror. I felt my ears would explode already, and I was about to go deaf. So, I screamed back: "No, thank you. It is already quite loud like this." The tuk-tuk driver looked amused. He kept on screaming. "I wanted to turn my vehicle into a little disco so that people can enjoy the music. The boxes behind you are new."

That was not the only time that I sat in a tuk-tuk with the music blaring loudly, but this one by far exceeded all my previous experiences. When I first sat down in the rickshaw to go to one of my interviews in the city, I noticed the happy sounds of Indian music. But once I entered, the enthusiastic driver turned up the music to such an extent that I really feared for my ear drums. I tried to cover my ears with the scarf I'd brought along, but it didn't change much. When he proposed to turn it up even louder—I thought he had already reached the maximum volume—I was terrified. But from his point of view, he likely just wanted to be hospitable and show his new client the new stereo system he had invested in and that his tuk-tuk had turned into an official "disco tuk-tuk."

Indian people quite often amazed me with their sense of innovation in everyday situations. I frequently saw vehicles that had somehow been reassembled, using all kinds of unusual items. For example, a bicycle would be transformed into a little shop by placing a counter on it. People would sell something or offer some kind of service from it. I often noticed such innovative stands and ideas during my stay in India. However, it was only recently that I came across a word that describes this kind of "innovative out-of-the-box thinking." In her insightful book *The Atlas of Happiness*, Helen Russell writes about the Indian concept of *jugaad,* a colloquial Hindi term that can be translated as "innovative fix." It refers to frugal innovation, improvisational ingenuity, and resourcefulness. In short, it means getting things done with what you've got, no matter what. Russell refers to her friend Fatema, who explained that having a *jugaad* attitude could be an asset. She would, for example, sometimes say at work: "I'll do some *jugaad,*" meaning that if faced with a challenge, she would figure something out and do her best to ensure a positive outcome. And if something did not go the way it was planned, she would not brood for long, but go to plan B. With the deep belief that there is always a way forward, one can reduce a lot of panic that can easily develop in stressful situations. And this holds true for personal and professional life alike.

Businesses in a variety of countries have taken up the *jugaad* approach as a new management style. Employees are encouraged to think outside the box and find innovative solutions with scarce means. Academics and people working in industries and businesses alike have tapped into this approach. The book *Jugaad Innovation: Think Frugal, Be Flexible, Generate Breakthrough Growth* by Navi Radjou, Jaideep Prabhu, and Simone Ahuja made headlines in business circles as many businesses sought to reach more growth with minimal resources.

But we should not glamorize the origin of the concept too much, either. It needs to be kept in mind that for many people in India, it was born out of scarcity, lack of opportunity, and a will to survive in difficult circumstances, and not so much for the conscious purpose of engaging in out-of-the-box thinking for innovation. For many people in India who live in poverty and who do not have certain opportunities, "*jugaad* thinking" is a basic survival need. Helen Russell concludes in her chapter on *jugaad* that practicing it from a stable position is desirable, while practicing it from a place of need is not. Manu Joseph, a journalist and novelist, goes even further, criticizing the "*jugaad* hype" in Western societies and companies. He points out that *jugaad*, in its original form in many Indian cases, is often something that results in borderline illegal, unethical, or dangerous behavior. For example, rickshaw drivers who put a wooden plank at the front and the end of their vehicle and start calling it a school bus.[i] He questions why big companies that have large budgets for innovation should not spend money on it—they don't need to be frugal. And in his view, such companies have done much more for humanity by investing than by cutting their innovation budgets.[25]

I certainly agree that it is not desirable if *jugaad* is practiced out of a need to survive in some way or if it is practiced in a dangerous way, putting lives at risk. Here, it is even more important to see how basic human needs can be met and regulations put in place so that dangerous *jugaad* versions are neither necessary nor practiced. However, as a personal principle and mindset, it can be very valuable. It reminds me of the mantra "Everything is 'figureoutable.'" This life philosophy is described in detail by Marie Forleo, a prominent American life coach, motivational speaker, and author in her book, *Everything is Figureoutable*. In it, she emphasizes that by adopting the right mindset, everything in life—no matter the challenge or the situation—is somehow "figureoutable." You just need to believe in it, get creative, roll up your sleeves, and work for it. This is very much like *jugaad* at its core. I love this practical "let's find a solution" approach. One of the motivational post cards in my office reflects this, too. It says: "If plan A does not work. Don't panic! There are still 25 more letters in the alphabet."

---

[i] Another dangerous *jugaad* method is "liquor *jugaad*," or liquor that is produced cheaply without taking necessary precautions. For example, the instance of "Punjab poisoning" in the summer of 2020, when consumption of such self-made liquor led to many deaths.

When talking to an Indian friend about the *jugaad* attitude, he pointed out, however, that a slight difference between *jugaad* and "everything is figureoutable" might be that *jugaad* is usually related to a problem that is external, not an internal motivational problem. So, *jugaad* is getting creative and resourceful and using whatever material or network you have at your disposal to find a solution to a concrete problem or challenge you face. Marie Forleo's principle can be used for external and for internal (e.g., emotional or mental) struggles and might also be used as a mantra to motivate yourself internally for a task. But the basic attitude behind both approaches is similar. You can find solutions by thinking outside the box. So, next time that you face a difficult situation or a challenge, it could be helpful to just remember: *Okay, everything is figureoutable. Let's do some* jugaad *and find a solution!*

Beautiful Lessons Learned from India

* **Approach the world and other people with curiosity and an open mind.** It can be very enriching to learn from others. Don't be shy to ask questions—there are no stupid questions, and you can always learn something new and valuable.

* **Welcome your guests with open arms, warmth, and appreciation**—as if they were a manifestation of God visiting your house.

* **Add a new sense to eating by doing things differently from time to time.** For example, enjoying a meal by using only your hands instead of cutlery. And get inspired by the variety of spices that can add so many different flavors to your food.

* **Be tolerant and open-minded when it comes to religious beliefs and spirituality.** People have different beliefs, but many of us believe in something higher than ourselves and in universal values like compassion, love, helping each other, etc. Focus on what unites us.

* **Include a spiritual practice—in a form that resonates most with you—in your life.** Spiritual practices can have lots of positive effects on the body, mind, and soul.

* **Adopt a *jugaad* or "I will figure it out" attitude.** It can be extremely powerful to think this way and tell ourselves we can and will find a way to make things work. Get innovative and creative when thinking about challenges or obstacles.

CHINA

Finding Balance and Flow

- ❖ **Balancing Confidence and Modesty**

- ❖ **Dynamism, Entrepreneurship, and the Joy of Bargaining**

- ❖ **Yin and Yang – Finding Balance and Flow**

- ❖ **The Importance of a Good Network or "Guanxi"**

---

first visited China in 2001. My brother had just finished high school, and he had dreamed of visiting China one day. For our family vacation, my parents decided to do something special: a three-week trip to China to honor the new chapter starting in my brother's life. We were blown away by the country's massive population. We traveled with a group of about 30 people. When we approached one of the cities on our tour, the Chinese guide who accompanied us said: "Now, we will approach a little city. It only has three to four million inhabitants." When we heard this, we had to laugh. Three to four million is the size of Germany's capital city, Berlin. In China, a city that big is considered a little city. Another Chinese guide accompanying us smiled and said, "In Germany, having 3 percent annual economic growth is praised as an economic miracle. In China, we have growth rates of almost 10 percent, on average."[i,1] These were just some of the remarks that reflected China's impressive size. Its presence on the global stage and in the global economy has become indispensable. Almost 19 percent of the world's population lives in China, meaning that almost every fifth person in the world is a Chinese resident.[2] Like India, these numbers feel somehow mind-blowing.

Back in 2001, I never imagined that I would one day live in that gigantic country. I found it interesting to learn about, but I never saw myself living there. Yet, with the job opportunity that came up for my husband, Antoine, in 2012, my life path turned unexpectedly in a new direction. And so, in the summer of 2013, I left my job in Geneva and joined Antoine, who had moved there some months earlier already, for a two-year adventure in Beijing.

Balancing Confidence and Modesty

I was sitting in the taxi, looking out of the window in the night sky. There were lots of blinking lights and advertising signs all over the place, covered with Chinese characters I couldn't identify. It seemed mysterious and magical. I felt as if I had entered a different world, a world where

---

[i] This remark was made back in 2001 when the Chinese economy was growing impressively and reached growth rates of about 9.5 percent several years in a row. Nowadays, and especially in the momentary crisis—trade wars and the fight against the Coronavirus in 2020—annual growth has dropped. Yet, despite this growth reduction, economic growth in China is still much higher than in countries like Germany.

my known belief systems, language, and communication skills would be shaken. I felt lost and, at the same time, excited to learn more about this giant country. I felt I needed to adapt if I wanted to get along in this completely different universe.

The taxi driver had made it clear that he did not speak any English and would only take us on the ride if we could make ourselves understood in Chinese. This was when my husband pulled out a visiting card with Chinese characters indicating the address we wanted to go to. We had tried to pronounce our desired address several times, but the taxi driver kept looking at us in a way that made it clear he did not understand. We probably made some mistakes with the pronunciation. Pronunciation is so complicated in the Chinese language that I admire non-Chinese people who manage to master it. In Mandarin Chinese, there are four different tones besides the neutral tone, and each syllable can be pronounced in one of these four tones or in the fifth neutral tone. Words change meaning, often quite drastically, according to how the syllable of a word is pronounced. Sometimes, I tried all the different tones when indicating an address to a taxi driver, and it often made me feel like I was in a weird pronunciation class or a comedy show with a hidden camera. Sometimes, when I was just about to give up, the taxi driver would laugh, nod, and say that he now knew where I wanted to go.

While sitting in the taxi with my husband, seeing the city pass by, I was amazed. This country was so different from all the countries I had lived in so far. It seemed powerful, and I realized that having the world's largest population gives a country power. Why should people speak English to you if more than 1.4 billion people speak Mandarin Chinese or one of the other Chinese dialects as their first language? I started to reflect on it. Then again, English is the international language of communication and business, and even though not everyone speaks it fluently, many people have some grasp of it. Millions of Chinese people speak impeccable English, too.

And yet, I found myself in situations where I was completely lost if I couldn't make myself understood in Chinese.[ii]

I understood how it must feel to be illiterate and how difficult it must be to manage daily life. During our time in China and Japan, I felt extremely dependent on others to be able to manage daily tasks. Whether it was to understand text messages I received from my mobile phone company or reading the instructions on the washing machine, at an ATM machine, or even on the automated Japanese toilets, I often resorted to trial and error. Sometimes I got the desired result. But I much preferred to take notes whenever someone explained the procedure to me so that I could replicate it on my own later on.

I found it an exciting, inspiring, and sometimes exhausting experience compared to living in other countries. And what stood out to me was the confidence that China displayed as a country. You could somehow feel the power and the presence that the country has in the world. China has been among the world's fastest-growing economies since it opened up to foreign trade and investment and introduced free-market reforms in the late 1970s. Impressive growth rates have enabled China to double its gross domestic product (GDP) on average every eight years.[3] Since China opened up to the world a few decades ago, it has managed to lift more than 800 million people out of poverty—representing the greatest anti-poverty achievement in history.[4] While China's per-capita income is still only around a quarter of that of high-income countries, it is now an upper-middle-income country, and the world second's largest economy.[5] On the military front, China's military ranks together with the military forces of the U.S. and Russia. And on the cultural level, China is one of the most ancient civilizations, with philosophical influences dating

---

[ii] Of course, this is the case in many countries. But for me personally, it was still different from everything I had known before. China and the Chinese language represented a completely new universe for me.

back thousands of years. Most Chinese people have an extraordinary amount of pride in and respect for their history. And much of that history is kept alive in daily living rituals and in societal and in business behavior. Many philosophical streams have shaped Chinese culture, including Confucianism, Taoism, and Buddhism. And while all these philosophical streams have shaped Chinese culture throughout time, it's often argued that the supreme ideology shaping Chinese society today is socialism with Chinese characteristics.[6,7]

Even though there is an extraordinary sense of confidence about China's history and its position in the world, many Chinese people display a high degree of modesty in personal life. For example, it is not very common that a Chinese person accepts a compliment with a simple "thank you." More often than not, people downplay the compliment by saying something like, *"Na li, na li,"* meaning "No, not really," or they return the compliment right away. Another common feature in Chinese work environments is that people will say, "I will do my best" when asked if they will achieve a set target. To some people from Western societies who are used to getting more straight-forward answers, such a response can sound confusing. However, in China, modesty is not merely about humility. Modest behavior and communication reflect the need to make sure that relationships are harmonious in a communal environment. Often people will downplay their accomplishments and skills and praise others to make other people feel better about themselves.[iii,8]

When reflecting more about this degree of Chinese modesty and politeness, I thought back to some conversations that I had with my father when I was younger. My behavior seemed to match the Chinese way. I would frequently say about a task, a plan, or a request: "I will try my best to achieve it." My father would often tell me that

---

[iii] Even though there are tendencies toward modesty in China, not everyone behaves like this, and people from younger generations are often happy to speak about their talents and show confidence publicly, as well.

I needed to show more confidence in myself and my capabilities, otherwise people would not have confidence in me either. So, when asked if I would achieve something by a specific date, I should just say "yes." Yet, it always felt more natural to me to say that I would do my best. Also, in terms of accepting compliments, I was a lot like many of the Chinese and often rejected or downplayed them. I later learned in lectures on self-confidence and business etiquette in Western surroundings that there is nothing bad about gracefully accepting a compliment with a simple "thank you" and a smile.[9]

It seems that, as with everything in life, it is about finding the right degree between self-confidence, politeness, and modesty. In today's world, some people in power display such a degree of confidence and even narcissism that it can be off-putting or even harmful. For them, a dose of some modesty and politeness could be valuable. But for many people, it can be beneficial as well to develop a sense of confidence in their accomplishments, learning to acknowledge them in front of themselves and others.

So, what can we learn from China in terms of confidence and modesty? Maybe that there are cultural differences when it comes to these attributes. In many Western societies, personal confidence is praised, while in many Asian ones, modesty and a harmonious communal environment play a more critical role. I personally think that it is valuable to develop confidence in ourselves, our dreams, and our capabilities to make our dreams come true. Confidence and a healthy belief in our capabilities can bring us very far—on a personal level and country-wide. And at the same time, a degree of humble politeness in our everyday interactions can be very valuable as well. The saying "Humble on the outside, confident on the inside" could be a guide to follow on a personal level, as it incorporates both attributes—modesty and confidence—in a friendly and balanced way.

Dynamism, Entrepreneurship, and the Joy of Bargaining

*"Every time I visit China, I am stunned
by the speed of change and progress."*

—U.N. Secretary-General António Guterres, 2019[10]

I could not agree more with U.N. Secretary-General António Guterres's statement, made in 2019 at the exhibition for the 70th anniversary of the founding of the People's Republic of China. When we lived in China, Antoine and I were often impressed by how quickly our daily surroundings changed. A new building here, a new road or subway station there, and restaurants opened and closed in our district continuously. When listening to some of my German friends' and family members' complaints about how long construction work often takes on German highways, I was all the more impressed to see how quickly new buildings or construction developed during our time in Beijing. Usually, when coming back to Beijing after a few weeks back home in Europe or a longer trip to India for my research, a new building had been constructed in our neighborhood or some café or restaurant I used to visit was no longer there. In some cases, I was happy about the new surroundings. In others, I was surprised and resented that a café or restaurant had been replaced with something completely different. Sometimes we joked that if we were to be away for a few months, we wouldn't even recognize our home street when we returned.

When my husband and I arrived in Beijing, we quickly got to know a lovely group of expats in their late twenties who had come to Beijing to set up their own businesses. One of them was half-Chinese and could take care of the necessary permits. We were impressed by the number of young entrepreneurs we encountered during our years in China. There seemed to be a general faith that if you did it right, you could start very promising businesses there due to the sheer possibility of scaling your services or products up to the huge market. My husband often talked to me about the possibilities that existed if you developed a product or a service that would even just please a fraction of the almost 1.4 billion people. Of course, China is not just one big, singular market but instead consists of many very diverse regional ones. Nevertheless, like the motto "Go West, young man," from the 1850s Gold Rush to California, nowadays it could be heard "Go East, young entrepreneur" because of the huge business potentials that exist if you know how to navigate the Chinese market and administration.[11] Understanding the subtle negotiation procedures in China can, however, be a completely different story. Even people who have impeccable Chinese language skills often prefer to have a native person with them as negotiations in China are as much about what is being said as about what is *not* being said. And the use of visual cues, indicating where a negotiation is going, can be challenging to understand for non-native Chinese.[12]

Another facet of the entrepreneurial spirit of many Chinese people is the love of bargaining. It is not only about getting a lower price. Instead, it is an art form. Chai and Chai argue in their book *China A to Z: Chinese Customs and Culture* that "Bargaining, to the Chinese, is like seduction to the French. The process is as important as the actual end result."[13] Of course, bargaining is common in many countries. But for me, it was always important in our everyday life in China.

My husband is a passionate bargainer who knows how to use the right mix of firmness, confidence, charm, and negotiation skills to usually get what he wants at reasonable prices. He also won't buy something if he is not convinced of the price. In contrast, I am not a natural bargainer at all, and I'm usually relieved if I can find a price tag somewhere and know it isn't necessary to bargain. For one, I find it very hard to estimate prices correctly; and secondly, I usually don't like to bargain since I feel uncomfortable doing it. I remember our many visits to all kinds of markets in Beijing: stalls of artwork, jewelry, souvenirs, calligraphy materials, DVDs, handbags, fruit, and anything you can think of. Antoine would regularly engage in the bargaining game by making use of the few Chinese sentences that we learned from the very beginning: "How much is it? Oh, that is way too expensive. I am not a tourist. I'm living here and I know that this is too expensive. So, what is your price for me?" Usually, this introduction would conjure up a smile on the merchant's face and then I knew that the game had started. There would be a lot of back and forth and all types of bargaining tricks in a mixture of Chinese and English. But to my surprise, Antoine and the merchants would usually not leave each other in a bad-tempered mood when negotiating had been particularly fierce. Instead, the vendors—men and women alike—would start laughing when sealing the deal and congratulate Antoine for his bargaining skills. Quite often, they would ask him which Chinese zodiac sign he was. When he said that he was a rat, they'd laugh and say that they now understood why he was so good at bargaining; The Chinese zodiac sign of the rat is considered to be very clever and thrifty.

For me, these bargaining trips were more stressful than anything else. Usually, I used a tip I'd received from some other expat friends who advised me to pay as much as I thought was reasonable for me, regardless of the asking price. If the item meant something to me, I would sometimes pay a price I considered reasonable, even if it might've been possible to bargain further. Yet, when it came to buying fruits and vegetables each week at the market, I often did not feel like bargaining each time. I decided to frequent a couple of stands where I got to know the people and where I was okay with their prices. To honor my loyalty to them, they often offered me a couple of extra fruits or new arrivals as a gift.

While I am not the best bargainer in the formal sense, I enjoy bargaining in other areas. For example, sometimes in restaurants, I like to change the menu and include something slightly different. Or, in a bar, I might ask if we could have one last round even though they are about to close. Or when I'm dealing with administrative issues in daily life. Sometimes it works and sometimes it doesn't, but I have noticed that some good will, humor, and charm can go a long way on these occasions.

When we moved back to Switzerland after our Asia stay and bought our first home, we planned to change it by opening the wall between the kitchen and the living room, and the renovations were scheduled in a tight timeframe. One day, I drove out to see the progress on our new kitchen. It needed to be finished the next day, since the painters were scheduled and the furniture was about to arrive. I stood in a state of shock when I entered the house and saw that the kitchen was far from finished. I looked at the man working on it, who didn't seem to be in the best mood. Cautiously, I asked him how it was going and if he thought that he would manage to finish installing everything before midday the next day. He grumbled back that there was no way he would finish the next day, since he'd been left alone. His colleague, who was supposed to help him, had been called to another construction site. He added that he would not even have time to come the next day to finish. I noticed that putting more pressure on this man was useless. So instead, I asked him if he was up for a little coffee break and a few biscuits—and he agreed happily. While we sat down amid the chaos with two cups of coffee—fortunately, the coffee machine was installed already—and some snacks, he talked about how unfair his job was. He was always under pressure about timelines with insufficient resources to be able to finish on time. And he was tired of it. I told him that I could understand his feelings very well. It must be hard to be in a position where you are always under pressure from your employer and customers alike. At the same time, I explained to him that now

I was in trouble since the painters would arrive the next day and the furniture a couple of days later. I just did not know how to manage it since the painters could only start their work once the kitchen was finished. After some reflection, he said: "You know what, I will put in an extra shift tomorrow morning and ask my boss to send me another person for a few hours so that by tomorrow afternoon, we should finish. We will make it work somehow." I cannot tell you how relieved I felt. I still had to call the painters and postpone for a day. But the attitude of the man changed so much that he was almost not recognizable. I am not sure if this could be called bargaining or if it was more about being empathetic and creating a connection. But I figured that some entrepreneurial thinking and bargaining, combined with charm and empathy, can help cross mountains for many situations. Like in our days back in China, when bargaining mixed with some charm and humor usually helped find a good compromise for everyone.

Yin and Yang – Finding Balance and Flow

When thinking of China and Chinese concepts, many people think of yin and yang. Its symbol is a circle divided by a curved line with one half of the circle being black, and one half being white. There is a white dot in the black area and a black dot in the white one, showing that each side carries the seed of the other one.[14] Yin and yang is a fundamental concept in Chinese society derived from Taoism.[iv] Originating thousands of years ago, it is also called the "law of balancing opposites". As for the meaning of yin and yang,

---

[iv] The terms *Taoism* and *Daoism* are often used interchangeably. Daoism is closer to the original Chinese character 道, which also means "the way." Taoism is the Chinese romanization version, i.e., the English version. In this book, I use the term Taosim.

it is believed that "the universe consists of these two fundamental, harmonious, yet opposite forces."[15] And such opposing forces exist in everything. Yin is often characterized as "an inward energy that is feminine, still, dark, and negative."[16] It is also a symbol for passivity and absorption. In the simplified Chinese characters, the second part of the character is reflected by the symbol for *moon*. Yang, in contrast, is characterized as "outward energy, masculine, hot, bright, and positive."[17] It stands for activity and in the simplified Chinese characters, the second part of the character is the symbol for *sun*. The two forces coexist and complement each other. And while they exemplify the dualist nature of things—like day and night, light and dark, active and passive, etc.—the concept shows that one cannot exist without the other. Wholeness can only be achieved if balance and harmony is found between these opposing forces. A misconception can be that women are more yin and men more yang. However, every man and every woman have yin and yang energies, and these keep moving all the time. In traditional Chinese medicine (TCM), it is believed that the essential life-force energy, also called *qi*, flows through every living thing and is responsible for health and physical, mental, and emotional harmony. For a smoothly flowing *qi*, yin and yang forces have to be in balance. The ever-turning wheel symbolizing yin and yang indicates that things can always turn and keep on changing.[18]

During our time living in China, Antoine and I often came in touch with the theory and the power of yin and yang. I was fascinated when I learned that yin and yang played a role when you choose the name of your child. Another thing that stood out to me was the careful consideration that friends and colleagues took whenever we visited a restaurant. In China, it is quite common that one person takes charge of the whole table's order and gives it to the waiter. Unlike the custom in many Western countries, where people order their own dish, in China, you usually order many different dishes and share them with everyone. This also explains why, for larger tables, there is often a rotating wheel on which the various dishes are placed so that everyone can easily access them. I was often impressed when going out for dining with Chinese friends or Antoine's Chinese colleagues. When someone assumed the task of ordering food for the whole table, they carefully selected the dishes to ensure a good balance. Usually, people would order some spicy food, some not so spicy food, some meat dishes, some vegetarian dishes, some greasy, some dry food, some hot, some chilled food and so on. I always thought that they were doing this to ensure that there would be something for everyone. And while this was probably one of the reasons, I later understood that balancing different forces in all kinds of actions and interactions plays a vital role in daily life in China. The careful selection of dishes represents a form of honoring yin and yang and finding a balance between them. Though, when it comes to yin and yang regarding food, it is less about the actual temperature or moisture level of the food itself, but about the energy properties and the effects on the body.[19]

I still have to laugh when thinking back to an anecdote from my teenage years when my parents, my brother, and I visited the U.S. One evening, we went to a beautiful Chinese restaurant owned by a Chinese couple in Las Vegas. We sat down and studied the menu, and we all decided that the duck dish looked particularly good. So, when the waiter came to take the order, we ordered the same duck dish four times. When we saw the waiter's surprised reaction and his hesitation to write down our order, we figured that something was wrong. He then explained that he would advise us to get a few different dishes to share. After listening to some of his recommendations for dish choices, we agreed. When the plates were served and placed on the rotating wheel on the table, we understood and laughed out loud at our lack of knowledge about Chinese eating customs. Those eating customs also represent the traditional community-centric society in China. Sharing a meal via the rotating wheel symbolizes the importance that is given to communal living in China.

The yin and yang concept, addressing the importance of balance and flow, made me think about other concepts related to creating a state of flow and living a purposeful life. *Flow* has been defined as a "mental state of operation in which the person is fully immersed in what he or she is doing, characterized by a feeling of energized focus, full involvement, and success in the process of the activity."[20] Some people refer to it as "being in the zone." The underlying feeling while being in a flow state often involves a sense of enjoyment, fulfillment, and skill. Mihály Csíkszentmihályi, one of the cofounders of the positive psychology movement, who coined the term *flow* within that movement, explains:

> *"The best moments in our lives are not the passive, receptive, relaxing times...The best moments usually occur if a person's body or mind is stretched to its limits in a voluntary effort to accomplish something difficult and worthwhile."*

> —Mihály Csíkszentmihályi[21]

And again, *flow* is all about having the right balance, a balance between the challenge at hand and the skill set at your disposal. If the challenge is bigger than the skill level, one can quickly become stressed or anxious. If, on the other hand, the skill level is higher than the challenge, one can quickly become bored or distracted. In the end, "inducing flow is about the balance between the level of skill and the size of the challenge at hand."[22] Experiencing flow in everyday life is an essential component for our creativity and well-being. The flow experience is a crucial aspect of the Greek concept of *eudaimonia* or self-actualization. Self-actualization occurs when we fulfill our unique virtuous potentials and live as we were naturally meant to live.[23] The interconnected counterpart of flow is stillness. To live with an enduring state of flow, we need to retreat into silence regularly, as well. For many people, meditation practices or prayer can help find this essential stillness in everyday life. Many inspiring and successful people emphasize the importance that meditation plays in their lives. The right balance between the two can help us find the "harmonious balance in both our external and internal worlds."[24] The Chinese philosopher Lao Tzu summarized this knowledge thousands of years ago when he said: "Be still like a mountain and flow like a great river."

The importance of finding balance and flow is omnipresent in many day-to-day activities in China. For example, acupuncture, one method of traditional Chinese medicine, seeks to restore the energy levels in such a way that the ailment, whatever form it takes, can be addressed. Tai chi, the internal Chinese martial art that integrates defense training, health benefits, and meditation, is another common activity originating in China. The philosophy behind tai chi is that meeting a brute force with brute force will lead to injuries on both sides. To avoid this, students learn to not directly fight or to resist an incoming force. Instead, they are asked to meet the force in softness and follow its motion. By remaining in physical contact until the incoming force of attack exhausts itself, it is possible to safely redirect it, meeting yang with yin.[25] Lao Tzu described this form of interaction as "the soft and the pliable will defeat the hard and the strong."

I often experienced a mental state of flow in China when I was learning to write Chinese characters. For my Chinese language class, I received a book with Chinese characters. It explained the meaning of the characters and the sequence of the various strokes to draw them. There were also a few pages with space to practice drawing the various characters. I loved this exercise. I could sit for hours in cafés drawing different characters and feeling very soothed and relaxed when finishing my homework. So I can understand why the Chinese art of calligraphy—the visual art of beautiful, decorative handwriting—is such an appreciated practice among many people. Sometimes, when Antoine and I strolled through the streets of Beijing, we could observe people engaged in calligraphy, painting Chinese characters in wonderfully elegant manners with ink on paper. And it often seemed as if they were in a different world. Every touch with the brush on the paper, every stroke of the character requires a lot of concentration. I had the impression that many people pursuing this art were in a complete state of flow.

I think that flow also plays a role when indulging in the pleasure of having a good massage. One of the things that I loved most during our stay in China was the possibility to get regular relaxing or restorative massages in one of the numerous massage centers. In comparison to the prices we knew from back home, they came at quite reasonable rates. I will always remember my very first Chinese massage experience when visiting Beijing in 2012 with Antoine. We went for a couple of weeks to explore the city and find out if we could imagine living there for a while. I was lucky that a good friend of mine was visiting Beijing at the same time to see his brother who lived there. While Antoine went to visit his company's office, my friend and I wandered around Beijing and ended up in one of the famous massage salons in the city. We opted for the Chinese massage version. I was expecting a relaxing massage, similar to the aromatherapy massages I had tried before. But the experience proved to be a very different one. The masseuse handed me some light pajamas to wear and as soon as I lay down, she started kneading and twisting me from head to toe. The points that she pressed hurt so much that I could barely avoid screaming and wondered what I had gotten into. My friend, who was attended by a masseuse who seemed to press even more strongly, could at some point not hold it back anymore and started making screaming noises. After the massage, we looked at each other and had to laugh about the experience.

However, over time, I started to appreciate the traditional Chinese massage. Even though they sometimes hurt when a specific body point was pressed particularly hard, I learned that these massages not only help release tension but also improve the energy flow of the body and create balance. And I loved the great, relaxed, yet energized feeling I had when I left. Several massage types can help to restore balance, or yin and yang, in our bodies. Some people even stress that having a massage therapist of the opposite sex is beneficial to rebalance our yin and yang energies.[26] No matter what the preference is in that regard, what could be a nicer way to restore inner body balance than indulging in a pleasant massage from time to time?

For our own daily lives, I think that it can be beneficial to think about where some more balance or equilibrated yin and yang energies are needed. It could be in any area of our life: from a relationship with a particular person in which we feel some imbalance to a room in our home that feels unbalanced. You can go into much more detail in terms of balancing your home with the Chinese *feng shui* concept, in which yin and yang play a role as well. It could also be related to the food we eat, to our emotional, mental, or physical well-being, and to about anything we deal with in our lives. Finding a balance between work, family, and leisure time, between a state of flow and a state of stillness, between speaking and listening, and between so many other things, is not always easy at first. But it can help us a lot in leading more fulfilling and happy lives. And the first step might be to reflect on the areas in our lives that could need some more balance. The Chinese concept of yin and yang can certainly be a helpful and inspirational guide in this endeavor!

The Importance of a Good Network or "*Guanxi*"

One of the core elements of the Chinese thought process is the one of connectedness. According to this line of thought, people are not necessarily born equal—the prevailing view in many Western societies—but they *are* born connected. A Chinese person is not "encouraged to think in an individualistic manner or attitude, and is never treated on a stand-alone basis."[27] Instead, it is believed that every person forms part of multiple networks, which can be anything from family, to work groups or social clubs. Without reference to others, a person has no identity. Confucian teachings, which have played an essential role in shaping customs and behavioral codes in China, emphasize the importance of adhering to specific social roles. Most of the roles or relationships have, according to Confucianism, a hierarchical element. Sons should obey their fathers, subjects their ruler, younger family members the elder ones, etc. However, relationships are also reciprocal. For example, "the filial piety of the son should be reciprocated by the love of the father, and the obedience of the subject [...] by the fairness of the ruler."[28] The only horizontal relationship is the one between friends, where trust plays an important role. People who are too concerned about their own achievements are not considered ambitious but rather aggressive or selfish. In such a line of thought, it is not unusual that people will, for example, accept jobs that they would not have chosen for themselves but that were desired options by their parents or even the state.

This is a very different thought process than the one we know in many Western states, where self-realization and living the life we want to live has come to be one of the proclaimed mottos of our time. While the Chinese way of thinking might seem restrictive in this regard, it has also been argued that the sense of belonging and patriotism that comes with it contributes to the contentment and happiness of people. Of course, times are changing. Over the past decades, with increasing influences from outside, some of these more traditional thought patterns have started to change in China. Yet, I found it very interesting to learn about the importance of connectedness and networks while living in China. The term *guanxi*, which translates to *network* or *connections*, plays a crucial role in this regard. Having a good *guanxi* is enormously important in business and personal life alike. If you want to generate a business deal, knowing the right people can be an incredible advantage over someone who does not know the right people or have the necessary *guanxi*. On a personal level, a good *guanxi* can also be of utmost importance. A good Chinese friend of mine was diagnosed with a severe form of cancer while I lived in Beijing. When the doctors at the public hospital told her about the diagnosis, they also said she would have to wait for a few months before starting the treatment since the waiting list was so long. For my friend, it was a question of life and death, as her cancer was aggressive and advancing quickly and her blood values deteriorated from day to day. Fortunately, her parents had a *guanxi* that could step in to support in this situation. Ultimately, a hospital was found where they were willing to schedule the operation and the treatment much quicker, thereby saving her life. I was so grateful when I heard about this. Yet, at the same time, I felt somewhat troubled by the fact that a *guanxi* was needed in this case to get the necessary treatment on time.

Reading about *guanxi* like this, it might give the impression it was a corrupt system. But it is far more complex than that, and *guanxi* activities, in general, can't be classified as being corrupt. On the contrary, *guanxi* is a "moral code prescribing proper social behavior within Chinese culture."[29] A good *guanxi* relationship develops over time through multiple interactions and exchanges. And it creates a web of reciprocal obligations and indebtedness. To maintain such relationships, each party needs to understand that they must fulfill their duties concerning these obligations.[30] It is hence a complex web of reciprocal giving and receiving, which can be in the form of a gift, a favor or any other support for the opposite party.

The building of a *guanxi* usually takes time and trust from both sides. If one party gives the impression of abusing the relationship, it can quickly lead to irritation or even an end of the relationship. One hindrance that can easily become a problem for foreigners wanting to do business in China is not properly understanding the importance of *guanxi* or behaving inappropriately if a Chinese person opens up their *guanxi*. If a friend or a business acquaintance in China facilitates the contact to a key person for a foreigner, the foreigner will do good to pay utmost respect to the person who did this favor and to the person he or she is introduced to. Usually, it is expected that this favor is returned at some point in time, usually on a larger scale. If these behavioral rules are disregarded, it is easy to lose the respect of the person who helped in the first place or to lose access to the *guanxi* that had been opened. It can be very tricky and complex to deal with such interwoven relationships if one is not used to the appropriate behavioral codes. That is why it can help to get advice from people who understand this custom and know how to politely and elegantly navigate these complexities. Of course, the line between legitimate *guanxi* practice, unethical *guanxi* practice, and blatant corruption can sometimes be blurry. But usually, *guanxi* is not about corruption but about reciprocity in terms of giving and taking in relationships.

I think that striving for connection and reciprocity when it comes to helping each other is in our human nature. And this is universal. Even though I was impressed by the frequent use of the term guanxi while living in Beijing, China is not the only country where such reciprocal relationships are common. In many Asian, Latin American, African, and Middle Eastern societies where communal living is viewed as a priority, the network effect—referred to as *guanxi* in China—is valued and forms part of everyday life. And while it is a concept practiced in similar forms in many countries around the world, I found it fascinating to notice its omnipresence in China. I learned that a *guanxi* is composed of several "circles of influence." One of these circles is the family, which can be the close nuclear family, but also the extended family and even people coming from the same region. Another one is the business or working circle. At the core of this circle are usually "the most commercially and strategically active relationships, including friends, business contacts, as well as government connections."[31] The circle's outer ring can also include colleagues, alumni, or members of the same club or association. People usually spend a lot of time and energy to nurture and grow these circles of influence. And then there is the "friends circle," which contains different types of friends: for example, the friends you go out with to eat and drink and to discover new restaurants, the friends you do sports with, the friends you do business with, the ones you talk and listen to, etc. Many Chinese people prefer to spend most of their time and energy in their various circles of influence. People not belonging to these circles or networks are regarded as strangers and are treated differently. While adequate behavior in the respective circles plays a vital role, behavior toward strangers can, in some cases, be marked by indifference.[32]

Reflecting on the complex concept of *guanxi*, I wondered how it works in Western society, where I grew up, and if we could learn something from it. As such, I find the idea that we are all connected beings and that we only exist in relation to this web of connections very appealing. I do believe that somehow everything is connected in this world. Our actions stand in close correlation to our environment. In Germany, there is the famous saying, stating: *"Wie man in den Wald hineinruft, so schallt es heraus,"* which can be literally translated as: "The way you call into the forest, is the way it comes back," meaning "what goes around comes around." If you spread positive energy, you are receptive to receiving good energy, as well. And if you are friendly to your environment, more often than not, you are treated in a friendly way as well. A lot of fascinating research is being done on the law of attraction and, on a more personal level, how to manifest specific things in our lives by getting the energy right.

Brené Brown, who has inspired millions of people with her research and thoughts on human nature, noted: "Connection is why we're here. We are hardwired to connect with others, it's what gives purpose and meaning to our lives, and without it, there is suffering."[33]

She also claims that "connection doesn't exist without giving and receiving. We need to give, and we need to need."[34] I think that we all can relate to the great feeling we have when we meet with people we feel connected to. A sense of understanding and appreciation for one another gives us joy and purpose in life. To feel part of something bigger than oneself is certainly something that helps us achieve a sense of connection and belonging. And for many Chinese people, their *guanxis* may represent exactly this.

No matter where we are living and no matter if we have heard about the *guanxi* concept before, every person has various circles of influence of which he or she is part. We all wear different hats. In my case, I am a wife, a mother, a daughter, a sister, an aunt, a friend, a colleague, an accountability buddy, a sports companion, a researcher, a writer, but also just Judith, a woman with her own dreams, visions, and desires. And throughout daily life, we shift between the various hats and responsibilities we have. And despite wearing different hats, we can remain true to our core self and our core values, no matter which role we play.

I can relate very much to the observation that many Chinese people feel most confident in their respective circles of influence. For me, too, it is important to have different groups and networks in different areas of life. These are first and foremost my close family and friends.

But then there are many other support networks. For example, my monthly women's support group where we talk about our dreams and hold each other accountable. Or the group of mothers from the nursery with whom I discuss issues related to our children or about life as a mom. Then there are writer and entrepreneurial support groups, sports buddies, the groups of close childhood friends, or the various groups of friends that meant so much to me in every place I lived. These circles and support networks are important for me and help me feel supported and understood in the various areas of my life. And even though it takes time and energy to create or find such supportive circles—especially if, like me, you move around a lot—it's absolutely worth it. The value of connections plays out as well when moving abroad. I have always found it incredibly helpful to learn from people who lived in the place I was about to move to. Their insider tips and hints often made the adaptation to a new place much easier and smoother.

Also, in terms of work, it has been shown over and over again just how important connections are now. What was for a long time negatively viewed as partisanship or cronyism is proven time and over again to be very important. If you know people in various places, opportunities can open up in the most unexpected ways. Some studies have shown that between 70 and 85 percent of people ended up in their positions due to networking.[35] Connecting with people and finding out about potential job fits is critical for many to find the job they are looking for. Having observed the competitive job landscape in Geneva for a while, I also noticed just how powerful a good connection can be. This doesn't mean that people need not be qualified for the job they apply for or what they aim to achieve. But the first door to show what you can do often opens through some sort of connection. Good connections also play a crucial role in entrepreneurial circles. I have met many entrepreneurs who help and support each other by inviting each other to their respective podcasts or events or by promoting each other's products.

So, what can we draw from this Chinese custom for our personal life? I believe that the Chinese *guanxi* or network custom can help us to consciously reflect on the networks we are part of or want to be part of. And to find ways to establish valuable networks for the various areas in our lives. Networks help us thrive and feel supported, and they provide opportunities to support and give positive energy to others in return as well!

Beautiful Lessons Learned from China

✳ **Be confident and hopeful on the inside and modest and polite on the outside.** The attributes of confidence and modesty hold different meanings in different cultures. Understanding these differences can help avoid misunderstandings. And combining both attributes in our daily lives can help us to live up to both of them in a healthy way.

✳ **Be entrepreneurial in your thinking and add a touch of bargaining and charm,** and you will be able to open up great opportunities in business and in personal life alike.

✳ **Work on restoring balance in areas of your life that feel unbalanced.** Balancing opposites can help us in achieving harmony. It could be about finding a balance between work and rest, between listening and speaking, or it could be about balancing our inner energies or our food intake. The Chinese yin and yang concept can give some inspiring insights in this regard.

✳ **Flow and stillness are complementary.** Challenge yourself and use your unique skill set to experience a state of flow in which you feel energized, creative, and fulfilled. And at the same time, take time to indulge in moments of stillness. It could be in the form of meditation, prayer, journaling, focusing on your breath, or being silently mindful of your surroundings. Stillness is the interconnected counterpart of flow.

✳ **Think about the connections and networks you want to establish or be part of on a personal and on a professional level.** We need connections and support networks. Many Chinese people are very good at navigating different webs of connections or guanxis. Think of support groups that can help you with your dreams and aspirations and in which you would like to engage actively, as well!

Chapter 9

JAPAN

The Land of the Rising Sun

❖ **Politeness and Respect in Everyday Life**

❖ **Striving for Perfection and the Appreciation of Imperfection or "Wabi-sabi"**

❖ **Healthy Living and Having a Life Purpose or "Ikigai:" Japanese Secrets for a Long and Happy Life**

❖ **The Importance of Community, of Finding your Tribe, and of Moments for Conscious Self-Care**

Japan, the Land of the Rising Sun, has fascinated me since I was small and listened to my father's stories about his frequent travel to Japan for business. I liked the expression "The Land of the Rising Sun" and always pictured a beautiful image of the sun rising in the very early morning over this country. The expression dates back about 1,400 years and was first used by the Sui Dynasty in China in 618 AD to describe Japan. Given that Japan was located East of the Chinese coastline, it gave the impression that the sun rose over Japan. As a consequence, people started referring to Japan as *Nihon* or sun origin. This nickname also inspired the country's national flag, which has a red point symbolizing the sun.[1]

When my husband and I lived in Beijing, my husband traveled often to Japan for business. Every time he came back home to China, he told me how much he liked Tokyo, the food, and the way of life in Japan. While I was fascinated by his stories, I had just started to really appreciate life in China. I had gotten used to the sometimes chaotic way of life in Beijing's streets and markets and had developed an appreciation for the country. When my husband suggested that Japan could be our next destination for a move, I had mixed feelings. On the one hand, many nice images popped up in my mind when thinking of Japan: cherry blossom trees, Japanese gardens, and images of geishas and women dressed in beautiful kimonos. On the other hand, I had also heard about the stiff, hierarchical system in Japanese society and the societal pressures that went along with it. I worried that I would feel constricted. I had always imagined myself returning to Central or Latin America one day since I loved the warm-hearted atmosphere shared by the people I had met while living there. I enjoyed the physical contact through hugs or kisses on the cheeks every day and feared that I could feel socially or personally isolated in a country like Japan. Yet, at the same time, Antoine and I considered it a beautiful lifetime opportunity to discover living in this fascinating country for a while. Also, business-wise it made sense for Antoine to move to Japan. So, after some long discussions, we decided to give it a try and, in the summer of 2015, we moved from China to Japan—the land of the rising sun.

Politeness and Respect in Everyday Life

I was sitting in an airport shuttle bus going from the large Narita airport outside of Tokyo to Tokyo's city center. The transit would take about an hour and a half, and I had just gotten comfortable in one of the bus seats. When the bus was about to leave, I looked out the window and paused in surprise. Next to the bus, a handful of Japanese people working for the bus company were standing, pressing their hands together in the typical way of respectful greeting in many Asian countries. When the bus set off to leave, all of them bowed down deeply, waiting until we had left the terminal. At first, I wondered if some high politician or respected person was sitting on the same bus, explaining this humble conduct. But with time, I learned that such respectful behavior is common practice with customers in almost any domain in Japan. It was a first taste of usual interactions of life in Japan.

My husband, his parents, and I visited Japan a year before our move, so I was touching Japanese soil for the second time in my life. In contrast to what I had feared experiencing, I was more than positively surprised by the country. The experience you have in a country often depends on the people you get to know. In Japan, I was lucky to quickly connect with a wonderful group of pregnant international and Japanese women via the Tokyo Pregnancy Group. I got pregnant in May 2015, a couple of months before our move to Japan. When researching doctors, hospitals, and support networks for English-speaking pregnant women in Japan, I discovered this group. It was the tribe that I needed to quickly feel at home in this new country. We regularly met at one of the group members' homes and learned about the health infrastructure and support for pregnant women in Tokyo. Usually, a health expert joined us, addressing such diverse topics as acupuncture, chiropractic, and doula services for pregnant ladies. On other occasions, people would inform us about child development stages or on how to find and apply for nursery places. The meetings were not only a great source of information to feel more comfortable in a foreign environment, but it was also the birthplace of a wonderful group of mama friends—in Japanese often referred to as *mamatomo*. The intensity of living in such a foreign environment during a life-changing period (being pregnant and becoming a mother) tied us very close together. The frequent meetings and exchanges via messages throughout the week, provided extra support for whenever we faced a challenge. It was a life-saver for me. It was one important experience that made my entry into this new life chapter in Japan much smoother and comfortable.

But then there was also the truly Japanese part that I started to love. My husband and I found a little apartment in a Japanese residential neighborhood, and we enjoyed the fact that we really felt like we were in Japan when stepping out of the house. In the beginning, I struggled quite a bit with the language and language-sign barriers. I remember trying to explain at the local supermarkets that I was looking for pasteurized milk since I was pregnant. Something so simple to explain in a language you master well, represented quite a challenge for me during my first weeks in Japan in a language that was completely new to me. Yet, with the help of Japanese translation apps, a few Japanese words that I picked up, and the good will of the people working in the supermarkets, I learned to find the items I was looking for.[i] Every little excursion to the supermarket, the pharmacy, the post office, or the bus stop to ask for directions became a little adventure. And while sometimes it was tiresome and I just felt like staying at home to prevent the hassles of communicating, I was also

---

[i] A Japanese friend of mine explained later to me that pregnant women in Japan are usually not very concerned about drinking unpasteurized milk. This could also explain why people in the supermarket did not really understand my concern in the beginning. The do's and don'ts of pregnancies vary a lot according to the country and the culture you are in—something that was fascinating to observe and experience.

very proud every time I managed to get some daily transaction done in this entirely new environment.

What stood out to me from the very beginning was the politeness and kindness the Japanese showered me with, no matter where I went. Usually, when entering a supermarket or the local pharmacy or even the 7-Eleven store next to our apartment building, several of the employees would shout out, "*Irasshaimase*," which can be translated to "welcome" or "please come in." Quite often, several employees or shop clerks would call out this welcome as soon as you enter the shop. The first time that several people shouted this when I entered a supermarket, I wondered if I had done something wrong. But soon, I understood the meaning of the term and was quite amazed by this formal, kind, and welcoming attitude toward customers. Also, on other occasions, I noted the omnipresent Japanese politeness and the respectful behavior toward customers. For example, I loved taking taxis in Japan. In Beijing, my experiences with taxi drivers had often been quite adventurous. If I didn't manage to pronounce the address correctly, I usually had to leave the taxi. On several occasions, taxi drivers even explained that they couldn't take me since my desired destination was not on their way where they were going. So, when in Tokyo, we called a taxi and the driver pulled up, I expected similar issues. Instead, I was impressed by the polite way taxi drivers would patiently listen to my attempts to explain the destination, sometimes handing me over a sheet with Japanese/English expressions if we faced a communication issue. Taking a taxi was much more expensive than in Beijing, so it was not something very common to do, but I remember how much I always enjoyed the experience. When the taxi stopped, the rear left door would often open automatically. Sometimes, I would find myself in a cab decorated with little white curtains or other neat details, so it felt more like entering a private limousine than entering a taxi. On some occasions, the taxi drivers even wore white gloves, which accentuated the impression to expect an exceptional experience. That is when I learned about the Japanese way of doing what you do with passion, rigor, and dignity. Taxi drivers in Japan would go out of their way to provide their clients with a memorable, pleasant experience. It seemed like a mixture of being polite and being proud of doing the job in the best possible way.

Politeness and respect are also shown on public transportation in Japan. When I took the airport bus shuttle service for the first time, I was surprised to hear and see an announcement specifying that people should put on safety belts, set their cellphones on silent, and not speak on the phone during the bus ride. While I could understand the security-belt part, I was quite surprised that I was not allowed to talk on the phone on a bus. And this rule holds for every public transportation system. You are allowed to listen to music using headphones or to play games on your phone. But it isn't well-regarded to disturb others with loud noise or loud conversations. So, despite hundreds or sometimes thousands of people being packed into the subway cars, especially during rush hour, the ride is usually a silent experience. It was something entirely new for me in comparison to my experiences in other countries. From India, with its constant noise level in the streets, to Beijing, where talking loudly was the common norm on subways, or on Geneva's trams where small musical groups would often entertain the whole wagon for a few stops—in addition to all the phone and live conversations going on. In comparison, the subways, buses, and trains in Japan were so silent that you could hear a pin drop on the floor. It made the public transportation rides in a city with almost 14 million inhabitants—and a surrounding metropolitan area of 37 million people—an enjoyable and not-too-tiresome experience.[2] It was still possible to speak to someone on the train or bus, but usually quietly. However, most Japanese people using public transportation seemed to indulge in some silent activity on their phone like reading news or playing games, reading a book, working, or just using the time to sit quietly or enjoy a nap. This respectful not-disturbing of other people traveling with them was something quite revealing about Japanese society.

I noticed a similar behavioral code when it came to respecting and protecting other people when being ill. It is common practice for people in Japan to wear a face mask when they have the flu or a cold to avoid spreading the bacteria and germs to others. In Beijing, I often saw people with face masks, and I had started wearing them myself on certain days when the city's pollution levels were particularly high. In Japan, I was told that wearing a face mask was mainly to protect each other from falling ill. When we lived in Japan from 2015 to 2017, it was not common among Europeans to wear face masks when they had a cold.[ii] One time, when my parents and my brother visited us in Tokyo, my mom was struggling with a cold and a runny nose. One afternoon, we were all on a subway and my brother had just asked me why so many people were wearing face masks. While I was talking to him about it, my mom got a sneezing attack and after sneezing a few times into her hands, she pulled out a tissue from her handbag and blew her nose. While this would have been completely normal behavior in Europe at that time, the Japanese people around us looked astonished. Public nose blowing is not usually done in Japanese society. It is much more common to hold your nose, something many Westerners might need to get used to. So, after seeing the many astonished looks following the sneeze attack, my brother exclaimed laughing: "So, I guess mom just did exactly what you are not supposed to do here." We quietly joked that we would probably have the entire subway wagon for ourselves if we continued behaving like this. My mom felt sorry when hearing about the nose-blowing etiquette. Behaviors and customs change from country to country and sometimes, even when you know the rule, it can be difficult to adhere to it. Yet, the nice thing about being a

---

[ii] The situation has changed, of course, since COVID-19 hit the world and wearing face masks has become a common norm across Europe and the Western world, as well.

foreigner in a country is that people often have a kind, tolerant eye toward you when they see that you are trying to adapt to the culture, even if you don't manage to succeed. My husband and I often said to each other that we were lucky to live in such a fascinating country without needing to adhere to all the cultural expectations in work and family life that most Japanese people do. In a way, we were always considered as slightly exotic outsiders anyway.

Also, in other everyday situations, a respectful attitude toward others and their belongings usually prevailed. I noticed it after one of my trips to Europe shortly after my move to Japan. When coming back to Tokyo, I went directly to a mall to meet my husband—with my large suitcases. I had seen a little bakery in the mall, which was so small that I didn't want to enter it with my huge suitcases and all my bags. A woman who seemed very nice was sitting at one of the benches in front of the bakery. I approached her and asked if she could watch my luggage while I bought a pastry. She agreed and added, smiling: "Of course, I do it with pleasure. But you don't need to worry about anything getting stolen. You are in Japan." I had heard that Japan was one of the safest countries globally, but I was still used to having an eye on my belongings as this is a wise thing to do in many countries. But with time, I became used to this sense of security. I think that—apart from the fear of earthquakes—I never felt as safe in my whole life as I did during my time in Japan. Usually, I don't enjoy walking through subway stations in the later evening hours. Yet in Japan, I had no problem taking subways, sometimes even with our baby, late in the evening. It just felt safe, and I enjoyed this feeling enormously. After a few months of living in Tokyo, I became used to leaving my phone on the table in a café when I would go to the toilet, or I'd leave my purse outside in the stroller when taking our little girl inside a playground. It had become so natural that when I left, I had to get used to being more cautious again outside of Japan.

Children in Japanese society are taught the importance of morality and respect. In the first years of school, teaching manners and helping children develop character takes a more important place than transmitting factual knowledge. A lot of emphasis is put on helping children learn to be generous, compassionate, and empathetic. Also, the transmission of qualities like grit, self-control, and fairness plays an essential part. A primary goal is to teach children from the beginning to respect other people and to be gentle to animals and nature. I found it fascinating to learn that in many Japanese schools, children take part in the school's daily cleaning activities. The period of *o-soji*, or cleaning, usually takes place after lunch. Students are then divided into small groups and given cleaning tasks like cleaning the classroom, the hallway, the windows, or the library that rotate throughout the year. Cleaning up together not only teaches students to work in teams and help each other; it also instills in children respect for their surroundings and the work that others are doing in a playful, respectful manner. [3,4] During my time in Japan, Antoine and I and our family and friends who were visiting us were all surprised by the respectful behavior displayed by children and teenagers we encountered. And we often said to each other that it was probably one of the most valuable things society could do: put emphasis on teaching qualities such as empathy, compassion, and respect for each other from an early age.

Striving for Perfection and The Appreciation of Imperfection or "*Wabi-sabi*"

Whoever has watched the documentary *Jiro Dreams of Sushi* knows what striving for perfection means. In this American documentary, recorded in Japanese, director David Gelb followed Jiro Ono, a sushi-restaurant owner who was in his mid-80s when the documentary was produced in 2011, and explained how Jiro relentlessly strived to make his sushi even more perfect. His son, at that time in his 50s, who is supposed to take over the restaurant one day, was for years "only" allowed to prepare the rice for the sushi. Careful attention was paid to preparing the rice in a way so that it would have just the right consistency for the sushi. Even though this way of living and working might seem quite extreme, I was impressed by the willingness and perseverance of people like Jiro and his son to perfect their work on a daily basis. It reminded me of an experience in China when I was told in a beginner's tai chi class that you could perfect your tai chi moves throughout your whole life.

Personally, I have been struggling with perfectionism and its consequences, as it can become so extreme that it creates blocks, complicates life, and makes it difficult to get things done. So, I need to follow a "get it done" or "progress over perfection" approach. What fascinated me more than the perfectionism of these Japanese sushi chefs was their humble attitude and their willingness to keep learning. I had the impression that many of the Japanese would deeply commit to whatever task they were supposed to do and would work to get it done in the best possible way and go all in. And they would do it in a humble, dignified manner.

In this context, the Japanese concept of "*kaizen*"—which stands for "change for the better" or a "continuous improvement"—comes in. It originated in the business environment in Japan after World War II. It was influenced by American business-advisory teams that had come to Japan to talk about quality management after the war had left many Japanese companies destroyed and people's morale devastated.[5] Masaaki Imai, who coined the term *kaizen*, and who is the founder of the Kaizen Institute, is quoted as saying that the message of *kaizen* is that no day should go by without some type of improvement in a company. The Japanese company Toyota, which also faced significant hardships after the war, is known to have implemented a kaizen strategy by focusing on constant, gradual improvements in terms of productivity. Employees play an essential role in suggesting and implementing these improvements. Imai observed that the idea of progressive change is not as common in Western societies, where often radical or abrupt transformations are undertaken.[6] But he emphasizes the immense power that progressive, incremental change can have. The *kaizen* concept is nowadays not only applied in diverse business environments but also in sports and in personal development areas. Instead of striving for immediate perfection, it promotes the very small, sometimes almost unnoticeable behavior changes that can lead to significant progress in the long term. Sarah Harvey, who wrote a very insightful book about the power of *kaizen* in changing our habits for the better, stresses how the tiniest steps in our habits or routines toward improvement we seek can be the best way to start to change or create new habits.[7]

I have noticed how powerful it can be to start with small, incremental steps when trying to change or set up a habit. For example, I want to implement a new habit of getting up earlier in the morning to have some restorative and energizing me time before the family hustle sets in. I read the inspiring book *Miracle Morning* by Hal Elrod, who, after researching some of the most successful and happy people, found out that what most of them had in common was a healthy morning routine to set them up for a great day. He developed a method of a variety of different activities to do first thing in the morning that can help to set you up for a more fulfilling and successful life. Hundreds of thousands of people have started practicing a miracle morning routine. And many take an hour or more to conduct their individual morning routines, which can include sports, meditation, reading, journaling, affirmations, visualizations, and any other person-specific rituals. I have been wanting to install a healthier morning routine for a while but have not acted upon it since I can't seem to force myself to get up an hour earlier, especially since our nights are still often interrupted by our little children. So recently, I came across some very helpful advice from one of the entrepreneurs applying a "miracle morning" routine. He claimed that it's often easiest to start small. For example, just get up 10 minutes earlier to implement a short daily morning routine. And then, add more time and activities once you become used to it and probably begin to really enjoy it. This was the hint that made me start a little morning routine for just a few minutes to give to myself time before starting the usual morning hustle. It can be anything from a short prayer or meditation to some stretching movements or a few thoughts jotted down in my journal. And with this in mind, I could also better understand what fascinated me during our time in Japan: that, rather than striving for perfection immediately, people aspired to become better in different areas of life gradually, but constantly with incremental steps.

While I have the impression that many people in Japan strive to perfect their tasks and give a lot of attention to detail, there is another widespread and essential concept that shows the appreciation of imperfection and incompletion. This concept is called *wabi-sabi*. *Wabi-sabi* comes from the Zen Buddhist concept of impermanence and constant flow and emphasizes the simplicity of things.[8] It is about seeing "the beauty in every aspect of imperfection in nature" and in things alike.[9] A broken teacup that is kept and repaired can be *wabi-sabi*. In fact, there is even a term, *kintsugi*, in Japanese that is used for describing the ancient Japanese art of repairing broken ceramics with metallic lacquer, dusted or mixed with gold, silver, or platinum powder. Instead of covering or concealing the cracks, they are celebrated by highlighting them in a beautiful way. Another delightful manifestation of *wabi-sabi* is the annual cherry-blossom celebration in Japan. It is referred to as *hanami*, which translates to "flower watching." During this celebration, people get together with family and friends for picknicks under the cherry trees. What is special about this custom is the philosophy standing behind it.

Cherry blossoms are a flower of the spring and stand for renewal and the fleeting nature of life.[10] Their life span is not very long. Shortly after the flowers have fully developed and their beauty peaks, the wind starts carrying them away. I remember that it often looked almost as if it had snowed when all the white and rose petals had fallen on the ground. This natural spectacle is a beautiful symbol for the evanescence and transience of life, which is very much in line with the *wabi-sabi* concept.[11]

Wabi-sabi has also become famous as a stylistic concept in art and architecture, where it stands for a plain, frugal design and simple, organic structures with asymmetry and signs of wear.[12] Many books have been written on the concept of *wabi-sabi*, highlighting the appreciation of transience, imperfection, and asymmetry. Author Helen Russell highlights and describes this concept as well in her book *The Atlas of Happiness*. She refers to a Japanese woman who explains *wabi-sabi* as follows: "It's like your grandmother. As an elder in the family, you have a lot of respect, and being 'old' isn't a bad thing in Japanese culture. It means you have a history, which adds value."[13] I found this explanation, applying the concept even to people, very telling. There is deep appreciation and respect for older people in Japan. And I often find that elderly people radiate a sense of pleasant, calm wisdom that they can transmit to others.

In Western Europe, I sometimes miss this appreciation for the old and the imperfect. I have the impression that we often want to "get rid" of everything and everyone that is not "functioning" to the fullest. This can be a shame since, on a material level, it can be a waste, and on an interpersonal level, so much can be learned when listening to the older generation. I understand and appreciate that adult-child relationships have shifted in the past decades more and more from an authoritarian style to a style in which mutual respect and cooperation are favored. Yet, at the same time, I do think that showing respect to the elderly for their life experiences and wisdom is something beautiful and valuable to do.

I came to value this sense of *wabi-sabi* for elderly people, particularly during the last years when my grandfather was still alive. I cherished my grandparents a lot. They were very supportive and loving with all their grandchildren. However, I only started to consciously realize how much wisdom and interesting insights my grandparents had when they got older. My mom's mom lived by some very basic but very true and comforting truths, which my mom and I keep reciting even today.[iii] And my father's father, to whom I referred earlier in the chapter on Germany, shared some of his insights and wisdom with us only when he reached his 80s. When he opened up about some of his experiences from World War II, I remember thinking that soon there would not be any survivors of the Second World War left, and that it was extremely precious to learn from those who had lived through it first-hand. In this context, the Japanese concept of *wabi-sabi* resonates a lot with me. Also, in terms of our consumer society—of which I am certainly part—and in which it is easier to throw away things than to repair them, it can be helpful to adopt a *wabi-sabi* approach from time to time. This way, we can learn to appreciate the imperfect yet beautifully unique nature of those things that show that they have a history.

[iii] Two of our favorite cited statements are: *"Die Ruhe, die man sich selber gibt, kann einem keiner nehmen,"* which can be translated to: "No one can take away the rest you give to yourself." And, when things seem to become overwhelming: *"Eins nach dem anderen, wie man die Klöße isst,"* which means: "One after the other, as you eat the dumplings."

Healthy Living and Having a Life Purpose or "*Ikigai*": Japanese Secrets for a Long and Happy Life

Japan is one of the countries with the highest life expectancies, with an average of 87 years for women and 81 years for men, as of 2019.[14] The Southern Japanese island archipelago of Okinawa, also known as the land of the immortals, is home to the highest rate of centenarians (people over 100 years old) in the world.[15] The Japanese diet is one reason why many Japanese experience good overall health. Most Japanese dishes do not include a lot of fat, but rather healthy fish and seaweed. Also, green tea, which has lots of antioxidants, is consumed frequently.[16] Yet, what is even more telling is that most of the Japanese don't overeat. One of the open secrets for a healthy life on the Japanese Okinawa islands is to only eat until you are 80 percent full—a stark contrast to many other countries in the world. There is an expression for this practice in Japanese: "*Hara hachi bu*," or stop eating when you are 80 percent full. This philosophy implies that you should push your plate aside when you are still a little bit hungry since "it takes about 20 minutes for the stomach to send signals to the brain that it is full."[17] So if you stop eating when you are just about to be full, you will feel completely satisfied 20 minutes later. This concept doesn't imply that you should be wasting food. Indeed, there is another saying in Japanese that there are seven fortune gods in every grain of rice and that it is, therefore, important to respect each rice grain. It's a saying often told to children, aiming to teach them that food should be appreciated and not wasted. One solution to be able to stop eating when you are 80 percent full, therefore, might lie in simply having smaller servings from the beginning.

When my husband and I moved to Japan, we were sometimes surprised by the seemingly small plates that were served. After finishing them, however, we usually felt completely satisfied. There is this saying that your stomach adapts to your eating habits and that it has the capacity to either grow or shrink according to the quantities of food it has become used to. What I loved in Japan was that often we were served several small plates or bowls when having a typical lunch menu. Somehow, the very fact of having little quantities on these plates made me eat more mindfully and slower in order to enjoy each bite. There is research showing that the simple fact of using smaller plates and bowls can lead to people consuming a third less than usual and still feel satisfied.[18]

That there are differences between countries in terms of meal serving sizes was something that my husband and I realized first-hand. During our stay in Japan, we organized a trip to Hawaii for our babymoon a few months before our first daughter was born. We considered it a golden opportunity to visit Hawaii, since it was only a few hours plane ride from Japan and we had wanted to visit the country for a while. When we arrived in Hawaii and went to one of the food trucks—there were many excellent food trucks, serving everything from burgers and garlic shrimp to international cuisines—we ordered, as usual, two plates. We were almost in shock when we saw the large quantity of food being served to us. After realizing several times that we could only finish about half our plates, we decided to order only one dish for the two of us for the rest of the journey. Japan on the one hand and the U.S. on the other might be two quite extreme versions when it comes to food quantities being served. And it was interesting for us to notice the difference so clearly.

Despite living in Japan, my husband and I struggled quite often to apply the "eat until you are 80 percent full" rule. Both of us love food, cooking, and eating out. And we love dessert. So even when we decided to go for a relatively light meal, we often did not refrain from buying a dessert somewhere else afterward. Or, when buying

frequently bought quantities that filled us much more than
ested 80 percent. Often, we ended up feeling like stranded
on their backs about to burst when we had enjoyed a meal
could not stop eating. It is not particularly easy to follow the 80
cent rule right away since it demands quite a lot of self-discipline
nd practice. But making efforts to try this from time to time and
to stop eating when we are pleasantly satiated can certainly have
a positive impact on our physical and mental well-being. A whole
body of research emphasizes the positive effects of "intuitive eating,"
stressing the value of listening to your body and its hunger and
satisfaction signals. This way of eating allows you to eat what feels
good to you, to feed your body when it is hungry, and to stop eating
when you start feeling satisfied.

In addition to the healthy diet tips that one can learn from the
Japanese, there is the beautiful Japanese concept called *ikigai*, roughly
translated in English to mean "the reason for living" or "meaning
for life." It can also be described as the Japanese form of the *raison
d'être*, and the concept is deeply ingrained in Japanese society in a
casual way.[19] Your *ikigai* is a personal driving force in everyday life.
People have described it as being the reason you get up for in the
morning. In Western societies, the *ikigai* concept has been brought
up in recent years in many books and coaching programs. Often it is
depicted as a Venn diagram, with people's *ikigai* at the intersection of
four components: what you love doing, what you are good at doing,
what the world needs, and what you can get paid to do.

—Source: *Forbes*,
based on diagram by Marc Winn[20,21]

Nicholas Kemp, *ikigai* coach and Japanologist, points out, however, that this interpretation of *ikigai* is a Western misinterpretation which doesn't correspond to the original use of the term in Japanese society.[22] According to him, for the average Japanese person, the concept of *ikigai* is important, but it is used in casual conversations without all the hype around it found in Western societies. And, maybe even more importantly, for Japanese people, their *ikigai* does not have to be linked to a profession or to making money. In fact, in most cases, it has nothing to do with the pursuit of making money. Instead, it is "a spectrum that includes all the things we value, from the little joys in life to the pursuit of life-defining goals."[23] And for many Japanese people their *ikigai* is related to family or community.

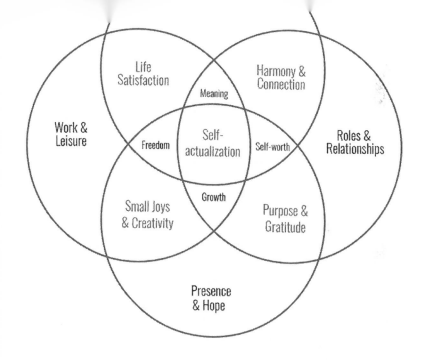

Life Satisfaction

Harmony & Connection

Meaning

Work & Leisure

Freedom

Self-actualization

Self-worth

Roles & Relationships

Growth

Small Joys & Creativity

Purpose & Gratitude

Presence & Hope

—"The Ikigai Framework" by Nicholas Kemp in cooperation with Prof. Akihiro Hasegawa

Hasegawa and Kemp stress that the Japanese do not use such a framework to *find* their *ikigai*. Their intention behind developing this framework is to show what *ikigai* means to the Japanese and to replace the misinterpreted *ikigai* framework circulating on the Internet. Kemp emphasizes that in order to understand your *ikigai*,

outer circles overlap with each oth

values are in line with our work, hobbies, or interests, we have life satisfaction. If we live our values in our roles and relationships, we are able to experience harmony and connection. If we are present and hopeful in regard to our roles and relationships, we experience a sense of purpose and gratitude. And being present in our work, interests, or hobbies provides us with the opportunity to recognize and savor the small joys of life and help us express our creative selves.

If we live and perceive our *ikigai* in these ways, we are likely to experience meaning, self-worth, growth, and freedom in our lives. And all of these aspects will lead to "self-actualization," the ultimate aspect of *ikigai*: knowing who you are and becoming the most honest, most true version of yourself.

I have heard stories of people whose *ikigai* was to take care of their sheep each day. For others, it is spending time with their families or with their grandchildren. And for others still, it's indulging in one of their hobbies or passions. What's important is that you feel that there is a purpose and a meaning in your life. A Japanese friend of mine explained to me that your *ikigai* can also change over your lifetime. When you become parents, your *ikigai* might be your children. At a different stage in your life, it might be related to a passion, a hobby, or a vocation. Or you might have several *ikigais*. Her grandmother's *ikigai* was, for example, to meet each Thursday night for family dinners with her children and grandchildren. People often live healthier and longer when they have a sense of purpose.

Thinking back to my grandfather, who created his own wine business and spent most of his days in the vineyards, I think that his *ikigai* was taking care of his vineyards and producing quality wine with lots of love and effort. Even in his 80s, a day would only have been a good day for him if he had at least been in his vineyards for an hour or two. The worst thing for him was to become bedridden in his final years since he could not live his *ikigai* anymore. I remember that during my last visit to him in 2015, my mom and I went to several of his vineyards and collected a few grapevines of green and red grapes and brought them to his bed. His eyes that had been marked by a lot of pain in the preceding months started to glow again, and while he tasted the different grapes, he told us in detail which grapes were ripe for collecting already and which grapes needed a bit more time. It was a wonderful image that I will always keep of him.

Thinking about one's *ikigai* in the Japanese sense can be a beneficial tool in digging deeper into what makes our daily life meaningful and purposeful. And there can certainly be different aspects that add meaning to our lives. The other interpretation of *ikigai*, described in the first illustration—despite the fact that it does not represent the original Japanese meaning—can also help reflect on how we can feel more fulfilled in personal and work life. Nowadays, many people are split between two seemingly conflicting wishes: one to live a purposeful life in which they feel they can somehow realize themselves, their talents, and make a positive contribution to the world, and one with the desire and necessity to make money so that they can take care of the monthly bills and enjoy a pleasant life. And here, the concept, which has sometimes been described as the "Westernized concept" of *ikigai*, can come in very handy. It means that you can address both these aspects if you find the intersection of what you love doing, what you are good at doing, what the world needs, and what you can be paid to do.

Lately, I have learned about many people who have started to do precisely this. For example, I recently came across Wired Creatives, recently renamed to The Creatives Platform, which is an education hub for people who want to establish or upgrade their online business using social media. It is run by a couple from New Zealand who started living their dreams on a daily basis. The man, Nat, had been a plumber in New Zealand, and while pursuing his job, he wondered how he could integrate more of his passion into his daily work life. He loved surfing and traveling, so he researched in detail how travel bloggers worked and combined their work and travel. After doing a lot of research and taking some first steps, he managed to combine his passion for traveling with his business. Today, he has tens of thousands of followers on social media and earns a six-figure salary by writing about his travels, advertising for certain travel products, and offering several online courses with his wife. His wife, Hannah, followed a similar path. She followed her partner on his travels and carved out her very own travel-writing niche, writing about traveling from an introvert's perspective. There are many stories of people who, at some point in their lives, decided they wanted more out of life and started working on their very own dream life—in the personal and the professional realm. This form of *ikigai* does not necessarily require that you build your own business, though it can. I believe that what counts at the core is that you do what you do every day with pleasure. Every job has its upsides and downsides. Yet, since many of us spend much of our life at work, it certainly helps if we work at something we believe in.

There are many books and workbooks out there that can guide us to reflect on this version of *ikigai*. To make the decision to live one's *ikigai* in this sense might sometimes be a bit scary. It is often a way that goes off the beaten path and might involve some risks and uncertainties. Yet, in the end, we have limited time here on Earth and it is worth trying to live our lives in a joyful, fulfilling, and meaningful way. Combining our talents, dreams, passions, and potentially, vocation and profession in some way might be the most powerful way to do this.

In her book *Daring Greatly: How the Courage to be Vulnerable Transforms the Way We Live, Love, Parent, and Lead*, Brené Brown describes how important vulnerability is for leading an authentic, wholehearted, fulfilled, and happy life. She explains in detail how the very effect of daring to do something you are passionate about is what takes you further. You might be successful or you might fail, but at least you dared it and won't regret that you did not take action at the end of your life. She explains how all great men and women failed many times before they achieved what they achieved. Failures are the necessary components that lead to success. Acknowledging our fear and embracing our vulnerability makes us stronger and more courageous. She is the best example of what she talks about. Her TEDx talk on vulnerability gained so much momentum that she became famous overnight and had to deal with all the advantages and disadvantages of this sudden fame. In a later TED talk, she explained how she learned to deal with this new role and how she lives with vulnerability on a daily basis. All of that makes her very authentic, and she has accumulated such a big community of fans that she recently released her own Netflix special.

To dare to do what you are passionate about, with all its joys, hurdles, and challenges, is something also advised by Bronnie Ware, the author of the eye-opening book *The Top Five Regrets of the Dying*. After working for years in a palliative care center, she wrote a blog entry—and later, a book—about what she learned from those dying people and their last thoughts, considerations, and regrets. The first regret that many had was that they wished they had lived a life true to themselves and not according to others' expectations. This is very much in line with finding and living your own *ikigai*.

I think it is worth taking some time to reflect on our *ikigai*, in the personal sense and, if we wish to, in the professional sense. It can help us become more conscious about what is important to us and live our everyday life with much more joy, fulfillment, and meaning.

The Importance of Community, of Finding Your Tribe, and of Moments for Conscious Self-Care

Appreciating the Value of Community

Another aspect that I viewed with fascination in Japan was the prevailing sense of community. In contrast to the emphasis on individualism and self-realization in many Western societies, in many Asian countries, community and group harmony always come before the individual. While this can be individually constraining at times, it can also help build a society in which harmony and the common good stand before individualism and self-interest. In Japan, it is quite a common practice for companies to reach a consensus before any major decision is taken. This practice can slow down the decision-making process. But it helps get everyone on board, consider various viewpoints before making a decision, and, once a decision is made, move forward with great clarity and speed.

Also, in everyday situations, this emphasis on group harmony plays out. For example, I was impressed when learning that after the Fukushima disaster that hit Japan in March 2011, there was no widespread looting in Japan, something which often happens after a natural disaster. Even though the high-magnitude earthquake, the following tsunamis, and the accidents in Fukushima's nuclear plants left millions of Japanese in darkness for days, with shortages of drinking water and food, no widespread looting was reported. Instead, most people waited patiently in line outside the damaged shops, accepting the food and drink rations available. It is even reported that in Tokyo, people still formed orderly lines at the subway after waiting for hours, as it had been closed down at the time of the quake. Commentators have explained this phenomenon by the degree of social order and discipline present in Japanese society and by the fact that people feel first and foremost responsible to the community.[24]

It was something I often thought about during our two-year stay in Japan. From the very beginning, we were informed by our embassies and by the city district office about several precautions and rules we should adhere to in the case of a major earthquake. I remember that it was a new situation for me. Japan is one of the countries with the highest earthquake occurrences globally. There are several thousand minor earthquakes per year, little tremors on a daily basis, and nearly 20 percent of large earthquakes (with magnitude 6 and higher) happening in the country.[25] When I felt the first earthquake in our apartment, noticing how the whole building started swaying back and forth, I was quite terrified. It became a common habit to look at our earthquake app whenever we noticed something trembling to check if it would be necessary to quickly look for rescue under the next table or chair. And we always had an earthquake bag prepared, standing next to our door, and a flashlight in our bedside tables in case the electricity went off.

And while the awareness that a major earthquake could happen at any moment was very real, I felt quite comforted by a couple of factors. One was that the Japanese government is trying everything to prepare and secure its citizens in case of an earthquake. Many buildings are constructed to bend but not break when a medium magnitude earthquake hits a place. And from young to old, the society is educated on how to behave in case of an earthquake. I remember that we had a workshop on this in the nursery where our young daughter went to play a few hours per week. They explained to us things like how to find your children and family members if an earthquake occurred and how electricity and telephone connections might not work for a while. It was still a scary scenario, but I felt reassured that there were plans that could be put into action in case of an emergency. In addition to these preparatory precautions, I was deeply reassured by the values and behavior of Japanese society at large. Even if a natural disaster was to occur, I felt reassured by the sense of community prevalent in Japanese culture that emphasized helping each other and not taking advantage of any such situation.

Finding Your Tribe or "Moai"

The importance that community plays can, however, not only be found at the broader societal level in Japan but also at a personal level. Researchers who visited Japan's Southern Okinawa islands in an attempt to untangle the secrets of the island's many centenarians report that being part of a community or a tribe—also referred to as *moai* in Okinawa—plays a significant role for people to lead healthy and happy long lives. It is one of the longevity traditions in this part of the world. A *moai* has been defined as "an informal social group of people who have common interests and look out for each other."[26] Or as "a group of lifelong friends" or "a social support group that forms to provide varying support from social, financial, health, and spiritual interests."[27] In past days, it was a tradition in Okinawa that parents would pair their children from an early age onward with a group of usually about five other children with similar interests or circumstances. This group would then commit to support each other for a lifetime. There have been cases in which *moais* lasted over 90 years.[iv]

In practice, such *moais* represent a social support network for individuals. People of a *moai* will be there if someone faces struggles in life, such as financial struggles, or if a child is sick, or a loved one dies. But they will also get together regularly—often several times per week—to meet, chat, and enjoy some common moments or a shared hobby together. People in a *moai* provide deep support and respect for each other. Being part of a *moai* and knowing that there is a safety net in good and bad times makes it much easier to go through the ups and downs that life brings.

Research has shown that positive social connections play a crucial role for people to feel happy and healthy. A study on social connectedness and longevity demonstrated that people getting together with groups with similar values and healthy habits and life goals are much more likely to experience less stress, feel happier, and live longer.[v,28] In recent years, there have been experiments on how such *moai* concepts could play out in the Western world. Dan Buettner, a National Geographic fellow and author, and his team have done extensive research on "blue zones," those areas in the world where people live on average longer and happier lives. The importance of positive friendships and surroundings was a common theme in all of

---

[iv] The term *moai* originated hundreds of years ago and initially referred to a village's financial support system, created to pool the resources of an entire village for major projects or for public works. *Moais* also functioned as mutual financial support networks. If an individual was in need of capital to buy some land or to take care of an emergency, people would come together and pool money to help that particular person of the group. Nowadays, the *moai* concept has been expanded to be a social support network or a cultural tradition for built-in companionship.

[v] The study also showed that the type of connection does not play a major role. It could be anything from a spousal relationship to a tight-knit friend group. What counts is the feeling of having a common bond and common values.

the blue zones. In an attempt to integrate some of the positive lessons from the blue zones in the U.S., Buettner has been cooperating with federal and state health officials to create *moais* in two dozen cities around the country. People interested in similar values or lifestyles are then put together and encouraged to hang out together for at least 10 weeks. For example, those who want to change health behaviors meet regularly to walk, socialize, or organize plant-based potlucks. Some of these initiated *moais* are now several years old and have been showing a healthy influence on members' lives. There is now even a term, walking *moais*, for groups where people get together regularly to walk and socialize.[29]

Even though I recognized the importance that community plays in Japan while living there, I only learned about the *moai* concept from Okinawa when doing some more research while writing this book. And I was fascinated by the research done on blue zones around the world and the positive lessons that we can learn from them. When reflecting on the *moai* concept, I could relate on many levels to the importance that good friends and positive, supportive networks play in our lives. And while I love the *moai* concept and I find it fascinating that some *moais* in Japan have lasted for more than 90 years, for many of us, it might be difficult to keep up such a *moai* in the same place for a lifetime simply because we might move or evolve on our life journey.

Therefore, I really like the idea that you can be part of different moais like you can be part of various networks or *guanxis* in China. Each of us wears many hats, and I believe that it can be beneficial to find or create *moais* for different areas of our lives. Finding your tribe, which can be related to a particular activity or situation in your life or might be a friends' group, is something precious in life. I know from experience that sometimes it can take time to set up a new tribe, especially if you moved and have to set up a new social network or build new friendships from scratch. When I was a child, my close tribe or support system consisted of my parents, my brother, and my two best friends. Whenever I was around them, I felt happy. And even though we are now living in different countries, the close bond created in these early years persists, and I know that I can call them at any moment in time. I have had similar experiences with people I got to know in the various corners of the world where I lived. And even though I can't see many of them in my everyday life, I feel that the saying, "Friends are like stars, you can't always see them, but they are always with you," holds very true for good friendships. With some close friends that range from my baby years up to my adult years, it does not matter if we don't see each other for months or even years. As soon as we meet, there is the same old appreciative connection that we share.[vi]

I noticed that attending activities where I could meet like-minded people helped me find my tribes in the different places I've lived. In China, it was through meetings with young entrepreneurs that we found our very unique friend group. In Japan, it was by attending activities related to pregnancy. And back in Switzerland, it was by attending activities for mothers and children and joining groups for entrepreneurs, writers, and women's networks. Some of my *moais* are online, some are offline, and some are both. One of my close "mama *moais*" that I joined in Tokyo has transformed from an in-person *moai* from our Tokyo times to an online *moai* since most of us are spread around the world at the moment. We still have the intention of meeting each other in person once every year or two years and these get-togethers are beautiful moments of deep connection. And while I love my global mama village, it has always been important to me to also find a few mothers I can connect with in the place where I am living, thus allowing us to meet more

---

[vi] There is also a Japanese expression, *osananajimi*, for lifelong friends whom you have since your early childhood days. While the *moai* concept seems to be more common in Japan's Southern Okinawa islands, *osananajimi* is an expression commonly used in other parts in Japan, as well.

regularly in person. Another tribe in my life are those people with whom I share a common love for writing. So far, I have met most of my author and writer colleagues only online. But since we have been interacting regularly via new collaboration technology, I feel like I know some of them very well. The Internet allows us to meet people we share interests, dreams, or aspirations with online and to interact regularly. Such online groups can be deeply inspiring as they can represent the type of tribe that you need at a particular point in your life. Nowadays, there exist groups for just about anything that could be of interest to you. And still, it has been shown that face-to-face meetings are critical for people to feel happy. It can take some time to find those tribes in which you feel accepted, supported, and respected—be it in the online or off. But it is worth searching for them or even creating them. And then to regularly surround yourself with people who inspire, encourage, and uplift you. Thinking of the benefits that tribes or *moais* have had on some of the oldest people on earth living in Japan confirms that regular social interaction with a group of like-minded people or friends seems to be one of the main ingredients for living a long and happy life.

Moments for Conscious Self-Care

But Japan is not only an example for community spirit and for the positive effects that supportive tribes can play in your life, but also for how to integrate conscious self-care moments into your everyday life. To be able to take care of others and be a supportive part of a community, it is essential to take care of yourself and your own needs as well. As the saying goes: we can't pour from an empty cup. And good, old plane-safety procedures remind us every time we hop on a plane: we need to put on our own oxygen mask first before we can help others. If we don't have any oxygen—or energy for that matter—we can't give energy and support to others. It is important to find these little self-care islands, which help us refuel our energy tank. In Japan, people have for centuries turned everyday activities into powerful practices of self-care, self-awareness, and self-cultivation. It can be any activity, from cooking, bathing, or walking to drinking tea, arranging flowers, or anything else. What turns such activities into self-care tools is doing them mindfully, consciously bringing attention to the activity, and enjoying it in the process.

One of the daily habits that I found fascinating to learn about while living in Japan was the ritual of many Japanese people of taking a hot bath in the evenings. In Japan, the ritual of engaging in a relaxing daily bathing routine comes close to a sacred ritual. Water has always played an important role in Japanese society. The country is not only surrounded by water, but the element is also respected as one of the life forces.[30] In most Japanese houses and apartments, you can find a bathtub or *ofuro*. In contrast to those we usually have in Western societies, Japanese bathtubs are often wider, shorter, and deeper. When Antoine and I went on our apartment-hunting trip, we were impressed that despite the relatively small apartment sizes in Tokyo, lots of importance and space was given to bathrooms. Instead of a small shower cubicle, you usually have a completely closed shower and bathing room separated by a glass door from the sink and the bathroom cabinets. It is common in Japanese tradition to first clean yourself (usually sitting on a little stool, soaping up and then rinsing yourself) before stepping into the hot *ofuro* afterward. It is said that it helps to relax and stimulates blood circulation and is an important moment of family communication as small children often join their parents in the *ofuro* on a daily basis. Since everyone enters the tub clean and the water can often be easily reheated with attached boilers, the same water is usually used by all the family members.[vii] The daily *ofuro* can be an individual self-care ritual or a pleasant family experience. In addition to the *ofuro* tradition, you can find

---

[vii] Since all family members usually use the same bathing water and because water is used very consciously in this ritual to reducing water wastage, water from the previous day is often used for cleaning or laundry purposes afterward.

many *sento* (public baths) and *onsen* (a luxurious form thereof) in Japan. Usually, the water taken for these baths comes directly from the mountains and is imbued with the natural minerals from the volcanic area where the *onsen* is located.[31]

But this daily bathing routine is not the only activity that Japanese people use as self-care or self-cultivation tools. Many other daily activities are used as a form of meditation and mindfulness. There is, for example, the practice of *ikebana*, the Japanese tradition of arranging flowers in a mindful, attentive way, to create something beautiful with nature. There is the tea drinking ceremony, *chado*, a beautiful practice rooted in Zen Buddhism that involves the choreographed ceremony of preparing and sharing a bowl of finely powdered green tea. Some people engage in *shodo*, classical Japanese calligraphy, to foster a meditative state of mind. And there is even a vegetarian cooking tradition, *shoyin ryori*, which employs mindful cooking, using fresh ingredients, and not wasting anything.[32] I also got to know many people who reach a meditative state of mind while doing origami, the Japanese art of folding paper in beautiful ways. These are some examples of small activities used in Japanese society to find a state of calmness and meditation in busy and often hectic everyday life. The presence of dignity and elegance, which seemed omnipresent to me when observing people in Japan, might be linked to little daily rituals that people undertake to take care of their physical and mental well-being.

What seems to be crucial in all these activities is fully indulging in the activity and letting yourself be taken away by them for a little while. I often admire how children manage to do this easily. When I observe our daughters play, it can be the most heart-warming experience to see how they indulge in the play world they are creating, forgetting about everything else around them for that moment. For parents of small children, it might sometimes be a little bit more difficult to fully concentrate on doing a task mindfully, simply because we are often interrupted by a request or a need from our little ones. Many might know that it can sometimes even be difficult to drink your coffee while it is still hot or to finish your line of thought in a conversation when your little ones start jumping around or calling for you. But I still believe that it's highly beneficial to carve out some silent or restorative moments for yourself, be they in the morning before your family is awake, in the evening when everyone is asleep, or at any time in your day that fits into your rhythm. It is about finding moments when you can consciously take care of yourself and your physical, emotional, mental, or spiritual needs. Many activities can be meditative when we bring our attention to them. It can also be great to look out for meditative, restorative experiences together with our kids. I love, for example, to consciously enjoy moments in nature with our daughters. It can be anything from observing a butterfly or a bird to looking out for beautiful flowers or leaves we could collect for a little flower arrangement. I also love coloring together with our girls. We sometimes put on some nice music or a story with our older daughter and just color next to each other, she in her coloring books, I in my adult coloring books, sometimes switching books with one another. This activity is like a meditation for us; it helps us calm down and regain energy at the same time.

Self-care can, of course, also be an occasional spa treatment or a shopping trip, after which you might feel relaxed, energized, or just better in your skin. I had such an episode in autumn 2018 when I was heavily pregnant with our second daughter and felt tired, exhausted, and irritable. At that point, I often did not have the energy to take good care of our young daughter who was two-and-a-half years old at the time, and my husband and I would easily end up arguing about minor stuff. When it became clear that I was facing pregnancy complications again and that I was supposed to rest as much as possible, I decided to take better care of myself to give the best of me to the baby growing inside me and to my family in general. I went for a couple of prenatal spa treatments with facials and massages, bought some new clothes that fitted comfortably and took time to sit down and read whenever I had a moment. After a week or two of taking better care of myself, I felt that I had a lot more energy and patience to deal with the daily tasks and enjoy the time with my daughter and husband. I felt that something had shifted within me and that I could take much better care of my family again after some good, restorative moments for myself. If you feel tired and depressed, it is hard to have the energy to take care of others who might need you.

Such occasional moments of indulgence are, of course, wonderful to have from time to time. But what seems to be even more critical is making little self-care moments a habit that can easily be included in our everyday lives at home. Recently, I learned in one of the women's networks I belong to about the power of micro-moments of self-care. The life coach talking about this topic encouraged us to make a list of little activities that could help us refill our energy tank throughout the day, even in the usual busyness and family hustle. These activities could include anything that might easily be integrated into our days. For example, it could be to take a few deep, conscious breaths or do some stretching or a few yoga exercises. It could also be to consciously prepare and then enjoy a good cup of tea or coffee. Or to listen to one of your favorite songs, to read a few pages in a book you want to read, or to listen to an inspiring podcast. It is really up to each of us to find activities that make us feel good, relaxed, calm, or inspire—anything that can help us refill our energy tank. When hearing about this "micro-moment" concept, I had to think back to a question that my parents used to ask me when I had a bad day or when I was in a low mood. Often, they would ask which little activity could help me feel better in the moment. Sometimes a good talk or letting out the emotions would be the recipe. Sometimes a short nap would work wonders. And sometimes journaling, some music, or some coffee and chocolate could turn the situation around. My mom used to say: "You can find yourself in situations where you feel like a frog in a high glass, not able to get out. The important thing is to create ladders that can help you out." Writing out or making a mental list of activities that can help us regain energy or just feel better can be extremely valuable. I have now put my personal list of micro-moments of self-care in a little kitchen corner where I can easily see it and remind myself of pausing for such moments from time to time.

The heart of the matter seems to lie in really enjoying the activity we choose, consciously and gratefully. Like many of the people in Japan who mindfully enjoy everyday activities, and thereby transform them into moments of self-care and self-cultivation—not in a selfish sense, but in a mindful, healthy sense that then allows people to stand up and support the community at large as well.

Beautiful Lessons Learned from Japan

✸ **Be polite and respectful with your surroundings:** little behavioral rules can make a huge difference and if all of us make some small efforts, the whole atmosphere can change for the better.

✸ **Keep learning and improving yourself and your craft continuously.** The Japanese *kaizen* concept promoting continuous, incremental steps for improvement can serve as an inspiration. Starting small can be the best way to make lasting changes in the long-term.

✸ **Take up a *wabi-sabi* approach for things, people, and life in general.** Perceiving and appreciating the imperfect and the traces that time has left can be beautiful and is worth cherishing and celebrating.

✸ **Try to apply the *hara hachi bu* approach from time to time.** Eating until you are 80 percent full can have great effects physically and mentally alike.

✸ **Think about your own *ikigai* or purpose in life.** It can be a personal driving force like people you love, a passion, or a hobby. Or it can be a deeper purpose found on a professional level.

✸ **Find or create your tribes of people who support and inspire you.** Having a group of people who support you through life's ups and downs is one of the secrets for leading a long and happy life for many centenarians in Japan's Okinawa islands.

✸ **Develop a community spirit, promoting cooperation and caring for each other in society.** We are much stronger together than if we turn against each other, especially in the face of hardship.

✸ **Include mindful moments of self-care and self-cultivation in your everyday-life.** If you show up for yourself with love and kindness, you can also show up for others with love and kindness!

CONCLUSION

*"Certainly, travel is more than the seeing
of sights; it is a change that goes on, deep
and permanent, in the ideas of living."*

—Miriam Beard

Beautiful Lessons from Countries Around the World

Traveling and living abroad changes us on a much deeper level than just the memories of the sites we may have visited. Seeing and observing how other people live, think, and behave can open up new horizons for our own thinking. We might begin to question some of our belief systems. Some of our beliefs might be strengthened or confirmed by our observations. I think that traveling and getting to know other countries and cultures is one of the most enriching ways to educate ourselves about the world, ourselves, and our core values. But what I appreciate the most are the wonderful connections you can make with people from around the world. Having friends in many countries makes the world seem small and very connected. I listen much more closely to news or statements about countries where I have lived or where I know people who are dear to my heart. Through traveling, your interest in countries or regions you traveled to is automatically awakened. Traveling and exchanging with others also shows us that people in the different corners of the world strive for similar kinds of things in their lives. Even if the ways to get there might be different according to cultural, familial, and personal environments.

This book set out to take you on a journey to various countries around the world and to point out some of the positive attributes and lessons that impressed me in each of them. In a time when many societies and the world as a whole seems to be quite polarized, I wanted to focus on some attributes that could reunite us and that could help us see the positive things that countries and cultures around the world have to offer. Of course, we face many challenges at the global and national levels. Yet, from time to time, it can be good to shift perspective and focus on the positive. This practice with countries is similar to the deliberate gratitude practices on a personal level that can help you to focus perspective on the positive things and relationships in your life. By doing this regularly, you can charge yourself with the necessary positive energy to keep working on what needs to be changed for the better. When we look at the world, I think that it can be very valuable to shift our focus to what we can learn from each other. And through the eyes of oneness, we can look at which areas in different countries and cultures can bring value to each other. Once we recognize this invaluable richness, it can become much easier to also find common ground in more challenging areas.

This book did not intend to enter in-depth political discussions. Rather, it attempts to point out valuable mindsets, concepts, and customs that could inspire each one of us on a personal level in our very own everyday lives. The summary boxes with the beautiful lessons learned from each country aim to provide some inspiration. And as mentioned earlier, it is really up to each of us to focus on what resonates with us. Despite the different topics that I chose for each country, there were some overarching themes that came up several times and I want to touch upon them in more detail in this conclusion.

Four Overarching Themes for Living a Happier, More Balanced, and Fulfilling Life

From all the beautiful lessons learned in the various countries, some kept coming up in different forms in multiple countries. There are lots of additional positive lessons that we could draw from each country. This book only provided a small, personal selection of some of the ones that came up in my mind when reflecting on my living experiences in the countries. From the ones mentioned in this book, I noticed four themes that kept showing up in one way or another.

1.) Meaningful Relationships

The first one is the need for meaningful relationships. No matter where I lived, people expressed the importance of meaningful relationships in order to live a happy and fulfilling life. I found that, in the end, experiences count more than things. Taking time to sit down and talk, enjoy meals together, and philosophize about life are some of the most precious moments you can share with family and friends. And while customs for this are different in each country, the need for these moments of connection is clearly prevalent everywhere. We humans are social creatures and need to feel connected and interact with others to be inspired, live through difficult moments, and celebrate and enjoy life together.

In France, it is common to sit down for hours with loved ones when having a meal. In Switzerland, the *apéro* concept is a highly convivial and easygoing opportunity to meet and converse. In the

Netherlands, the notion of being *gezellig* emphasizes the importance of just spending a nice moment together without getting stressed out about it. In Mexico and India, people are so hospitable that they even welcome strangers with open arms. Supporting and spending quality moments not only with the nuclear family but also with the extended family plays an extremely important role in most families that I spent time with in these countries. In China, we could see how important different network circles are in personal and professional life alike. The whole concept of *guanxi* is based on the presumption that we are born connected and can only exist in connection with others. In Japan, I shared the importance of having a supportive tribe, and this can be extended to having several supportive tribes in different areas of our lives. Also, people's *ikigai* or purpose in life is often related to meaningful relationships and community. In the U.S., connection is often created by addressing people you meet in a casual, friendly manner. And a lot of emphasis is often put on engaging in team activities and fostering team spirit. And from my upbringing in Germany, I learned how valuable it is for children to grow up in a loving, supportive environment. Providing children with roots and wings is something wonderful that many parents from around the world are striving for.

Meaningful relationships with people—be they family, friends, acquaintances, or strangers—play an enormously important part in our daily lives. Investing some of our time and energy in the development and nourishment of such relationships is one of the best ways to feel fulfilled, supported, and connected in good times and bad.

2.) Positive, Healthy Mindsets and Attitudes

Another feature that I could observe in each country was the ability of people to adopt positive, healthy mindsets and attitudes, particularly in challenging situations. Developing a positive attitude or mindset is, of course, something very personal to work on and mindsets cannot be generalized from individuals to an entire country. But there were some widespread attitudes in the different countries that I found very inspiring.

In the Asian context, many attitudes impressed me. I personally loved to learn about the *jugaad* principle in India. It is the idea that, with some creativity and resourcefulness, you can find a solution to any problem and that every challenge you face is somehow "figureoutable." I also appreciated the curiosity and the thirst for learning that many people displayed. Our brains crave novelty. If we keep up our curiosity to learn, we can experience immense personal growth throughout our lives. In the Chinese context, I loved learning in more detail about yin and yang and the value that balancing opposite forces can play in the most diverse areas of our lives. If we adopt a mindset in which we learn how to balance different forces and energies in our lives—in any area of life—we can experience much more balance and well-being. Another mindset that I enjoyed was that, with confidence, humor, and charm, you could go a long way when negotiating. Negotiating itself was not seen as something bad, but rather as a game to play, and I appreciated the humor that often came along with it. I was also impressed by many Chinese people's ability to adapt quickly to new situations and surroundings as things can move very quickly in that country. In Japan, I loved the omnipresent mindset of completing the task at hand with diligence and a sense of pride and honor. I was also impressed by the concept of *kaizen*, the continuous striving for incremental improvement. I believe that this attitude can take us very far if we adopt it in our daily lives. And at the same time, I loved the appreciative approach of many Japanese people toward the incomplete, the imperfect, the old, and the broken: *wabi-sabi*.

In the European context, I loved learning in more detail about the French concept of *savoir vivre*—taking joy in sitting down to pleasantly savor the food you are eating and connecting with loved ones at the same time. In Switzerland, I was impressed by people's ability to just slow down and enjoy—be it in nature or in everyday situations. Slowing down and appreciating the beauty of the moment can completely change how you perceive daily life. I also appreciated the tendency in the country to find ways to cooperate and find compromises. This happens in the political realm, domestically and internationally, but also when building bridges between different sectors (like industry and the academic sector). The underlying premise that we can get better results if we cooperate is an attitude that can also help in our personal lives. What impressed me in the Netherlands was many people's ability to not take things too personally and to live life as you please, without thinking too much about what others might think. If we live in alignment with what is important to us, according to our values and our own definition of success, it is much easier to experience happiness and fulfillment. I also appreciated the general attitude that things don't have to be complicated to be nice and that simplifying structures and chores at home can help experience life with more lightness and ease. And what I appreciate in my home country, Germany, is that people do not shy away from confronting themselves with shortcomings from the past. Instead, a lot of effort is put into analyzing and understanding the root causes that led to a particular situation and learning from it for the future.

The U.S., for me, represents a country where people think big and dare to dream, then go after their dreams. The very act of allowing yourself to think big can be the first step toward a bright future. The growth mindset, putting a lot of emphasis on the intention and the efforts being made, has proven to be an extremely helpful mindset to encourage children and adults alike. It creates an optimistic foundation and helps us remind ourselves that it's good to dream big and find ways to achieve our dreams. And in Mexico, I sincerely appreciated the underlying belief of many people that things happen for a reason and that we will never be alone when facing challenges. Many people have a deep faith that, even if we face struggles or difficulties from time to time, we will be fine in the end. It is a very reassuring attitude that can help enormously in accepting the ups and downs of life with good faith and hope.

The importance of adopting healthy mindsets cannot be underestimated. Often, we are our own harshest critics, and I know from experience that it can be easy to fall into a negative spiral of thinking. I am still working on adopting a more positive mindset. Becoming aware of limiting beliefs or negative self-talk is often the first step to be able to actively change it afterward. The positive mindsets and attitudes that I observed in many people in the various countries where I lived are just a few examples. But they inspired me and I want to make conscious efforts to integrate them more in my daily life and in my daily decisions.

Robin Sharma, one of the world's top leadership and optimization advisers, states it similarly with his three-step success formula. He says that the first step is to gain better awareness so that in the second step, you can make better choices, and, in the third step, achieve better results.[1] I believe that it can be very valuable to reflect on the areas in our lives where we are struggling and to think about options that can help us transcend these struggles. And adopting positive mindsets, no matter which ones resonate most with us at a particular point in time can be a perfect start to this journey.

There is a famous saying, attributed to multiple sources, which goes:

> *"Watch your thoughts for they become words;*
> *watch your words for they become actions;*
> *watch your actions, for they become habits;*
> *watch your habits for they become your character;*
> *watch your character for it becomes your destiny."*[2]

217

So, let's start influencing our destiny for the positive by adopting beliefs and thoughts that can help us on our journeys toward more happiness, fulfillment, and purpose in our lives. And try to uphold a positive outlook, curiosity, open-mindedness, self-acceptance, and self-confidence whenever possible.

3.) Self-Care and Taking Time to Unwind

The third theme that I noticed when going through the chapters was the importance of taking time to unwind and for conscious self-care moments. This is not in a selfish sense, forgetting about other important people in our lives, but instead, in a natural sense, understanding that if we want to be able to give love and kindness to others, we need to do the same for ourselves. I have experienced it several times myself that when you reach rock bottom and are tired, exhausted, and feel depressed, it is just not possible to take care and be present for others and for the ones that matter most to you. We cannot pour from an empty cup. So taking the time to fill our own cups, even via minor daily rituals, is something essential that will be hugely beneficial for ourselves and for those around us.

The countries discussed in this book give several inspiring examples of how we could do this. In Japan, many people step into a hot bath or *ofuro* in the evening to relax. Or they integrate little activities, like cooking a nice meal, making a beautiful flower arrangement, or making and enjoying a good cup of tea consciously. I loved the idea that you can just integrate little micro-moments of self-care into your daily rituals. And there is no prescription for it. It can be anything that gives you a jolt of joy or well-being. What counts is to do and enjoy them consciously, allowing them to recharge you on a daily basis.

In the chapter on France, I touched on the idea of creating our own personal wellness islands. The Provence region has fascinated countless artists. The special sunlight and the beautiful nature create a perfect environment to get creative and experience a state of flow. Innumerable beautiful artistic works have been created in this region. And while we might not be able to hop on a plane and go to Provence in order to get inspired, I think that we can all create our own Provence-like wellness islands in or around our homes. Having places where we feel peaceful and at ease can create wonders for our well-being and for our personal and professional endeavors alike.

Finding a state of flow—the special state when we feel in our element and work with ease on things that are important to us—also plays a crucial role for our creativity, self-actualization, and well-being. In China, I learned more about the yin and yang concept and the importance of balancing out different forces to achieve a healthy flow. The flow can be related to physical issues, for example, by using different traditional Chinese medicine methods to stimulate a good energy flow in our bodies. But it can also relate to other areas in our life, like balancing our food intake or engaging in activities that set us in a state of flow. And of course, massages can likewise be highly beneficial as a self-care tool that can help us unwind and regain energy. Also, a practice like yoga, which had its origin thousands of years ago in India, can be beneficial in this regard.

Another self-care tool is going out regularly to enjoy nature. Lots of studies have shown the positive effects that nature outings have on our well-being. During my time in Switzerland, I realized the vital role that nature plays in many peoples' lives. There are innumerable outdoor activities that you can do in Switzerland, during any season of the year. And while the beautiful landscapes in Switzerland lend themselves well to breathtaking views, we can do our best to connect with nature anywhere, no matter where we live. It can be by having a forest walk, a walk through the flower fields, or when living in a city, by visiting a park or just enjoying the presence of trees. I know from experience that it can sometimes be hard to push ourselves to go outside, especially when we love making ourselves comfortable at home. Yet, I believe that it is worth taking such moments from time to time, to just breathe in the fresh air and enjoy all the beautiful things that nature has to offer.

People in the Netherlands have shown me how to integrate these kinds of nature outings naturally in everyday life, simply by getting on a bike. Biking as a means of transportation naturally allows you to include outdoor and nature excursions daily. And at the same time, it adds moderate physical exercise to your day. Studies prove that a moderate daily amount of exercise not only helps us to stay fit, but also releases endorphins that make us feel happy. Not every country lends itself as well to biking as the Netherlands. But there are many options for adding a moderate amount of physical exercise into our daily rhythm.

Another excellent tool for unwinding can be to listen to music we enjoy. In Mexico, I often observed the positive effects of happy, upbeat music on my mood. And if you dance along with your friends or family, it amplifies this feeling. The chapter on Germany addresses the importance of taking time to celebrate and enjoy life. One of the mottos for many people in my home country is to work hard and party hard. Taking time to unwind is not only beneficial but also essential to being able to have the energy and strength to commit to daily responsibilities.

No matter which self-care tools or ideas we choose—and we can select many—it should be something that resonates with us and that makes us feel good. And if we consciously take a little time for these important moments, we can experience more joy, balance, and fulfillment on a daily basis.

4.) The Belief in Something Bigger and in a Life Purpose

And finally, a fourth theme emerged in many of the country contexts. The belief in something or some part of our being that is bigger and vaster than ourselves. This can take the form of religious or spiritual beliefs and practices. It can also relate to our own life purpose and the belief that we can contribute to something bigger and make a difference in the world. It can be related to our family, our work, or a larger cause we believe in and work for.

In Mexico, where large parts of the population are Christian, I found it comforting to see how God is included in the most common everyday interactions. Their beliefs seem to give many people a sense of strength and purpose. In India—where polytheism is widespread—I was impressed by the openness to different beliefs and the engagement with spirituality on a daily basis. Even though there are many different faith and belief systems in this world, many people believe in something higher that is not fully explicable. It can be in the form of a God or a redeemer or in the forces of the universe or of nature. But realizing that we are part of something larger than ourselves can be very comforting and provide us with inner calm and a feeling of support and unlimited possibilities.

And we might, at some point in our lives, ask ourselves questions about the meaning and purpose of life and of our lives in particular. I believe that every person is here for a reason. And that every person is valuable and worthy. We sometimes just need to dig a little deeper to find out what gives purpose and meaning to our lives. This can be personally or professionally or both. In the Germany chapter, I touched on the positive effects that having a sense of purpose in one's life can play for people who have to face incredible hardships. Victor Frankl's logotherapy or existence analysis gives some interesting insights into questions we can ask ourselves to dig deeper into our very own life purpose. In the Japanese context, the concept of *ikigai*, or the reason for being, fascinated me. For many Japanese people, the term *ikigai* is something very natural that they grow up with. In recent years, the *ikigai* concept has become popular in Western societies. In the chapter on Japan, I discuss two different approaches toward *ikigai* and share two different Venn diagrams in this regard. They each have a different focus, but both of the diagrams and the questions that go along with them can help us in our reflections about our life purpose and how we can live it on a daily basis.

Bringing It All Together

The four themes referred to above kept
showing up throughout the book.
This illustration depicts how these themes come together.

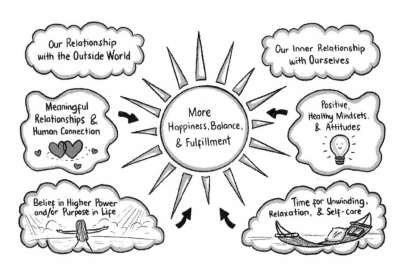

If we keep working on developing good, nurturing relationships with ourselves and with the outside world, we can experience a lot of joy, balance, meaning, and purpose in our lives. Many of us can probably improve our inner self-talk, remind ourselves of positive mindsets, and take time for the things that contribute to our well-being. And at the same time, the joy and meaning that come from interacting with other people and feeling part of something bigger cannot be underestimated.

The different country examples provided some ideas and suggestions on what types of mindsets or behaviors we could include in our daily lives. The underlying aim of the book goes, however, one step further and encourages you to approach other countries and cultures with a sense of curiosity and open-mindedness and to develop an appreciation for the many different ways of how we can live a happy, balanced, and fulfilling life. Ultimately, the feelings of happiness, meaning, fulfillment, and balance come from deep within ourselves and from our attitudes and our approach to life. On our path to strengthen positive attitudes and meaningful connections, examples from the most diverse corners of the world can help us realize that there are many tools we can use along the way.

Where to Go from Here

I sincerely hope that you can take away some inspiration from this book for your own life. And even more, I hope you keep your eyes open and look for the beautiful, sometimes hidden treasures that you can appreciate about your home country or that you encounter when traveling or living abroad. I invite you to create your own "beautiful lessons" list of attitudes, mindsets, values, or customs that you appreciate personally or that you observed in people or countries, including your home country. Consciously listing such things can help us integrate them more intentionally in our lives.

And even if we don't have the possibility or the desire to travel physically, there are many other ways to learn from different countries. We can travel through books, stories, documentaries, and movies. I enjoy reading nonfiction books, but I also love to read fiction stories that weave in some historical events or common customs and mindsets of people in a particular country into a story. We can learn a lot by just reading a good book. Movies can also give us an opportunity to travel and be entertaining and educational at the same time. We can also start learning a new language as a way to gain a deeper understanding of the connotations used in a language or culture. We can listen to songs and melodies from around the world. And we can order food or cook dishes from various country cuisines. I love to have some ingredients at home to cook Thai dishes that a close Thai friend has taught me. And recently, we enjoyed a delicious Nigerian meal prepared by my Nigerian brother-in-law. He and my sister-in-law explained to us how eating this particular food with our hands makes it even more enjoyable. Savoring this food and the different spices gave us the chance to travel to the country in our imagination.

There are many options that we can use to travel with our senses and our imagination. And realizing that most people in this world do care for others and do have very similar hopes and dreams is a very comforting revelation. If we consciously contemplate and share customs, concepts, and mindsets that have helped us and that could help others live a happier, more balanced, and fulfilling life, we can spark an inspiring exchange among people around the world. So, let's open our eyes, learn from each other, and enjoy the beauty the world has to offer!

EPILOGUE

While revising my book and writing the conclusion, the world as we knew it changed dramatically. The COVID-19 pandemic hit the world in 2020 with a force barely anyone could have imagined possible. Within weeks, borders were closed in Europe and across the globe. People all over the world were sent into lockdowns and, for a while, an almost complete travel ban existed. A health crisis hit many countries and an economic one followed right behind it. The lives of people across the world were turned upside down, with shops, schools, and workplaces closed. Many people, and especially those already living in vulnerable situations or with previous health conditions, faced incredible hardships. A sense of insecurity has permeated people's lives in countries and societies across the world. And mental health issues, including feelings of depression and anxiety, have risen, and I have certainly experienced such feelings.

We are still in the process of understanding this new world. But at the moment of writing this, it is clear that, despite borders opening slowly again, something has shifted in our travel behavior. At the moment, many people think twice before stepping onto a plane and the world seems to be undergoing more profound changes in terms of how we see nature and our lives here on Earth. It might be that, despite the hardships and the heartbreaking personal tragedies that come along with the crisis, we can also learn something from it.

What is it that is essential in our lives? What do we absolutely not want to miss? What can we let go of?

For my own little family and me, the pandemic situation has led to a complete change of our family rhythm. Never in our lives have we spent so much time with the four of us together. My husband, who used to travel at least a week per month for work, was suddenly home and could join us for breakfast, lunch, and dinner. Our young daughters were also home, and with no childcare support for several weeks, we had to adapt our family routine. In order to stay sane, my husband was quick to do some *jugaad* and figure out a new pace for work and family time that worked well for all of us. And I, who had wanted to integrate more nature activities with the family into our lives for a long time, suddenly had the chance to do so on a daily basis. In Switzerland we were only semi-confined, so it was still possible to take walks with the close family outside. I went out frequently with the girls to keep the general mood up. We became close friends with the horses and ponies in a nearby field, as we visited them frequently. We had picnics in places we had never visited before to keep a distance from other families. And we consciously tried to focus on the positive things that we had as often as possible in order to improve our mental state of mind. And while we dearly missed and continue to miss seeing our families and friends regularly, we did not miss the hectic everyday rhythm we were used to before the pandemic. The world slowed down, and to some extent, we appreciated the newly found calmness. We started to have online *apéros* and virtual coffee meetings, dance parties, and yoga sessions. Lots of new online experiences and opportunities were created to suit people's needs.

I kept reflecting on the role of intercultural experiences in this new world. And I've come to believe that despite the travel restrictions and the change in travel behavior for years to come, countries from around the globe can still keep inspiring us. We can reflect on those countries we visited already and about the aspects that we appreciated and that we would like to bring home in some way. And we can learn about and experience countries in many other forms beyond physically traveling there ourselves. We can do this by talking to people from different countries, watching documentaries or movies, reading, trying out new cuisines, or listening to music from abroad.

And at the same time, we can appreciate our home countries, our home regions, and our very close home circles. Some of the mindsets that we enjoyed abroad can transform our experiences at home, and they can serve us well when rediscovering the beauty at home. I increasingly notice how taking the same wide-eyed, curious perspective I often adopted during my travels abroad can be just as beneficial when at home. I try to pay more attention to all the beauty surrounding me. While we cancelled our summer travel plans in 2020, we still tried to engage in excursions near home. We visited zoos and farms with animals native to Switzerland, and our daughters loved it. We also discovered a beautiful swimming pool close to my husband's hometown with an amazing view of the lake and the mountains. And I increasingly stop to take in all the wonders that each place near our home has to offer us.

As mentioned earlier, I believe that, eventually, feelings of happiness, balance, and fulfillment come from deep within ourselves and our attitude of how we approach life. On our path to strengthen positive attitudes and behaviors, examples and tools from the most diverse corners of the world can help us along the way. And I hope that this book has provided some inspiration for that!

ACKNOWLEDGEMENTS

The writing of this book was a journey that I could never have done alone. I am grateful to so many people and circumstances, and I'd like to express my gratitude to a few of them over here:

I am grateful for...

o   My wonderful husband, Antoine, who actually came up with the idea that I should write a book and who supported me from the very first day, encouraging me, brainstorming with me, pushing me, and inspiring me! I love you to the moon and back and am so happy to share my life with you. You are interwoven with my life and this book. Thank you for reading each chapter, for giving me valuable feedback, and for celebrating each little step on my author's journey. Thank you for supporting me in all my dreams and aspirations whole-heartedly, for believing in me, and for making life so much more beautiful. *Je t'aime, mon a.d.m.v*!

o   Noelie and Elisa, our sweet, empathetic, loving, kind, and strong-willed daughters: you bring me joy and laughter every day, and you teach me how to marvel at little things in everyday life. Your presence motivated me to reflect on life and on the way I want to live. And you inspired me to sit down and write about the positive things that this world has to offer and that I wanted to share with you. Both of you have wonderful, unique personalities, and you can always count on my unconditional love and support.

o My wonderful parents. As we have often said: "It must have been a match in heaven." You are the best parents I could have ever imagined. Since the very first day of my life, you have been showering Lutz and me with unconditional love and support. Mama, you are like a soulmate and I love our conversations so much. No matter where, we always enjoy the time together and can talk, reflect, and laugh for hours without seeing the time pass by. Papa, I love talking with you about politics, geography, philosophical questions, and, actually, any topic. It is so inspiring, and I can't tell you how much I appreciate the lightness and humor you bring to life. Thank you for having instilled in all of us the appreciation for traveling and for learning about other countries and cultures. Both of you have been some of my most avid cheerleaders for this book project and were among the first ones to read it completely. Thank you for everything! You are both just wonderful, and I love you deeply.

o My dear brother, Lutz, who added so much joy to my childhood and teenage years, who is one of my best personal counselors, and who always has an open ear for anything going on in my life. You are the perfect big brother, and I am so grateful to have you in my life.

o My dear sister-in-law, Armelle, and my lovely niece and nephew, Anaïs and Joshua: you are such wonderful, considerate, and empathetic beings. I love conversing with you, diving into deep philosophical discussions, and spending time together.

o   My wonderful family-in-law from my husband's side: Béatrice, Gérard, Léonie, Dennis, and my lovely nephews, Arthur and Louis: you have all welcomed me with open arms since the very first day. I could honestly not have found any better family-in-law. I love spending time with you, hanging out together, and you show me constantly how wonderful it is to enjoy life and nature together. Thank you for all your love and support in good times and in challenging times and for all the beauty you add to our lives.

o   Léa, who has become like a family member. Without your precious support with Noelie and Elisa, none of this would have been possible. Your kind, gentle, eternally patient, and loving nature is contagious and makes our everyday life much more beautiful. Thank you for all the wonderful, deep conversations. I love that we have the same values, and I could not be more grateful that our paths have crossed!

o   My wider family from the Mosel Valley and my friends from around the world who are like a "heart family" for me. I can't mention all of you personally, but I hope that every one of you knows how important you are for me. A special thank you to Franzi and Hannah for having been at my side for almost my entire life, no matter how far the geographical distance. You are like stars for me. We can't always see each other, but I know that you are always there. Susanne, for endless, long discussions about the meaning of life, for belly laughter, and for being a very present part of my personal development journey. Kim and Philippe and Mady, for the long, beautiful friendship we have. Helena, for having stepped into my life recently and for the soul connection we share; and for all the nice moments with your lovely family as well. Isa, Bambi, Sinile, Sole, Irene, Claudia, Katharina, Charles and Gwen, Chiara and Antoine, Grégoire, Andrea,

Sophie, Clare, Ekci, Dorothee, the wonderful "Epe group" of long-time friends, and so many more for always asking how it is going with my book and for encouraging me on my journey. My wonderful Mexican friends who are like family for me. All the dear friends whom I met in the various countries and places I lived in. I have so many beautiful memories from all of you in my heart—you were the ones who made me enjoy each place I lived in so very much.

o   My friends and the wonderful people who encouraged me to pursue my dream of writing a book and who helped me in the book-writing process: Odile and Hanna, you were some of the first to plant the seed for the book. Alessandra, you were the one who helped me water the seed. Olena, we shared prenatal yoga practices with each other and also our view of how we want to live life and motherhood. Our conversations inspired me deeply in the pursuit of writing this book. Tasha, you were one of my first cheerleaders when you learned about my book project and your loving nature inspires me constantly. Carmela, Pauline, Armelle, Avis, Stacey, Emi, Daisy, Nick, and Rishabh: you all took the time to read my chapters on your home countries and provided me with immensely helpful feedback. Thank you for being wonderful friends and book contributors at the same time.

o   The women's networks and sisterhoods I am part of: when women come together to dream and support each other, magic happens. I couldn't be more grateful for the wonderful Driven Woman group, for Hanna and Lisa from TAC She, for the amazing, wild Global Mama Village group, and for the various mom groups I am part of. We listen to each other, share our joys and struggles, and find ways together to move forward, each in her beautifully unique way. I cannot tell you how much our exchanges and conversations mean to me.

o   My amazing, inspiring accountability buddies, Kate and Colleen. Without our weekly calls, I would have been lost so many times. I love our brainstorming sessions, the laughter, how we keep each other on track, and how we dive into the unknown together, holding hands as we jump. I can't wait to continue this journey with both of you.

o   My editor, Debra, who accompanied me during this book-writing journey from the very beginning. I have learned so much by talking to you and by brainstorming with you. Your intuitive, calm nature and your gentle guidance in terms of story-telling and bringing my message across in a reader-friendly way have been invaluable. You had so much patience and good-will with me and my work. Thank you for all your valuable comments, corrections, and edits and for having played a very important part in making this book project a reality.

o   Eva, we met on the last steps of my book journey. Thank you for your kindness, your availability, your eye for detail and for giving my book the final touch. And Meredith, thank you for having introduced me to Eva.

o   The wonderful ladies from the Writers' Circle. Our monthly get-togethers not only inspired me and taught me a lot about the writing and publishing world, but they also held me accountable to keep advancing with my writing. I can't wait to read all of your books!

o   Chandler, Marcy, Michelle, Scott, and the whole team and community of the Self-Publishing School. You have opened new horizons for so many people. Without the great support from all of you, I think I would never have pushed this book to the finishing line. Thank you for making people dream big and go for it!

o   The great minds who created the cover design for the book and who did all the formatting. Your patience has been incredible and it has been a real pleasure working with all of you.

o   You, my dear reader, who took some of your precious time to join me on this journey. I deeply hope that you enjoyed the book and that some of the beautiful lessons that I learned in the various countries can provide positive inspiration for you and your daily life, as well. I would be honored if you joined me on the journey of spreading a sense of curiosity and appreciation for what we can learn from countries, cultures and people around the globe. I think that deep inside, we all have a lot in common and that we can inspire and encourage each other on our various, beautifully unique—and at the same time connected—life paths.

FREEBIE

Don't forget to pick up your free workbook to help you identify the things you loved most about your travels and create your own "beautiful lessons list" at:

https://judithfuhrmann.com/free-workbook/

ABOUT THE AUTHOR

Judith Fuhrmann is originally from Germany, but identifies herself as a global citizen. From an early age she developed a passion for traveling, visited nearly 50 countries, and lived in nine of them. She holds a Ph.D. in Development Studies, with a focus on human development, and worked for many years in academia. After her second maternity leave, she decided to pursue one of her passion projects and write a book on the beautiful lessons learned while living in different countries. Judith Fuhrmann believes in the power of people learning from each other and moving forward as humanity, together. She lives with her husband and their two small daughters in Switzerland and enjoys traveling, music, reading, spending quality time with family and friends, and a good glass of wine.

A SMALL REQUEST

*R*eviews are key when building excitement and credibility for a book, and as an independent author, reviews are critical.

If you enjoyed this book, it would be wonderful if you could leave your honest review on Amazon, Goodreads, or other relevant websites where you can leave book reviews.

This will help me spread my message that every country in this world has something beautiful to offer and that we can embrace the positive to live a more joyful, balanced, and fulfilling life.

BIBLIOGRAPHY

Here is a list of the books that I refer to and mention, sometimes various times, throughout my book and that I can highly recommend:

- Brown, Brené. *Daring Greatly: How the Courage to Be Vulnerable Transforms the Way We Live, Love, Parent and Lead.* U.S.: Avery, an imprint of Penguin Random House. Previously published as a Gotham Books hardcover, 2012.
- Byrne, Rhonda. *The Secret.* U.S.: Atria, an imprint of Simon and Schuster, Inc., 2006.
- Chai, May-lee & Chai, Winberg. *China A-Z. Chinese Customs and Culture.* New York: PLUME, Penguin Group, 2007.
- Chopra, Mallika. *100 Questions from my Child.* New York: Rodale, 2007.
- Clear, James: *Atomic Habits: An Easy and Proven Way to Build Good Habits and Break Bad Ones.* New York: Avery, an imprint of Penguin Random House, 2018.
- Collins, Jim; Hansen, Morten T. *Great by Choice: Uncertainty, Chaos, and Luck—Why Some Thrive Despite Them All.* New York: Harper Business, 2011.
- Downs, Robyn Conley. *The Feel Good Effect.* California/ New York: Ten Speed Press, 2020.

- Ellis, Yi S. & Ellis, Bryan D. *101 Stories for Foreigners to Understand Chinese People.* Beijing: China Intercontinental Press, 2012.

- Elrod, Hal. *The Miracle Morning. The Not-So-Obvious Secret Guaranteed to Transform Your Life Before 8 AM.* US: Hal Elrod International, 2017.

- Fannin, Rebecca A. *Startup Asia. Top Strategies for Cashing in on Asia's Innovation Boom.* Singapore: John Wiley & Sons (Asia) Pte. Ltd., 2012.

- Forleo, Marie. *Everything is Figureoutable.* U.S./U.K.: Portfolio/Penguin, an imprint of Penguin Random House, 2019.

- Garcia, Hector: *A Geek in Japan: Discovering the Land of Manga, Anime, Zen, and the Tea Ceremony.* Tokyo: Tuttle Publishing, 2011.

- Gates, Melinda. *The Moment of Lift: How Empowering Women Changes the World.* U.K.: Bluebird, an imprint of Pan Macmillan, 2019.

- Haihua Zhang & Baker, Geoff, *Think like Chinese.* Sydney: The Federation Press, 2008.

- Harvey, Sarah. *Kaizen : La Méthode Japonaise du Petit Pas Pour Changer Toutes ses Habitudes.* Paris: Hugo: New Life, 2020.

- Hollis, Rachel. *Girl, Wash Your Face: Stop Believing the Lies About Who You Are So You Can Become Who You Were Meant to Be.* Nashville, Tennessee: Nelson Books, an imprint of Thomas Nelson, 2018.

- Kaiser, Karin. *Fettnäpfchenführer Indien. Be happy oder das no problem-Problem.* Meerbusch: Conbook Medien GmbH, 2012, 2013.

- Louv, Richard. *Last Child in the Woods: Saving our Children from Nature-Deficit Disorder.* Chapel Hill, North Carolina: Algonquin Books of Chapel Hill, 2005.

- Nath Hanh, Thich. *Anger: Wisdom for Cooling the Flames.* New York: Riverhead Books, 2001.
- O'dea, Clare. *The Naked Swiss: A Nation behind 10 Myths.* Basel: Bergli Books, 2016.
- Pasricha, Neil. *The Book of Awesome.* New York: G.P. Putnam's Sons, an imprint of Penguin Random House, 2010.
- Radjou, Navi; Prabhu, Jaideep; Ahuja, Simone. *Jugaad Innovation: Think Frugal, Be Flexible, Generate Breakthrough Growth.* San Francisco: Jossey-Bass, 2012.
- Rubin, Gretchen. *The Happiness Project: Or, Why I Spent a Year Trying to Sing in the Morning, Clean My Closets, Fight Right, Read Aristotle, and Generally Have More Fun.* New York: HarperCollins Publishers, 2009.
- Rubin, Gretchen. *Outer Order, Inner Calm: Declutter and Organize to Make More Room for Happiness.* U.S./New York: Harmony Books, an imprint of the Crown Publishing Group, a division of Penguin Random House, 2019.
- Russel, Helen. *The Atlas of Happiness: The Global Secrets of How to Be Happy.* Great Britain: Two Roads, an imprint of John Murray Press, 2018.
- Taran, Randy. *Emotional Advantage. Embracing All Your Feelings to Create a Life You Love.* New York: St. Martin's Essentials, 2019.
- The 14th Dalai Lama; Tutu, Desmond; Abrams, Douglas Carlton. *The Book of Joy: Lasting Happiness in a Changing World.* New York: Avery, an imprint of Penguin Random House, 2016.
- Ware, Bronnie. *The Top Five Regrets of the Dying: A Life Transformed by the Dearly Departing.* London: Hay House, 2012.

REFERENCES

Chapter 1 - Germany

1 Many people have used this saying in one form or another. Another closely related one is: "There are only two lasting bequests we can hope to give our children. One of these is roots, the other, wings." While the "quote investigator" traces this saying back to the journalist, author, and newspaper editor, Hodding Carter, in the U.S. who quoted a "wise woman" in the book *Where Main Street Meats the River* in 1953, this saying has been taken up in various forms around the globe ever since. Some even trace the quote back to Johann Wolfgang von Goethe. For more information on the origin of this saying, please have a look at: https://quoteinvestigator.com/2014/08/12/roots-wings/

2 This sentence used by my grandmother has been quoted very often by my mom. For more information on where this aphorism originated, please have a look at: https://quoteinvestigator.com/tag/john-a-shedd/#return-note-7781-1

3 "Viktor Frankl," *The Viennese School of Existential Analysis and Logotherapy*, accessed Feb. 2021, https://www.gle-uk.com/viktor-frankl

4 For more information on the typical *"Prussian virtues,"* please see: BLPB, "Preußische Tugenden. Längst vergessen oder wieder erwünscht?" *Brandenburgische Landeszentrale für Politische Bildung*, June 2012, https://www.politische-bildung-brandenburg.de/ausstellungen/preu%C3%9Fische-betrachtungen/preu%C3%9Fische-tugenden

5 This quote is often attributed to Aristotle. Yet, while Aristotle made statements along these lines, it was the philosopher Will Durant, who coined this expression in his book *"The Story of Philosophy"* (1926) in which he chronicles the work of history's greatest philosophers.

6   John Maxwell, "It all comes down to what you do daily," accessed Oct. 2019, https://www.johnmaxwell.com/blog/it-all-comes-down-to-what-you-do-daily/

7   *"The 20 Mile March"* is a concept that was developed by Jim Collins in his book *Great by Choice* (2011). For more information on this concept, please see: https://www.jimcollins.com/concepts/twenty-mile-march.html

8   Rachel Hollis, *Girl, Wash Your Face. Stop Believing the Lies About Who You Are So You Can Become Who You Were Meant to Be* (Nashville: Nelson Books, 2018), 58/59.

Chapter 2 - USA

1   "Largest countries in the World 2021," last accessed Jan. 2021, http://worldpopulationreview.com/countries/largest-countries-in-the-world/

2   Gillian M. Sandstrom, Elizabeth W. Dunn: "Social Interactions and Well-Being: The Surprising Power of Weak Ties," *Personality and Social Psychology Bulletin*, 2014 Jul; 40(7): 910-922. doi: 10.1177/0146167214529799. Epub 2014 Apr 25.)

3   Victor Mather, "Great Moments in Cheerleading: Could the Olympics be next?" *The New York Times*, Dec. 8, 2016, https://www.nytimes.com/2016/12/08/sports/great-moments-in-cheerleading-could-the-olympics-be-next.html

4   Carol Dweck. "The Power of Believing that You Can Improve." Filmed December 2014 at TEDx Norrköping, Sweden. Video, 10:11. https://www.ted.com/talks/carol_dweck_the_power_of_believing_that_you_can_improve/transcript?language=en

Chapter 3 - Mexico

1   *"Potluck"*. Wikipedia, accessed Oct. 2019, https://en.wikipedia.org/wiki/Potluck#:~:text=The%20word%20pot%2Dluck%20appears,the%201930s%20during%20the%20Depression.

2   Kevin Clarke, "Mexico is home to world's second largest Catholic population." *America. The Jesuit Review*, Feb. 11, 2016, https://www.americamagazine.org/content/dispatches/pew-looks-state-mexicos-catholics

3   Alison Lesley, "81% of Mexican adults are Catholic and more facts on religion in Mexico." *World Religion News*, Feb. 16, 2016, https://www.

worldreligionnews.com/religion-news/81-of-mexican-adults-are-catholic
-more-facts-on-religion-in-mexico

4   This statement stems from Yehudi Menuhin, one of the great violinists of the 20th century.

5   David Mills, Jenna Flannigan, "Does music affect your mood?" *Healthline. Health News*, updated April 13, 2017 (referring to Lancet review study from 2015 – https://doi.org/10.1016/S0140-6736(15)60169-6). https://www.healthline.com/health-news/mental-listening-to-music-lift s-or-reinforces-mood-051713#3

6   David Mills, Jenna Flannigan, "Does music affect your mood?" *Healthline. Health News*, updated April 13, 2017, https://www.healthline.com/health-news/mental-listening-to-music-lifts-or-reinforces-mood-051713#3

7   Ibid.

Chapter 4 - Netherlands

1   Katja Brokke, "'We have nothing to hide' – Why Dutch people don't mind you peering into their homes," *CNN Travel*, updated April 14, 2020, https://edition.cnn.com/travel/article/dutch-windows/index.html

2   EF EPI (Education First, English Proficiency Index), "The world's largest ranking of countries and regions by English skills. Based on test results of 2.2 m adults in 100 countries & regions," edition 2020, accessed Feb. 2021, https://www.ef.com/wwen/epi/

3   Colleen Geske, *"12 Reasons why Dutch moms are the happiest. Unlocking the secrets of Dutch parenting,"* Nov. 29, 2016, https://stuffdutchpeople-like.com/2016/11/29/12-reasons-why-dutch-moms-are-the-happiest/

4   Peter Adamson, "Child well-being in rich countries. A comparative overview." Innocenti Report Card 11. *UNICEF Office of Research*, April. 2013, unicef-irc.org/publications/pdf/rc11_eng.pdf

5   Mark Wagenbuur, *"Dutch Cycling Figures,"* Bicycle Dutch, Jan. 2, 2018, https://bicycledutch.wordpress.com/2018/01/02/dutch-cycling-figures/

6   Ibid.

7   ITDP (Institute for Transportation and Development Policy). "How Cycling can Save Cities Money and Emissions," Nov. 12, 2015, https://www.itdp.org/2015/11/12/how-cycling-can-save-cities-money-and-emissions/

8   Ibid.

9   Courtney Connley, "American workers burn 140 fewer calories than they did in 1960 – here's how much exercise you should get each day," *CNBC*.

Make It. Nov. 13, 2018, https://www.cnbc.com/2018/11/13/2018-us-gu idelines-recommend-150-minutes-of-movement-each-week.html

Chapter 5 - France

1   Henry Samuel, "UNESCO declares French cuisine world intangible heritage," *The Telegraph*, Nov. 16, 2010, https://www.telegraph.co.uk/news/ worldnews/europe/france/8138348/UNESCO-declares-French-cuisin e-world-intangible-heritage.html

2   OECD, "Gender equality. Balancing paid work, unpaid work and leisure," *OECD. Better Policies for Better Lives*, March 5, 2018, http://www. oecd.org/gender/balancing-paid-work-unpaid-work-and-leisure.htm

3   Tim Radford, "Scientists discover secret that keeps French slim: eat less of everything," *The Guardian*, Aug. 25, 2003, https://www.theguardian. com/world/2003/aug/25/health.france

4   Kathleen M. Zelman, "How the French stay slim. An American dietitian explores the 'French Paradox': staying slim on a no-deprivation diet," *Nourish by WebMD*, accessed in Oct. 2019 at https://www.webmd.com/ diet/features/how-the-french-stay-slim#1

5   "French cuisine named a 'world intangible heritage,'" *Mail & Guardian*, Nov. 16, 2010, https://mg.co.za/article/2010-11-16-french-cuisine-na med-a-world-intangible-heritage/

6   Patrick A. Coleman, "6 Scientific Reasons Family Dinners are Important for Your Child," *Fatherly. Health & Science / Nutrition*, Feb. 8, 2017, https://www.fatherly.com/health-science/6-reasons-eating-family-dinner/

7   Katie Kelly Bell, "The Most Important Meal of the Day: The Family Dinner," *Forbes*, Aug. 11, 2014, https://www.forbes.com/sites/ka tiebell/2014/08/11/the-most-important-meal-of-the-day-the-family-dinner/#3dce0122b172

8   Patrick A. Coleman, "6 Scientific Reasons Family Dinners are Important for Your Child," *Fatherly. Health & Science / Nutrition*, Feb. 8, 2017, https://www.fatherly.com/health-science/6-reasons-eating-family-dinner/

9   Hugh Schofield, "Why does France insist school pupils master philosophy?" *BBC News, Paris*, June 3, 2013, https://www.bbc.com/news/ magazine-22729780

10 Gaëlle Le Roux, "Are French students taught to be more philosophical?" *France 24*, June 16, 2011, https://www.france24.com/en/20110616-franc e-baccalaureate-exams-philosophy-europe-curriculum-university

11 Ibid.

12 Hugh Schofield, "Why does France insist school pupils master philosophy?" *BBC News, Paris*, June 3, 2013, https://www.bbc.com/news/magazine-22729780

13 Ibid.

14 Archives Gouvernement, "17 Mars 1808 Infographie. Napoléon crée le baccalauréat, premier grade universitaire," *Gouvernment de la République française*, https://www.gouvernement.fr/partage/10047-napoleon-cree-le-baccalaureat-premier-grade-universitaire

15 Gaëlle Le Roux, "Are French students taught to be more philosophical?" *France 24*, June 16, 2011, https://www.france24.com/en/20110616-france-baccalaureate-exams-philosophy-europe-curriculum-university

16 Ibid.

17 Ibid.

18 Jamie Cat Callan, in: Felicia Czochanski, "8 Secrets to Dating like a French Woman," *Well + Good*, Feb. 13, 2018, https://www.wellandgood.com/good-advice/french-woman-dating-tips-parisian-charm-school-jamie-cat-callan/slide/2/

19 Felicia Czochanski, "8 Secrets to Dating like a French Woman," *Well + Good*, Feb. 13, 2018, https://www.wellandgood.com/good-advice/french-woman-dating-tips-parisian-charm-school-jamie-cat-callan/slide/2/

20 "12 Beauty Tricks that Make French Women so Naturally Charming," *Bright Side*, accessed Nov. 2019, https://brightside.me/inspiration-girls-stuff/12-beauty-tricks-that-make-french-women-so-naturally-charming-721260/

21 "Vincent van Gogh in Provence," *Avignon & Provence*, accessed Nov. 2019, https://www.avignon-et-provence.com/en/celebrities-provence/vincent-van-gogh-provence

22 Anne-Marie Simons, "The Light of Provence," *Bonjour Paris. The Insider's Guide*, Oct. 22, 2010, https://bonjourparis.com/archives/light_provence/

Chapter 6 - Switzerland

1 Richard Louv, in: Madhuleena Roy Chowdhury, "The Positive Effects of Nature on your Mental Well-being," *Positive Psychology*, Dec. 28, 2020, https://positivepsychology.com/positive-effects-of-nature/

2 Ibid.

3   Jamie Feldmar, "Gardening could be the hobby that helps you live to 100," *BBC. 100 Year Life. Longevity*, Dec. 10, 2018, https://www.bbc.com/worklife/article/20181210-gardening-could-be-the-hobby-that-helps-you-live-to-100

4   Julie Myerson, "Gardening: the secret of happiness," *The Guardian*, March 26, 2011, https://www.theguardian.com/lifeandstyle/2011/mar/26/gardening-secret-of-happiness-julie-myerson

5   "ANE Elternbrief. 11 Monate. Die Welt hat Ecken und Kanten," *Arbeitskreis Neue Erziehung (ANE)*, e.V., Berlin, www.ane.de

6   There are different stories circulating about this anecdote with Thomas Edison, but all of them exemplify the importance of perseverance. The Quote Investigator has traced this dialogue between him and his associate, Mallory, back to a tale written in 1910, called: *"Edison. His Life and Inventions."* For more information, please see: https://quoteinvestigator.com/2012/07/

7   Alexandra Kohler, "Berner sind Langsam," *Neue Zürcher Zeitung (NZZ)*, March 31, 2014, https://www.nzz.ch/panorama/montagsklischee/berner-sind-langsam-1.18272907

8   "Singapore has world's fastest walkers," *Sunday Morning Herald (SMH)*, May 3, 2007, https://www.smh.com.au/lifestyle/singapore-has-worlds-fastest-walkers-20070503-gdq1ww.html

9   "SWISS APERO. Das Geheimnis der Schweizer Gelassenheit," *Falstaff*, March 8, 2018, https://www.falstaff.de/nd/swiss-apero-das-geheimnis-der-schweizer-gelassenheit/

10 "The world leader in innovation. An international R&D and innovation hub," *GGBa (Greater Geneva Bern area)*, accessed, Nov. 2020, https://www.ggba-switzerland.ch/en/advantages/the-world-leader-in-innovation/

11 Ibid.

12 Ibid.

13 Ibid.

14 Clare O'dea, *The Naked Swiss. A Nation behind 10 Myths.* (Basel: Bergli Books, Schwabe Publishing, 2016).

15 Ibid, 78.

16 "Where the web was born," *CERN*, accessed Nov. 2020, https://home.cern/science/computing/where-web-was-born

17 Clare O'dea, *The Naked Swiss. A Nation Behind 10 Myths.* (Basel: Bergli Books, Schwabe Publishing, 2016), 82.

18 "City Statistics portraits 2020: core cities. Geneva: core city," *Confédération Suisse, Federal Statistical Office*, accessed Jan. 2021, https://www.

bfs.admin.ch/bfs/en/home/statistics/cross-sectional-topics/city-statistics/city-portraits/geneva.html

19 "City Statistics portraits 2020: agglomerations. Geneva: national agglomeration," *Confédération Suisse, Federal Statistical Office*, accessed Jan. 2021, https://www.bfs.admin.ch/bfs/en/home/statistics/cross-sectional-topics/city-statistics/agglomeration-portraits/geneva.html

20 "Fact and Figures about International Geneva," *Confédération Suisse. Federal Department of Foreign Affairs (FDFA)*, accessed after last update on Jan. 15, 2021, https://www.eda.admin.ch/missions/mission-onu-geneve/en/home/geneve-international/faits-et-chiffres.html

21 Marcus Vetter, "The Forum. Behind the Scenes of the World Economic Forum in Davos", Political Documentary, Theatrical Release, Germany, Nov. 6, 2019, accessed Jan. 2020, https://www.theforum-film.com/#film

22 Thich Nhat Hanh, *Anger: Wisdom for Cooling the Flames.* (New York: Riverhead Books, 2001).

Chapter 7 - India

1 "Future of Consumption in Fast-Growth Consumer Markets: INDIA," *World Economic Forum (WEF) in collaboration with Bain & Company*, 2018, accessed Oct. 2020, http://www3.weforum.org/docs/WEF_Future_of_Consumption_Fast-Growth_Consumers_markets_India_report_2019.pdf

2 "Challenges and opportunities emerge as India becomes third largest consumer market by 2030," *Bain and Company*. Press Release, Jan. 8, 2019, https://www.bain.com/about/media-center/press-releases/2018/wef-india-consumption-report/

3 "Competitiveness: Catching the next wave. India," *Deloitte*, Nov. 2014, accessed Oct. 2020 https://www2.deloitte.com/global/en/pages/about-deloitte/articles/india-competitiveness-report.html

4 Arun Janardhan, "Michael Perschke / For India, the horn is a category in itself," *Mint*, March 25, 2012, https://www.livemint.com/Companies/Z7coc0vtsWtfHLqWA5hBcM/Michael-Perschke--For-India-the-horn-is-a-category-in-itse.html

5 Samuel Osborne, "India to overtake China as most populous country within a decade, UN report finds," *Independent*, June 22, 2019, https://www.independent.co.uk/news/world/asia/india-china-population-2050-un-report-a8970531.html

6   "Tamil Nadu Population 2021," *World Population Review*, accessed Feb. 2021, https://worldpopulationreview.com/territories/tamil-nadu-population

7   "Uttar Pradesh Population," *World Population. India Population*, accessed Feb. 2021, http://www.populationu.com/in/uttar-pradesh-population

8   Milan Vaishnav, Jamie Hintson, "The World's largest election, explained," *Carnegie Endowment for International Peace*, accessed Nov. 2019, https://carnegieendowment.org/publications/interactive/india-elects-2019

9   Ian Jack, "India has 600 million young people – and they are set to change our world," *The Guardian. Opinion India*, Jan. 13, 2018, https://www.theguardian.com/commentisfree/2018/jan/13/india-600-million-young-people-world-cities-internet#:~:text=About%20600%20million%20people%2C%20more,country%20has%20more%20young%20people. /

10 H. Plecher, "India: Age distribution from 2009 to 2019," *statistica*, Oct. 20, 2020, https://www.statista.com/statistics/271315/age-distribution-in-india/

11 IBEF, "Spices Industry and Export in India," *India Brand Equity Foundation*, last updated Jan. 2021, https://www.ibef.org/exports/spice-industry-indias.aspx

12 "The Enchanting World of Indian Spices," *Tea, Coffee and Spices of India*, accessed Oct. 2020, https://teacoffeespiceofindia.com/spice/

13 Karin Kaiser, *INDIEN. Be happy oder das 'no problem' Problem* (Meerbusch: Conbook Medien GmbH, 2012, 2013), 231.

14 Srijan Shukla, "Indian food fourth most popular in the world, a study of cuisine trade finds," *The Print*, Aug. 29, 2019, https://theprint.in/world/indian-food-fourth-most-popular-in-the-world-a-study-of-cuisine-trade-finds/283119/

15 Don R. Crawley, "Treating Guests (and Customers) like God," *The Compassionate Geek Blog*, Jan. 20, 2016, https://www.doncrawley.com/treating-guests-and-customers-like-god/

16 "Madurai, the Athens of the East," *Walk through India*, accessed Oct. 2020, http://www.walkthroughindia.com/around-the-world/madurai-athens-east/

17 Karin Kaiser, *INDIEN. Be happy oder das 'no problem' Problem* (Meerbusch: Conbook Medien GmbH, 2012, 2013).

18 Ibid.

19 Rachelle Williams, "5 Physical Health Benefits of Spirituality," *The Chopra Center*, July 19, 2019, https://chopra.com/articles/5-physical-health-benefits-of-spirituality

20 Ibid.

21 Chad E Cooper, "The importance of spirituality versus religion for living a Legendary Life," *Thrive Global*, March 8, 2019, https://medium.com/thrive-global/the-importance-of-spirituality-versus-religion-for-living-a-legendary-life-e038554e4492

22 Ibid.

23 Itai Ivtzan & Sivaja Jegatheeswaran, "The Yoga Boom in Western Society: Practitioners' Spiritual vs. Physical Intentions and Their Impact on Psychological Wellbeing," *Journal of Yoga and Physical Therapy* 5, no. 3 (2015). Doi: 10.4172/2157-7595.1000204

24 Ibid.

25 Manu Joseph, "'Jugaad', India's most overrated idea," *Mint*, Aug. 18, 2018, https://www.livemint.com/Leisure/2c3sntdHfJ8Py2tWxEqgcN/Jugaad-Indias-most-overrated-idea.html

Chapter 8 - China

1 Wayne M Morrison, "China's Economic Rise: History, Trends, Challenges, and Implications for the United States," *CRS Report. Congressional Research Service,* updated June 25, 2019, https://www.everycrsreport.com/files/20190625_RL33534_088c5467dd11365dd4ab5f72133db-289fa10030f.pdf

2 "Countries in the world by population (2021)," *Worldometer*, accessed Jan. 2021, https://www.worldometers.info/world-population/population-by-country/

3 Wayne M Morrison, "China's Economic Rise: History, Trends, Challenges, and Implications for the United States," *EveryCRSReport,* accessed Feb. 2021, https://www.everycrsreport.com/reports/RL33534.html#_Toc12530866

4 UN, "Secretary General's remarks on the occasion of the 70th anniversary of the founding of the People's Republic of China [as delivered]," *United Nations Secretary-General. Statement*, Sep. 26, 2019, https://www.un.org/sg/en/content/sg/statement/2019-09-26/secretary-generals-remarks-the-occasion-of-the-70th-anniversary-of-the-founding-of-the-peoples-republic-of-china-delivered

5   IBRD/IDA, "The World Bank in China," accessed Nov. 2020, https://www.worldbank.org/en/country/china/overview

6   Zhang Haihua & Geoff Baker, *Think like Chinese* (Sydney: The Federation Press, 2008), 24.

7   Michael A. Peters, "The Chinese Dream: Xi Jinping thought on socialism with Chinese characteristics for a new era," *Educational Philosophy and Theory* 49, no. 14 (2017): 1299-1304, https://doi.org/10.1080/00131857.2017.1407578

8   Yi S. Ellis & Bryan D. Ellis, *101 Stories for Foreigners to Understand Chinese People* (Beijing: China Intercontinental Press, 2012).

9   Jacqueline Whitmore, "How to gracefully accept a compliment," *Huff-Post*, Oct. 4, 2015, https://www.huffpost.com/entry/how-to-gracefully-accept-_b_7042718

10 UN, "Secretary General's remarks on the occasion of the 70th anniversary of the founding of the People's Republic of China [as delivered]," *United Nations Secretary-General. Statement*, Sep. 26, 2019, https://www.un.org/sg/en/content/sg/statement/2019-09-26/secretary-generals-remarks-the-occasion-of-the-70th-anniversary-of-the-founding-of-the-peoples-republic-of-china-delivered

11 Rebecca A. Fannin, *Startup Asia. Top Strategies for Cashing in on Asia's Innovation Boom* (Singapore: John Wiley & Sons (Asia) Pte. Ltd., 2012), 16.

12 Yi S. Ellis & Bryan D. Ellis, *101 Stories for Foreigners to Understand Chinese People* (Beijing: China Intercontinental Press, 2012), 161.

13 May-lee Chai & Winberg Chai, *China A-Z. Chinese Customs and Culture* (New York: PLUME, Penguin Group, 2007), 13.

14 Jun Shan, "The Meaning of Yin and Yang" *ThoughtCo*, Aug. 28, 2020, https://www.thoughtco.com/yin-and-yang-629214

15 Zhang Haihua & Geoff Baker, *Think like Chinese* (Sydney: The Federation Press, 2008), 5; 14.

16 Jun Shan, "The Meaning of Yin and Yang." *ThoughtCo*, Aug. 28, 2020, https://www.thoughtco.com/yin-and-yang-629214

17 Ibid.

18 "Ying and Yang explained: For Balanced Health and Flow," *Wu Wei Wisdom*, YouTube video, Aug. 25, 2017, https://www.youtube.com/watch?v=Q8K7Ia-Oj3g

19 Diana Danko, "Yin and yang in the kitchen," *Alimentarium*, Oct. 26, 2016, https://www.alimentarium.org/en/magazine/nutrition/yin-and-yang-kitchen

20   Rosie Tanabe, "Flow (psychology)," *New World Encyclopedia*, last revision, April 14, 2017, https://www.newworldencyclopedia.org/p/index.php?title=Flow_(psychology)&oldid=1004315

21   Mike Oppland, "8 Ways to create Flow according to Mihaly Csikszentmihalyi," *PositivePsychology.com*, accessed Feb. 17, 2021, https://positivepsychology.com/mihaly-csikszentmihalyi-father-of-flow/

22   Ibid, with reference to: Jeanne Nakamura & Mihaly Csikszentmihalyi, *Flow theory and research*. In C. R. Snyder & S. J. Lopez (Eds.), *The Oxford Handbook of positive psychology* (Oxford: Oxford University Press, 2009), 195-206.

23   Catherine Moore, "What is Eudaimonia? Aristotle and Eudaimonic Well-Being," *PositivePsychology.com*, Sep. 1, 2020, https://positivepsychology.com/eudaimonia/

24   Patrick Zeis, "The Yin and Yang of Stillness and Flow," *Balanced Achievement*, July 9, 2018, https://balancedachievement.com/balachieve/stillness-and-flow/

25   "Tai Chi chuan," *Shibuiswords.com*, accessed Feb. 2021, http://www.shibuiswords.com/chuan.htm

26   Yi S. Ellis & Bryan D. Ellis, *101 Stories for Foreigners to Understand Chinese People* (Beijing: China Intercontinental Press, 2012), 203.

27   Zhang Haihua & Geoff Baker, *Think like Chinese* (Sydney: The Federation Press, 2008), 17.

28   May-lee Chai & Winberg Chai, *China A-Z. Chinese Customs and Culture* (New York: PLUME, Penguin Group, 2007), 41.

29   Jacob Harding, "Corruption or Guanxi? Differentiating Between the Legitimate, Unethical, and Corrupt Activities of Chinese Government Officials," *Pacific Basin Law Journal*, 31(2) (2014): 130. Accessed Sep. 2020, https://escholarship.org/uc/item/0p8650mm.

30   Ibid, 131.

31   Zhang Haihua & Geoff Baker, *Think like Chinese* (Sydney: The Federation Press, 2008), 105.

32   Ibid, 101.

33   Brown, Brené, *Daring Greatly: How the Courage to Be Vulnerable Transforms the Way We Live, Love, Parent and Lead* (U.S.: Gotham Books, a member of Penguin Group, 2012), 8.

34   Dana Staves, "The Best Brené Brown Quotes on Vulnerability, Love, and Belonging," *Book Riot*, April 16, 2018, https://bookriot.com/2018/04/16/brene-brown-quotes/

35   "How Many Jobs are Found Through Networking, Really?" *Payscale*, April 6, 2017, https://www.payscale.com/career-news/2017/04/many-jobs-found-networking#:~:text=The%20Most%20Common%20Way%20to%20Find%20Work&text=Some%20experts%20say%20that%2070,percent%20or%20even%2085%20percent.

Chapter 9 - Japan

1   "Why Japan is Known as Land of Rising Sun?" *Maps of World*, July 26, 2017, https://www.mapsofworld.com/answers/world/why-is-japan-called-land-of-rising-sun/

2   "Tokyo Population 2021," *World Population Review*, accessed Feb. 2021, https://worldpopulationreview.com/world-cities/tokyo-population

3   "Why is the Japanese Education System the Envy of the World?" *Lichfield Cathedral School,* accessed Nov. 2020, https://www.lichfieldcathedralschool.com/why-is-the-japanese-education-system-the-envy-of-the-world/667049.html

4   "Should School Children Clean Their Own Schools? Japan Thinks So," *Bright Vibes. Amplify The Good in the World,* accessed Nov. 2020, https://brightvibes.com/833/en/should-children-clean-their-own-schools-japan-thinks-so

5   Sarah Harvey, *Kaizen: La Méthode Japonaise du Petit Pas Pour Changer Toutes ses Habitudes* (Paris: Hugo: New Life, 2020), 27.

6   Ibid, 27- 29.

7   Sarah Harvey, *Kaizen: La Méthode Japonaise du Petit Pas Pour Changer Toutes ses Habitudes* (Paris: Hugo: New Life, 2020).

8   Héctor García, *A Geek in Japan: Discovering the Land of Manga, Anime, Zen, and the Tea Ceremony* (Tokyo: Tuttle Publishing, 2011), 41.

9   "Why is it Difficult to Understand what Wabi-Sabi Means?" *Sakura News*, Oct. 15, 2019, https://www.kyoto-ryokan-sakura.com/what-wabi-sabi-means/

10   Erina Takeda, "Significance of Sakura: Cherry Blossom Traditions in Japan," *Festival Blog*, April 9, 2014, https://festival.si.edu/blog/2014/significance-of-sakura-cherry-blossom-traditions-in-japan/

11   "What is Hanami: The Fun Way Japanese Enjoy Sakura Viewing." *Live Japan,* March 31, 2019, https://livejapan.com/en/article-a0000708/

12   Lula Bornhak, "Ich bin nicht perfekt - so what? Mit Wabi-Sabi Makel zelebrieren," *Fuck Lucky Go Happy,* July 3, 2018, https://www.fuckluckygohappy.de/ich-bin-nicht-perfekt-so-what-mit-wabi-sabi-makel-zelebrieren/

13 Helen Russel, *The Atlas of Happiness: The Global Secrets of How to Be Happy* (Great Britain: Two Roads, an imprint of John Murray Press, 2018), 156.

14 "Life Expectancy for Japanese Men and Women Rises in 2019," *Nippon. com*, Aug. 17, 2020, https://www.nippon.com/en/japan-data/h00788/

15 Tom Levitt, "People in Okinawa Live Longer than Almost Anyone on Earth. Here's What They Eat," *Huffpost*, Feb. 21, 2019, https://www.huffpost.com/entry/okinawa-japan-longevity-diet -eat_n_5c6b107fe4b01cea6b883962

16 Héctor García, *A Geek in Japan: Discovering the Land of Manga, Anime, Zen, and the Tea Ceremony* (Tokyo: Tuttle Publishing, 2011), 77.

17 Sanjay Gupta, "The Land of Immortals: How and What Japan's Oldest Population Eats," *CNN Health*, May 21, 2019, https://edition.cnn.com/2019/04/05/health/japan-okinawa-food-diet-hara-hachi-bu-chasing-life-gupta/index.html

18 "Hara Hachi Bu: Einfach Weniger Essen," *Wellness*, accessed Feb. 2021, https://www.wellnessverband.de/wellness-freunde/wellness_beratung/essen_und_trinken_hara_hachi_bu_okinawa.php

19 Marion Tilly, "What Ikigai Means and How to Find Yours," *The Institute of You*, https://instituteofyou.org/what-ikigai-means-and-how-to-find-yours/

20 The Venn diagram has been taken up by many media outlets and the one pictured here comes from the following article in *Forbes*: Chris Myers, "How to Find Your Ikigai and Transform Your Outlook on Life and Business," *Forbes*, Feb. 23, 2018, https://www.forbes.com/sites/chrismyers/2018/02/23/how-to-find-your-ikigai-and-transform-your-outlook-on-life-and-business/

21 Marc Winn, "What is Your Ikigai?" *The View Inside Me: The World Changing Blog by Marc Winn,* May 14, 2014, https://theviewinside.me/what-is-your-ikigai/

22 For more information on how this "Westernized version" of ikigai emerged, have a look at Nicholas Kemp's detailed explanation: https://medium.com/@support_35468/ikigai-is-not-a-venn-diagram-cca7abba323

23 Ibid.

24 Elizabeth Stuart, "Discipline in the Face of Disaster: No Looting in Japan," *Deseret News*, March 14, 2011, https://www.deseret.com/2011/3/14/20179195/discipline-in-the-face-of-disaster-no-looting-in-japan

25 "Factbox: Japan's Many Earthquakes," *Reuters*, July 17, 2007, https://www.reuters.com/article/us-quake-japan-factbox-idUST32929520070717

26 Sanjay Gupta, "The Land of Immortals: How and What Japan's Oldest Population Eats," *CNN Health*, May 21, 2019, https://edition.cnn.com/2019/04/05/health/japan-okinawa-food-diet-hara-hachi-bu-chasing-life-gupta/index.html

27 Aislinn Leonard, "Moai—This Tradition is Why Okinawan People Live Longer, Better," *Blue Zones*, accessed Oct. 2020, https://www.bluezones.com/2018/08/moai-this-tradition-is-why-okinawan-people-live-longer-better/

28 Ibid.

29 Tara Parker-Pope, "The Power of Positive People: Are Your Friendships Giving You a Boost or Bringing You Down?" *The New York Times*, July 10, 2018, https://www.nytimes.com/2018/07/10/well/the-power-of-positive-people.html

30 "Ofuro: Die Japanische Badewanne," *Japan Experience*, July 16, 2017, https://www.japan-experience.de/zu-wissen/japan-verstehen/ofuro-baden-in-japan

31 Héctor García, *A Geek in Japan: Discovering the Land of Manga, Anime, Zen, and the Tea Ceremony* (Tokyo: Tuttle Publishing, 2011), 50.

32 "8 Japanese Routines for a Happy and Healthy Life," *Ritulas*, April 1, 2019, https://www.rituals.com/en-nl/mag-rituality-the-japanese-way-of-life.html

Conclusion

1 Robin Sharma, "The 3 Step Success Formula + the Habit Installation Protocol," accessed Feb. 2021, https://robinsharma.com/nation/v2-the-3-step-success-formula/

2 This quote and similar versions of it, have been attributed to a wide array of different persons. For more information on this, please see the following article by the *Quote Investigator*: quoteinvestigator.com/2013/01/10/watch-your-thoughts/